Finding Fun & Friends in Washington

An Uncommon Guide to Common Interests

ROBERTA GOTTESMAN, Editor
ROBERTA MASTERS, Associate Editor, Second Edition
MICHELLE VANNEMAN, Associate Editor, First Edition

Copyright Piccolo Press 1992, 1994
Alexandria, Virginia

To Ken and Deborah, the best friends a mother could have

Piccolo Press, 901 King Street, Suite 102, Alexandria, VA 22314; 703/519-0376

ISBN 0-9631756-1-0

Finding fun and friends in Washington: an uncommon guide to common interests/ Roberta Gottesman, editor, Roberta Masters, associate editor, second edition.

Printed and bound by Victor Graphics
Design and layout by Irene Kiebuzinski with assistance from Britt Engen-Skalsky
Cover design by Wordscape, Washington, D.C.

The Second Edition

Published and edited by . . . . Roberta Gottesman
Revised by . . . . Roberta Masters

We gratefully acknowledge the following first edition contributing editors who paved the way for this book:

MICHELLE VANNEMAN
  Athletics and Outdoor Adventures
  Culinary Washington
  Education
  Historic Washington
  Literary Washington
  Personal Growth
  Photographic Washington
  Political, Civic, and Nonpartisan Organizations
  Volunteer

CATHERINE SENTMAN
  Arts
  Dance
  Gardening
  International Organizations
  Parks, Recreation and Community Centers

MARY ANNE PUGLISI
  Athletics and Outdoor Adventurses
  Gardening
  Parks, Recreation and Community Centers

ROBERTA MASTERS
  Animals
  Miscellaneous

Endorsements

"I was new in Washington and I was so happy to find this book! It really helped me meet people when I joined a bicycling club and group of symphony supporters."
— Dr. Brigit Kovacs, medical researcher from Germany

"As a lifelong resident, I was pleasantly surprised to discover so many opportunities I'd never heard of before. And the book is a must for newcomers. I gave my clients copies of the first edition as a Holiday gift."
— Barbara Simon, real estate agent with Long & Foster

"If you're suddenly single and don't know where to turn, this book is an invaluable resource."
— Carol Randolph, Executive Director of New Beginnings

"No Single should be without this book. It offers intelligent choices for intelligent Singles."
— Bert Finkelstein, President, Capital Area Singles

"Great resource for the outdoorsman."
— Gary Sturdevant, Engineer

Contents

Editor's Note

The inspiration for the first edition of our book came from the personal experience of a staff member of Piccolo Press. As a newcomer to the area, she wanted to meet new, interesting people. Because she had enjoyed tooling around with a hammer and nails since childhood, she choose to join Habitat for Humanity, a group dedicated to building homes for low-income families. At Habitat, she discovered a great group who shared a committment to helping others. After raising the beams and putting up the walls, they went out for drinks. This led to new friendships.

Her experience pointed out a great need in the metropolitan area for an insider's guide to the exciting programs, activities, and on-going events offered by hundreds of organizations within and outside the Beltway.

Since the publication of our first edition two years ago, we have heard from hundreds of people who used our book as a roadmap to new friendships, creative endeavors, and community involvement.

This book is a key to discovering the wealth of fascinating activities available for every conceivable interest around Washington. It can also serve as a way to meet new people in a safe environment.

With this insider's guide you can discover your creative talents with music ensembles, theater groups, and art leagues; join in team sports or learn to rock climb on the banks of the Potomac. The categories profiled include clubs devoted to artistic, historical, musical, athletic, outdoor, educational, and culinary pursuits, along with endless opportunities for community service. We've also added a chapter for animal lovers.

The second edition of *Finding Fun & Friends* has been expanded to include new topics and activities, some of which our readers have provided. We want the book to continue to be a reflection of the community. If you know of a unique club, society, organization, or publication that should be included in Finding Fun & Friends, please let us know so that we might feature it in future editions. Just send a note with the organization's name and address to us at Piccolo Press, 901 King Street, Suite 102, Alexandria, Va. 22314.

We welcome the use of *Finding Fun & Friends* in fundraising efforts by organizations in the community because without them, this book would not exist. If your group is looking for a new way to supplement its coffers or finance a scholarship fund, please call us at 703-519-0376.

Introduction

This is not a book for tourists. *Finding Fun and Friends* is a guide for those of us who live here. How and where Washingtonians can find fulfilling leisure activities — and friends to share them with — is the subject of this book. Our philosophy is simple — seek out activities and programs that interest you, and others in the group will welcome you on board. You'll soon discover how much you have in common with those who share an enthusiasm for the project at hand.

The organizations profiled in the book offer hundreds of opportunities for socializing. We have not included singles groups. We believe that by joining a group of others with common interests relationships will blossom and grow.

The sites of these diverse programs vary from backstage at the Kennedy Center to the Hungarian Embassy, and from the National Zoo to local archaeological digs. Many activities are sponsored by renowned organizations such as the Smithsonian Institute. Other programs are coordinated by smaller, community-based groups and by local chapters of national associations. We especially recommend exploring opportunities at local departments of parks, recreation, and community centers. We have tried to be geographically evenhanded throughout the book, including organizations in Washington D.C., Maryland, and Virginia.

Some of these programs are well-known and others are more difficult to track down. We provide telephone numbers and/or addresses, as well as short descriptions of the activities, membership information, fees, and everything else to get you going.

Many groups offer membership privileges such as invitations to special events. For example, by volunteering for some of the organizations supporting the arts it is possible to enjoy benefits such as free tickets and artist receptions, enabling active volunteers to live an upscale lifestyle on a shoestring budget. Before joining any of these groups, you may want to request a recent newsletter or attend an upcoming event.

We have also included a host of "Media Alerts" to update you on newspapers, books, and other local publications that cater to specific interests.

Whatever your particular inclinations, *Finding Fun & Friends* has something for everyone from kayaking to contra dancing.

Important Note: Every precaution has been taken to verify the information in this book, however, programs and telephone numbers change, organizations move, and the unexpected happens. Always call before attending a meeting or event.

Animals
Our Furry Friends

Animals have long been a source of companionship for those of us of the human persuasion, and the Washington area offers a variety of organizations for pet owners. From fish to felines, fillies to fidos, animal lovers will discover fellow afficionados in the metropolitan area. There are opportunities to learn about different breeds and species of pets, to assist in one of the many local animal shelters or volunteer at the Zoo, to observe various animals in the wild, and to share pets with those less fortunate.

We have included information on dogs, cats, horses, birds, fish, llamas and bats in this chapter. The National Zoo has an active volunteer program for those interested in participating in ongoing projects with their exotic residents. For additional information on volunteering with animals, see the *Volunteer* chapter.

Finding A Furry Friend

As you read this, thousands of animals await a loving owner in the metropolitan area humane societies and shelters. Adopting an animal from one of the many local shelters could mean saving the life of a dog or cat. The animal shelters and rescue leagues included here have various fees and stipulations for adoption.

District of Columbia Animal Shelter
1201 New York Avenue, NE
Washington, DC
202/576-6664

Washington Animal Rescue League
71 Oglethorpe Street, NW
Washington, DC 20012
202/726-2556

Washington Humane Society
7319 Georgia Avenue, NW
Washington, DC 20012
202/333-4010

Prince Georges County Animal Control
8311 D'Arcy Road
Forestville, MD
301/499-8300

Animal Welfare League of Alexandria
910 South Payne Street
Alexandria, VA 22314
703/838-4775

Fairfax County Animal Shelter
4500 West Ox Road
Fairfax, VA 22030
703/830-1100

Montgomery County Animal Shelter
14645 Rothgeb Drive
Rockville, MD 20850
301/279-1823

Dogs

"Man's best friend" is found in all shapes and sizes; for those interested in purebred prize-winners, scores of local groups exist for specific breeds. We have included a handful to illustrate the types of activities offered.
Others can be reached by contacting the American Kennel Club, which can also tell you where to find specific breeds of puppies for sale in the metro area.

American Kennel Club
51 Madison Avenue
New York, NY 10010
212/696-8200

The Greater Washington Dalmatian Club
c/o Sue Sommerfield, Secretary
213 Moncure Drive
Alexandria, VA 22314

Made up of individuals who have a strong interest in the Dalmatian breed either as exhibitors, obedience trail competitors, conscientious breeders, or those who own Dalmatians solely as companions. GWDC holds regular monthly meetings, an annual awards dinner, an annual crab feast, and various fundraising activities throughout the year. Guests are welcome to attend a club meeting. Dues are $10 per year, and include the monthly newsletter *On the Spot*. Request an information packet from the address given.

Northern Virginia Dog Lover's Club
1913 North Key Boulevard, #573
Arlington, VA 22201
703/276-9043

This newly formed group is for those with and without dogs who would like to join other dog owners in monthly outings to area parks. Anyone interested in making new friends is welcome to accompany the group. There is no membership fee or requirement other than a love of dogs.

Potomac Basset Hound Club, Inc.
823 Spring Valley Drive
Fredericksburg, VA 22405
703/373-0721

Owners, breeders, and lovers of Basset Hounds in the Washington area may apply for membership in this group. The Club encourages education in the breeding of purebred Basset Hounds; they protect the interests of Basset Hounds in the ring and in the field by conducting specialty shows, tracking tests, and obedience and field trials. Meetings are held bi-monthly. Members receive the club newsletter, *The Lowdown.* Prospective members must attend two PBHC sponsored events and must have their applications signed by two PBHC sponsors. Membership dues are $10.

Pug Dog Club of Maryland, Inc

14249 Briarwood Terrace
Rockville, MD 20853
301/871-8063

The Pug Dog Club of Maryland, Inc., was founded in 1959 by a handful of dedicated Pug lovers and breeders, some of whom are active members today. The approximately 85 members from several states come together for meetings six times a year, and those members who cannot attend are kept informed through the club newsletter. Membership is $10 per year.

 Media Alert! *The Dog Owner's Guide to Washington,* by Mary Edington Rand, has all the vital information dog owners in D.C., Maryland, and Virginia need to know: everything from pet stores to apartments that accept pets is covered in this helpful paperback, which is available in local bookstores.

Obedience

If you want to avoid being dragged down the street by your new pet, and ensure that "Spot" learns his manners, a class is in order. Additional trainers can be found by consulting your veterinarian, local humane society, or animal shelter.

Capital Dog Training Club of Washington, Inc.

1453 Wasp Lane
McLean, VA 22101
301/587-K9K9 (5959)

The Capital Dog Training Club has been in existence since 1938, and works to promote the sport of dog obedience training. The Club provides training classes at all obedience levels for the general public and active members of CDTC. CDTC also has a Demonstration Team, which consists of well-mannered pets who show off their skills at schools, nursing homes and other places. Owners of dogs who enjoy catching tennis balls might be interested in the Flyball Team. Membership in CDTC costs $65 per year, and all members must pass a ten-week training course and a proficiency test. Members are invited to the club's awards and trial dinners.

Cats

Elusive and independent like their animals, cat owners with pure breds will have to contact the Cat Fanciers of America headquarters to find out about the local cat clubs. They were very finicky about being included in this chapter! C.F.A. also sponsors an annual Cat Show in Washington for those who would like to admire the variety of the species.

Cat Fanciers of America
1805 Atlantic Ave.
P.O. Box 1005
Mansquin, NJ 08736-0805
908/528-9797

Cat owners with very friendly felines who would like to take their pet and brighten the days of residents in health care facilities should continue reading:

Volunteer Opportunties for Pets and Their Owners

Scientists have found that petting and playing with animals benefits humans both mentally and physically. The following organizations welcome pet owners and their animals to join them in outings to local care facilities for the institutionalized, for seniors, and for at-risk youth. Readers interested in working with horses should read the section at the bottom of the page for volunteer opportunities. The *Volunteering* chapter lists additional animal-related volunteer organizations that do not require participants to own a pet.

Lend-A-Paw Relief Organization
P.O. Box 4864
Falls Church, VA 22044
703/536-8809

This multifaceted humane program is dedicated to solving the pet overpopulation problem in Northern Virginia. LAP is at work in the community providing rescue and adoption of cats and kittens, spaying and neutering programs, emergency pet relief, human education, and pet facilitated therapy to the elderly and children. Volunteers can help with adoption fairs, foster pets waiting to be adopted, and can participate in many other activities supporting LAP.

People-Animals-Love (PAL)
4832 MacArthur Boulevard, NW
Washington, DC 20007
202/337-0120

PAL is a non-profit volunteer organization that uses people and their pets to brighten the lives of institutionalized individuals. Volunteers bring their pets to visit hospitalized children, as well as residents of nursing homes and hospices. PAL also has a newly evolving program that uses animals to positively influence the lives of young people who are at-risk. PAL volunteers also come together for an annual December holiday party and for a summer picnic, both of which give them the opportunity to socialize with other volunteers and swap stories. There is no membership fee; the only requirement is a willingness to make visits to sick and/or elderly individuals with a well-mannered, healthy pet.

Horses

A horse, of course, is a source of pleasure and independence for many in the area. Whether your interest is sitting astride the saddle, walking alongside a physically challenged rider, or watching the majestic performance of dressage, area horse clubs will meet your needs. Volunteer opportunities to work with neglected horses and in therapeutic riding programs are found at the end of this section. For additional horseback riding experiences, see the "Outdoor Adventures" chapter.

Capitol Hill Equestrian Society (CHES)
1199 Longworth House Office Building
Washington, DC 20515
202/828-3035

Join this organization and you may be saddling up for a trail ride next weekend. Equestrians of all riding levels enjoy events and excursions that include moonlight, overnight, and all-day picnic rides, as well as trips to horse farms and horse shows, a fall steeplechase party, and lectures on polo, jousting, and training. CHES also schedules monthly meetings, and publishes a monthly newsletter featuring a lengthy list of area horse activities and information on lessons, and leasing, boarding, buying, or selling horses. Members often receive discounts at area supply shops and on lessons at participating stables. CHES's 300 members pay annual dues starting at $25.

Rock Creek Park Horse Centre
5100 Glover Road, NW
Washington, DC 20015
202/362-0117

This public horseback riding facility includes a main barn housing 30 school horses and 30 privately owned horses, four outdoor rings, and one indoor arena, and offers escorted trail rides, group and private riding instruction, and boarding services. The facility also runs a summer day camp, a working student program, and an Equestrian Team that competes at local horse shows. Call the number above for a current semester schedule and to make trail ride reservations.

The Potomac Valley Dressage Association
9807 Bristol Avenue
Silver Spring, MD 20901
301/299-7093

Maryland is the home of the nation's second oldest and the third largest dressage club, the Potomac Valley Dressage Association. The Association hosts two annual competitions recognized by both the American Horse Show Association and the U.S. Dressage Federation, and organizes more than 20 dressage schooling shows in Maryland. All members are eligible to participate in the extensive schooling show program, the Active Junior/Young Rider program, the local chapter/group system, monthly board meetings, and the annual Meeting and Awards Dinner. Members also receive the *PVDA Newsletter*, and can use the Association's large educational video library. Membership starts at $15.

Volunteer Opportunities For Horse Lovers

The organizations included here are for those who want to help physically challenged and learning disabled children develop confidence and strength in therapeutic riding programs, and for those interested in helping neglected horses and large animals recuperate from abuses.

Equine Rescue League
P.O. Box 4366
Leesburg, VA 22075
703/771-1240

A less publicized but very important animal rights issue is the neglect and abuse of horses and other large animals in the greater Washington area. The Equine Rescue League provides care, rehabilitation, training, and adoption to qualified persons for horses and other large animals at their 66 acre farm shelter in Leesburg, Virginia. There are volunteer opportunities available, and membership in the League starts at $20 per year. Visitors are welcome to the farm Wednesdays through Sundays from 10:00 a.m. until 3:00 p.m. by appointment only.

Lift Me Up!
P.O. Box 104
Great Falls, VA 22066
703/759-6221

Lift Me Up! is a non-profit service organization dedicated to providing a safe and challenging program of therapeutic riding for people with disabilities. Volunteers work as sidewalkers, leaders, and horse caretakers during numerous sessions each week. The organization sponsors two main fundraising events each year: a horse show in July, and a Ride-A-Thon in October. Social events for volunteers include a holiday party in December and other informal gatherings. Most events are in the Great Falls area, and there are no membership fees.

National Center for Therapeutic Riding
5110 Glover Road, NW
Washington, DC 20015
202/362-4537

Retirees, students, housewives - anyone having weekday hours free and an interest in working with horses is welcome to volunteer at the Center. Eight week sessions are offered in Rock Creek Park for school children from the metropolitan area with a variety of disabilities; adults are needed to help with the riding program and care for the horses. Previous experience is not necessary.

Other Lively Possibilities

If your enthusiasm for a childhood goldfish or parakeet has grown into a lifelong interest in birds or fish, there is a group for you. If you have never felt the common fear of bats getting caught in your hair because you understood they have sonar and respected them for it, or if llamas have always held a special place in your heart, you are not alone in Washington!

Bats

American Bat Conservation Society
P.O. Box 1393
Rockville, MD 20849
301/309-6610

Yes, bats. This group is dedicated to educating the public and supporting conservation efforts for species of North American bats. Informal "close encounters of the bat kind", field trips to observe local bats, and formal lectures are offered to members. Volunteer projects include school outreach programs, bat rescues, and caring for the ABCS resident bat colony. Annual dues are $15.

Birds

For additional information about birdwatching clubs and organizations, see Birdwatching in the *Outdoor Adventures* chapter.

National Capital Bird Club
7011-A Manchester Blvd., Suite 107
Alexandria, VA 22310
703/339-1544

This group of more than 100 aviculturists hold monthly meetings to discuss various topics related to the care and breeding of birds in captivity. All levels of involvement are welcome, from breeders to bird owners. Annual dues are $12.

Media Alert! The Rockville Animal Exchange publishes a seasonal newsletter, "424-PETS" with information on scheduled Sunday afternoon classes on the care of various pets, as well as upcoming events which include a Blessing of the Animals on Memorial Day weekend, a Pet Birthday party in August, and lectures on topics like Parrot Psychology. Round table events are held for bird owners. The newsletter is available by calling 301-424-7387.

Ferrets

Loudon Area Ferret Fanciers (LAFF)
P.O. 2371
Leesburg, VA 22075
703/430-6329

More than 100 families belong to this group which meets monthly in Northern Virginia. LAFF hosts an annual championship show for ferrets in addition to fun matches whth games and contests for the furry members. Conservation of the black-footed ferret is another cause this group supports. Annual dues are $20 per family.

Fish

Potomac Valley Aquarium Society
5809 Lane Drive
Alexandria, VA 22310
703/971-0594

This social and educational non-profit organization promotes the aquarium hobby. There are over 100 members in the greater Washington-Baltimore area, and they range in aquarium experience from beginners with a single tank to fish breeders with dozens of tanks, and in interests from freshwater to saltwater. Regular monthly meetings are currently held in Fairfax City, and other events held all over the area include fish shows, weekend workshops, special tours, and dinners. Membership is $12 per year, and non-members are invited to attend a monthly meeting to see if they enjoy it. An admission charge may be asked of non-members at special events, but you may also attend these on a trial basis.

Llamas

Llama Association of Mid-Atlantic States
Loony Toon Llamas
Route 1, Box 232
Roundhill, VA 22141
703/777-3252

This exotic animal is typically equated with mountainous regions further south, but surprisingly, more than 110 members belong to this group. Llama ownership is not mandatory for membership, but an admiration for the graceful animal is required. Llamas are said to have a calming effect on humans, and the group is interested in sharing their knowledge with inner city and at-risk youth. Presentations for schools, hospitals, and nursing homes are offered, as well as free tours of the ranches. ⚜

Arts
From Studio to Stage

Becoming a patron or participant in the Washington creative community is as easy as picking up the telephone. Since the prestigious Kennedy Center opened in the mid-1960s, area theaters, symphonies, choruses, museums, and other arts organizations have flourished in the capital. Today, accomplished amateurs may share a stand with professional players in many local orchestras. Vocal ensembles welcome thousands of singers each year. More than 80 community theaters offer year-round performances with the help of area residents on and offstage. Community bands encourage musicians of all ages to tune up the old clarinet and join in concerts, tours, and special programs. Film aficionados view exclusive screenings at the city's film clubs. Visual artists can gather inspiration in Washington's 60 or so museums, then spotlight their own talent in local galleries, arts centers and leagues. Specialized organizations bring together those who focus on a particular medium.

Novice musicians, actors, and artists may develop their talents at a number of local arts centers, including Glen Echo Park, the Levine School of Music, the Art League, and the Capitol Hill Arts Workshop. And the Smithsonian Associate Program and other continuing education programs offer a number of innovative introductions to the arts.

Patrons of the arts are vital to Washington. Their energy and inventiveness contribute to a thriving community of professional arts organizations (profiled at the end of the chapter under "Fan Clubs"). Enthusiastic members often help to organize educational and community outreach projects, and they enjoy behind-the-scenes programs such as pre-performance galas, meet-the-artist receptions, and special invitations to dress rehearsals and exhibition openings.

This chapter vividly paints the creative scene in Washington for anyone interested in expanding his/her cultural horizons. The profiles here combined with the additional resources at the end of the chapter should be of assistance. Your involvement is limited only by your imagination.

For further information:
Consult the resources in *Education* for courses in the arts and humanities.
See *Parks, Recreation, and Community Centers* for courses in the arts and humanities, studio classes, performance opportunities, and dance programs offered at your local community center. Many centers also offer gallery exhibitions and performing arts programs artists at often surprisingly-low ticket prices.

Patrons of the arts will find additional opportunities for creative volunteering described under "Volunteering for the Arts" in *Volunteer.*

Media Alert! The *Washington Post* "Style" section and Friday Weekend provide information on current performances and programs. The *City Paper*, a free weekly distributed on Thursday afternoons to bookshops, restaurants, and businesses throughout the city, is also an important source of information on arts happenings.

Multidisciplinary Arts Organizations

Several of Washington's cultural institutions are so rich in diversity that they cannot be conveniently labelled. These organizations sponsor programs in more than one arts field, and offer classes, performances, and social events. These are often the centers that celebrate the interdisciplinary nature of the arts, and explore the constant exchange between the visual and performing arts and between the artist and the arts lover.

Arlington County Cultural Affairs Division
2700 South Lang Street
Arlington, VA 22206
703/358-6960 Office
703/358-6966 Arts Hotline

Arlington's Cultural Affairs Division coordinates: over 130 free summer concerts at the Lubber Run Amphitheatre, Crystal City Waterpark, Arlington Courthouse Plaza, Gateway Park, Bluemont Park and in many Arlington neighborhood parks; more than 300 performances annually at the Gunston Arts Center's two theatres, and over 100 at the Thomas Jefferson Theatre; master workshops and open studios in pottery, printmaking, and papermaking at the Lee Arts Center, and a mini-gallery that exhibits the artists' work; six annual visual arts exhibitions at the Ellipse Arts Center, and a film and chamber music series. The Gunston Arts Center also provides rehearsal space, dance studios, and set and costume shops for Arlington's 18 performing arts groups. The groups include community, professional, and children's theatre, dance, opera, Spanish and French language theatre, choral, symphonic, and barbershop music. The quarterly *Arlington Artsletter* provides arts information and a calendar of upcoming events. Call for a free introductory copy, or $5 for an annual subscription.

The Arts Club of Washington
2017 Eye Street, NW
Washington, DC 20006
202/331-7282

Behind one of the most beautiful doorways in Washington is the mansion that was once the residence of President James Monroe and is now the home of the Arts Club of Washington. Founded in 1916 to promote the arts in Washington, the club accepts members in the fields of architecture, dance, drama, industrial arts, literature, museology, music, painting and graphic arts, pictorial photography, and sculpture. The membership is comprised of both artists and art admirers, all of whom have access to the club's facilities and programs. The club features a continuing series of exhibitions in the gallery space of the Monroe House and the adjoining house at 2015 Eye Street. The club also hosts a regular noon-time concert series and co-sponsors the D.C. One Act Play Tournament each year with the D.C. Department of Recreation. Formal dinners on Thursday evenings are a favored tradition of the Arts Club. A presentation following the meal may include a play, light entertainment, or a general discussion of an arts topic. Many members use the club for private social functions. The Arts Club is affiliated with the Salmugundi Club and the National Arts Club in New York City. Annual dues begin at $300.

Athenaeum (Northern Virginia Fine Arts Association - NVFAA)
201 Prince Street
Alexandria, VA 22314
703/548-0035

In the course of its 140-year history, this Greek Revival building in Old Town Alexandria has served as a bank, a Union Army Commissary, a pharmaceutical storehouse, and a Methodist Church. Its present uses are almost as diverse, as the NVFAA presents art shows, dance classes, theatre productions, and a lecture series. Social events include exhibition openings, a Christmas party, fall and spring fundraisers, dances, and cocktail parties. The NVFAA's more than 900 members help produce these activities and volunteer in several capacities. Annual dues start at $15 for students and seniors, and entitle members to participate in all activities and events held by the NVFAA at the Athenaeum.

Capitol Hill Arts Workshop (CHAW)
545 7th Street, SE
Washington, DC 20003
202/547-6839

Every afternoon and evening the facilities at CHAW are filled with adults and children enjoying an array of arts programs. More than 25 classes for children and almost as many for adults offer dance (from New York jazz to ballet and swing), drama, studio arts, and private musical instruction. Studio classes feature pottery, sculpture, drawing, and watercolor.

District of Columbia Arts Center (DCAC)
2438 18th Street, NW
Washington, DC 20009
202/462-7833

"Taking risks is a serious thing—it's silly to be safe" claims one staff member at DCAC, a multi-disciplinary performing and visual arts center where formal theater, performance art, and exhibits by local and international artists constantly display the challenges and rewards of exploring the avant garde. Life drawing classes for beginners, programs for youth at risk, and process-oriented programs for established artists provide opportunities for all interested in non-traditional aspects of the arts. The only performing arts space in Adams Morgan, DCAC considers itself an "alternative space," and its 50-seat theater and 1100 square-foot gallery are in almost constant use. The center relies on the energy and contributions of its 400 members, who pay annual dues that start at $20.

Folklore Society of Greater Washington (FSGW)
c/o D. Nichols
307 Broadleaf Drive, NE
Vienna, VA 22180
703/281-2228

Music, song, dance, crafts, tales, and lore — in short, almost every aspect of folk culture — are brought to life by this exuberant, 2800-member society. The myriad programs include weekly contra, square, and international (Balkan, Israeli, Greek, etc.) dances, monthly open sings, Sacred Harp singing, Gospel sings, and other programs of music and lore. Special events feature concerts in members' homes, retreats, workshops, storytelling, and an annual Chesapeake Dance weekend. Two annual festivals bring together the various aspects of the Society and provide an ideal way to sample the diversity. A comprehensive newsletter provides descriptions of upcoming FSGW programs and a calendar of events scheduled throughout the metro area (including the activities of more than a dozen local pubs, clubs, and coffeehouses). Membership is $18 for individuals and $27 for a family.

Georgetown University
School for Summer and Continuing Education
Washington, DC 20057-1038
202/687-5942

Georgetown University's unique and innovative programs in the arts have included music, theater, and art appreciation classes such as The Culture and Art of Early Russia, Mozart's Bicentenary, and The Classics in Performance: From Page to Stage, a behind-the-scenes course which follows the local Shakespeare Theatre through rehearsal and performance. Acting, improvisation, and audition workshops, Theater Games, and Play Labs allow performers both new and experienced their chance at stardom. Singers of all levels may perform the leading roles in scenes from operas, operettas, and musicals at Georgetown's "Music Theater Workshop," and aspiring artists can draw, photograph, paint, and otherwise create at the University's studio arts program. As with most arts education courses, class fees range from $55 to $165. Call the number listed above for a course catalogue.

Glen Echo Park
7300 MacArthur Boulevard
Glen Echo, MD 20812
301/492-6282; 301/492-6229

Glen Echo Park began in 1891 as a local educational center, later became an Amusement Park, and today sponsors one of the largest cultural programs in the Washington area. The Park offers a comprehensive program in the studio and performing arts, including over 500 classes a year in ceramics, dance, drawing, glass, enamels, fibers, metals, music, painting, prints, photography, sculpture, T'ai Chi, theater, woodworks, and special workshops. Popular classes for beginners and the more practiced include Contra Dancing, Oil Painting, Portrait Sculpture, and Thursday Night Actors. Special workshops feature Gardening and Holiday Mask-Making. Classes and workshops, taught by accomplished artists and professionals, are generally scheduled on weekends and weekday evenings. Glen Echo Park also sponsors concerts, theater and dance performances, puppet shows, gallery exhibits, open artist studios, festivals, and special events. Call the number listed above for a course catalogue.

The Jewish Community Center of Greater Washington (JCC)
6125 Montrose Road
Rockville, MD 20852
301/881-0100

As presenter, producer, and educator, the JCC is among a handful of Washington institutions that offer performances and classes in virtually every facet of the arts. A special sense of community prevails here, where almost a dozen different performance series offer programs in dance, theater, and music. The School for Performing and Visual Arts enrolls over 2000 students of all ages and skill levels. Cartooning, calligraphy, and Mazzuzah case making are among the unusual offerings in a catalogue that also includes all forms of drama, dance, music, and the fine arts.

Performance Plus
The Kennedy Center
Washington, DC 20566-0001
202/416-8811

Go backstage and beyond with adventures in lifetime learning and the performing arts. Performance Plus offers discussions, demonstrations, lectures, and courses with creators, performers, directors, and noted authorities in the arts. These events are listed in the *Kennedy Center News Magazine*, or for a complete listing call the number listed above.

Smithsonian Institution Associate Program (Resident)
1100 Jefferson Drive, SW
Washington, DC 20560
202/357-3030

This nationally-renowned program offers an astounding array of performing arts events, film screenings, studio arts classes, and lectures, seminars, and tours related to the arts. The Smithsonian's Campus on the Mall includes courses and forums in art and architecture, the performing arts, and other special topics. See *Education*.

Strathmore Hall
10701 Rockville Pike
North Bethesda, MD 20852
301/530-0540

The bustle of Rockville Pike seems part of another world once one enters the quiet elegance of Strathmore Hall, a turn-of-the-century mansion that is now Montgomery County's cultural arts center. Concerts, lectures, art exhibitions, tea musicales, literary lunches, and special events draw artists and audiences from the entire metropolitan area. The 300 members of Strathmore receive discounts, advance ticket sales, invitations to special events, and the *Strathmore Muse-letter*. Volunteers staff the information desk and provide production support for concerts and other events. New Professionals For Strathmore meets bi-monthly for networking and helping with Strathmore events.

Music

Music is a common tongue for many in this international city, which has one of the highest concentrations of orchestras and choruses in the nation. This means that for all who have some talent and enthusiasm, there is a place to play an instrument or lend a voice. Washington is also becoming known as a chamber music center and several organizations are helping to coordinate the ensemble playing of avocational musicians. Community bands perform year-round, and a number of unusual ensembles offer a chance to try your hand at the balalaika or the koto. Music lovers who want to participate without drawing a breath or a bow should consult the possibilities under "The Fan Clubs" at the end of the chapter.

Media Alert!

Those interested in rock, jazz, and popular music will do best to keep an eye on the *City Paper* for advertisements by bands needing players and players needing bands. Also, several clubs in the area sponsor "open mike" nights, and these are great opportunities to meet your fellow musicians.

In addition, one of the area's centers for music, instruments, and information is Dales's Music at 8240 Georgia Avenue in Silver Spring (301/589-1459). They not only have the area's largest selection of sheet music, but also a knowledgeable and helpful staff and terrific bulletin boards.

Music Societies and Organizations

The following organizations range from small, specialized societies to large community programs, but almost all of them welcome beginners and advanced players, and include both instruction and performance opportunities in several musical genres from classical to contemporary. Jam with a jazz club, join an ad hoc chamber music ensemble, or perform your rendition of Für Elise before an audience of fellow learners. These organizations also offer innovative workshops, theory and masterclasses, community outreach programs, and a host of other special events. Never be afraid to ask about the level of playing, and if in doubt, go listen to a performance, a rehearsal, or a meeting.

Adult Music Student Forum (AMSF)
15408 Hannans Way
Rockville, MD 20853
301/929-1885

Most beginning music students are children, but for those enterprising souls who begin the adventure in adulthood, the AMSF offers performance opportunities, special events, lectures, a newsletter, and a chance to share the joys and struggles with other novice players. Informal recitals in members' homes serve as an introduction to performance, and formal recitals at Annunciation Catholic Church provide a public forum. Professional musicians and instructors offer lectures focusing on topics that have included "Emotions in Performance" and "The Art of Practicing." The membership fee is $25 and there is a small additional charge for lectures.

Friday Morning Music Club
7012 Partridge Place
Hyattsville, MD 20782
202/333-2075

One of the oldest clubs of its kind in the country, the Friday Morning Music Club was founded in 1886 "to promote musical culture among its members and in the community." The club's 800 members include associate members, who are non-performing music lovers, as well as performance members, who are auditioned singers, instrumentalists, composers, and conductors. These members perform in the Club's Friday noon-time concerts held in the Sumner School Museum at 17th and M Streets in Washington, D.C. Other concerts are scheduled on a regular basis at the Strathmore Hall Arts Center in Rockville and the Chevy Chase United Methodist Church in the District. The Club sponsors its own chorale and orchestra, and encourages members to form chamber ensembles. Associate members may also perform in private performances, and professional coaching is offered for piano, chamber, and vocal music in members' homes. The Club also sponsors community outreach programs, which have included the Washington International Competition, Concerts in Schools, Music for Shut-ins. All concerts are free and open to the public. Membership fees are $37.

George Washington University Chamber Music Registry Program
Department of Music
B-144 Academic Center
Washington, DC 20052
202/994-6245

Are you a violist in search of a string quartet? Or a harpist looking for a flutist? A singer pining for a pianist? If so, this consortium of chamber musicians can help put you in contact with your colleagues. Instrumentalists and vocalists of all levels are welcome to join the registry program, and you need not be a member of the George Washington University community to join. In addition to placing musicians in appropriate ensembles, the program provides monthly coaching sessions and a directory of local chamber musicians. There is a nominal registration fee, and an additional charge for coaching.

Levine School of Music
1690 36th Street, NW
Washington, DC 20007
202/337-2227

This community music school does everything possible to bring music into the lives of busy Washingtonians. In addition to lessons in all instruments and voice, classes in music theory and history, and opera workshops, the school offers several innovative programs. Drop In! classes require no long-term commitment or registration fee, and include African American Vocal Traditions with Sweet Honey in the Rock, Choral Sing-ins, Community Voice, and Chamber Music Weekends. Try It! classes, with no charge for the first class, include Tap Dance, Sightreading for Singers, and Voice Class. Registered adult students can play, sing, or listen with other students at Friday Nighters, informal gatherings with potluck munchies held every six weeks. The school has over 2000 students of all ages, with a number of family-oriented programs that include both young students and their parents. A Professional Studies program has recently been developed to train teachers in piano pedagogy and early childhood music.

Montgomery County Chamber Music Society
1206 Floral Street, NW
Washington, DC 20012
202/726-0392

Amateur musicians who enjoy playing with other instrumentalists and wish to sharpen their sight-reading skills will want to know about this organization, which has fostered community chamber music for more than 20 years. Members meet weekly at Montgomery College in Rockville and participate in two "ad hoc" ensembles during the evening. More regular rehearsals are held for ensembles planning to perform in retirement communities, nursing homes, and for private parties. An extensive music library is constantly expanding, thanks to the nominal dues paid three times a year.

Potomac River Jazz Club
3608 35th Street, NW
Washington, DC 20016
703/698-PRJC (7752)

The 1500 members of this club are devoted to preserving and encouraging jazz, including the New Orleans, Dixieland, and Chicago jazz styles as well as Ragtime and Blues. A monthly open jam session in Falls Church gives all attendees a chance to play. At the club's concert/dances, club members perform and dance to the tunes of Armstrong, Morton, Beiderbeck, and other jazz greats. The club also helps to publicize the events sponsored by the two dozen jazz bands in the area. There are club members of all ages, but almost half of the fans are in their 60s. The club's newsletter is full of information on local events and personalities. Annual dues start at $20.

The Washington Balalaika Society
400 Madison Street, #2103
Alexandria, VA 22314
703/549-2010

Members of this group share a common enthusiasm for the folk music of Russia, Ukraine, and Eastern Europe. The heart of the Society is a 20 member Russian Folk Orchestra utilizing traditional instruments which include the balalaika, the domra (a type of mandolin) and bayan (button accordion). Most of the members started out playing the violin, piano, guitar, or mandolin and progressed to the more exotic instruments. Experienced teachers train novices of this music genre, and within a short time you can be one of the performing ensemble. Experienced bass, oboe, and percussionists, vocalists and dancers are sought after. Weekly rehearsals are in McLean, and concerts are given throughout the year. Non-musicians are welcome as members. Annual dues are $15.

The Washington Conservatory of Music
P.O. Box 5758
5144 Massachusetts Ave. NW
Washington, D.C. 20016
301/320-2770

A number of National Symphony Orchestra members and other professional musicians are on the stellar faculty of the Washington Conservatory. In addition to private lessons, there are ensembles, classes, and workshops for all ages.

Washington Recorder Society
5510 Oakmont Avenue
Bethesda, MD 20817
301/530-6386

The Washington Recorder Society brings together 100 recorder enthusiasts twice a month for group practice sessions at the Chevy Chase Presbyterian Church. Once a month the session is preceded by a half-hour concert performed by music specialists who play the recorder, viol da gamba, krumhorn, sackbut, percussion, and other instruments. Alternate meetings are preceded by a social hour. Special workshops offer technical instruction, and a joint workshop with the Washington Viola da Gamba Society provides a chance to play in mixed consorts.

Washington Toho Koto Society, Inc.
10230 Green Forest Drive
Silver Spring, MD 20903
301/434-4487

The long, narrow stringed instrument known as the koto is one of Japan's most eloquent instruments, and its music ranges from traditional to contemporary. About 60 koto players are part of the Washington Toho Koto Society, which has participated in the opening ceremonies of the National Cherry Blossom Festival for a decade, and has played at the Japanese embassy at the request of the Emperor and Empress of Japan. The kimono-robed musicians at the annual spring concert are a diverse international group, proving that you do not need to be a native of Japan to master the instrument.

Choral Ensembles

No matter what your musical interest—classical, jazz, pop, ethnic, or folk—if you can carry a tune, there is an ensemble in Washington that can offer you a chance to sing outside the shower. While musicianship requirements vary from group to group, most ensembles are interested primarily in the sound and blending possibilities of your voice (you do not have to be a soloist!), and in your ability to learn music accurately. Sight-reading is a definite plus (and in some cases a requirement), but a good ear is perhaps your best asset. Most ensembles audition prospective members at the beginning of September, though many also audition in January and on an ongoing basis. Potential Lucianos, Placidos and Josés please note: conductors are always searching for tenors! The following ensembles are among the best known in Washington; prospective singers, however, should not neglect to consult the local choruses to be found in the lists below.

Cantate
5808 Valerian Lane
Rockville, MD 20852
301/330-4156

This highly selective chorus of 40 voices performs not only in Washington, but has taken its broad repertoire of American music, choral jazz, and sacred and secular music to audiences in Europe. Founded in 1985 by conductor Phyllis Isaacson, the chorus rehearses weekly on Wednesday evenings in Bethesda. The six annual concerts (two each in December, February, and May) are held at Bradley Hills Presbyterian Church and in other locales including Georgetown University's Gaston Hall. In addition, "runout" concerts are performed throughout the year by special request. Auditions are held on an ongoing basis, though most are scheduled in August and September. Members pay annual dues of $30 and purchase their music and concert attire.

Cathedral Choral Society

Washington Cathedral
Wisconsin & Massachusetts Avenues, NW
Washington, DC 20016
202/537-5527

Like the glorious Gothic cathedral where it rehearses and performs, this 200-voice chorus is virtually a Washington institution. The Society held its first rehearsal in 1941 only one week after the attack on Pearl Harbor, and featured its first performance, Verdi's Requiem, the following spring. Today, rehearsals for the Society's four annual concerts are scheduled on Monday evenings from September through May under the direction of conductor J. Reilly Lewis. In addition to its regular concerts, the Chorus participates in a number of outreach programs which include performances with the D.C. Youth Orchestra. During the summer, a non-auditioned ensemble of 80 voices rehearses and performs American music with choir members from the District's inner-city churches. The Cathedral Choral Society is one of the most social of Washington ensembles; in addition to the customary post-rehearsal adjournment to a nearby restaurant, the Society features fundraisers, theater parties, a walk-a-thon, and an annual benefit. Members pay annual dues of $35 and purchase their own music; choir robes are lent by the Society. With nearly 100 volunteers and an active Women's Board, the Cathedral also offers many opportunities for non-vocal participation. (See *Volunteer*).

Choral Arts Society of Washington

4321 Wisconsin Avenue, NW
Washington, DC 20016
202/244-3669

If you have longed to add your voice to the final chorus of Beethoven's Ninth Symphony, there may be no better opportunity than with the 180-member Choral Arts Society. Founded in 1965, today this symphonic chorus presents its annual four-concert season in the Kennedy Center Concert Hall, and joins the National Symphony Orchestra for additional performances. Directed by Norman Scribner, the ensemble presents masterpieces of choral literature and well as occasional world premieres. Weekly rehearsals are held on Tuesday evenings at St. Alban's Episcopal Church on Wisconsin Avenue. A small chamber group, Singers for All Seasons, performs monthly programs at locations such as local retirement and nursing homes. Chorus members purchase their own music and rent their concert attire. Auditions are held in late August and early September.

Choral Society of the World Bank

1818 H Street, NW
Washington, DC 20433
202/473-1584

Though sponsored by the World Bank and the International Monetary Fund, this international chorus is open to all singers who are able to attend the Tuesday lunchtime rehearsals. The 40 members rehearse at both the World Bank and the IMF, and perform Christmas and Spring concerts in both locations. Though the repertoire is mainly classical, there is also an attempt to present the music of varied cultures. Departures from standard choral music have included excerpts from *Die Fledermaus* and staged productions of Gilbert and Sullivan operettas. Outreach programs have been offered at Children's Hospital, the Veterans Administration Hospital, and local nursing homes.

Nevilla Otteley Singers
409 Rittenhouse Street, NW
Washington, DC 20011
301/589-4049

This enterprising ensemble, often joined by the Takoma Park Symphony Orchestra, explores the music of minority composers in addition to a standard repertoire. Since conductor Nevilla Otteley founded the group in 1981, she has led the Singers in concerts throughout the metropolitan area, as well as touring the Midwest and Barbados for a performance of Scott Joplin's opera Treemonisha. The 45 members rehearse weekly on Monday evenings for six annual concerts. There is a $50 membership fee, and auditions are held in the fall, January, and April.

Oratorio Society of Washington
1690 36th Street, NW
Washington, DC 20007
202/342-6221

In addition to its own subscription concerts at the Kennedy Center, this 180-voice chorus frequently appears with the National Symphony Orchestra. Conductor Robert Shafer leads the chorus in traditional and contemporary repertoire, and prepares the ensemble for performances led by many of the world's greatest conductors, including Sir Neville Marriner, Seiji Ozawa, Mstislav Rostropovich, Charles Dutoit, and Zdenek Macal. Rehearsals are held on Monday evenings at St. Ann's Church at Tenley Circle in the District. Members of the chorus participate in the Society's community outreach program which presents free concerts to groups with special needs. Members pay annual dues of $60 (music included) and provide their own concert attire.

The Paul Hill Chorale
5630 Connecticut Avenue, NW Suite 200
Washington, DC 20015
202/364-4321

This 150-voice chorus is one of the major Washington choral ensembles. The regular season concerts of choral masterpieces at the Kennedy Center are led by Paul Hill. In the years since its founding in 1967, the Chorale has performed many times with the National Symphony Orchestra under an impressive list of international conductors. The Chorale also has a professional chamber ensemble that performs under the name The Washington Singers.

Other choral ensembles to consider:

DISTRICT OF COLUMBIA:

Capitol Hill Choral Society
Riverside Church
680 I Street, SW
Washington, DC 20024
301/320-4192

25 member chamber ensemble; classical, contemporary

Friday Morning Music Club Chorale
8934 Bradmoor Drive
Bethesda, MD 20817
301/530-8583

45 members; classical and contemporary

Gay Men's Chorus of Washington
P.O. Box 57043
Washington, DC 20037
202/338-7464

140 members; classical, Gospel, Spiritual, religious, contemporary

Lesbian and Gay Chorus of Washington, DC
P.O. Box 65285
Washington, DC 20035
202/546-1549

3 annual concerts; variety of music from classical to contemporary

Moyé Ensemble
5243 Kenstan Drive
Camp Springs, MD 20748
301/449-4065

35 members; religious, gospel, spiritual, contemporary; rehearse in Southeast's Liberty Baptist Church

MARYLAND:

Bethesda Chamber Singers
9314 Edmonston Road, 203
Greenbelt, MD 20770
301/587-5756
16 members; classical, religious, contemporary

Bowie Sounds of Music
13319 Yarland Lane
Bowie, MD 20715
301/262-5471

17 women's voices; patriotic, easy listening, religious

New Century Singers
The Colonnade, Suite 1213
2801 New Mexico Avenue, NW
Washington, DC 20007
202/298-7526

40 members; American music

Thomas Circle Singers
1226 Vermont Avenue, NW
Washington, DC 20005
202/546-7282

32 members; classical, contemporary

Washington Men's Camerata
2828 Connecticut Avenue, NW Suite 908
Washington, DC 20008
202/265-8804

48 members; classical music for men's choruses

The Washington Revels Chorus
P.O. Box 39077
Washington, DC 20016
202/364-8744

Annual Christmas Revels; May Day Street Fair celebrations.

Washington Saengerbund
2434 Wisconsin Avenue, NW
Washington, DC 20007
202/585-7383

140 members; classical, German folk, contemporary

Cantigas Chorale
Church of Our Lady of Lourdes
7500 Pearl Street
Bethesda, MD 20814
301/718-0507

30 members; classical music of Latin America and Spain

Chesapeake Chorale
P.O. Box 1037
Bowie, MD 20718
301/262-5911

60 members; classical repertoire

MARYLAND, continued

Circle Singers
P.O. Box 30708
Bethesda, MD 20814
301/229-7768

20 members; choral chamber music

Con Viva Musica
P.O. Box 496
Bowie, MD 20715
301/390-0746

15 members; classical, jazz, showtunes

Harmony Express
210 Randolph Road
Silver Spring, MD 20904
301/622-3574

Close harmony for women's voices; show tunes, popular music of the 1920's and 30's

Heart of Maryland Chorus
Sweet Adelines International
11021 Marcliff Road
Rockville, MD 20852
301/230-1444

50 women's voices; barbershop harmony, programs are choreographed.

The Knights of Harmony
S.P.E.B.S.Q.S.A.
3304 Saville Lane
Bowie, MD 20721
301/577-3679

Men's voices; barbershop harmony

Laurel Oratorio Society
P.O. Box 696
Laurel, MD 20725
301/498-4254

75 members; classical and contemporary

Maryland Choral Society
P.O. Box 902
Clinton, MD 20735-0902
301/961-7131

90 members; classical, lighter repertoire, American music

Masterworks Chorus and Orchestra
P.O. Box 677
Bethesda, MD 20827
301/365-2855

100 members; classical

Musikanten
P.O. Box 34855
Bethesda, MD 20817
301/530-9596

20 members; all kind of music

New Dimension Singers
2827 Calverton Boulevard
Silver Spring, MD 20904
301/572-7364

18 women's voices; showtunes, blues, ballads, fully choreographed

Polyhymnia
c/o Jim Klumpner
506 Deerfield Avenue
Silver Spring, MD 20910
301/565-0314

17 members; varied classical programs

Prince George's Choral Society
6611 Kenilworth Avenue, Suite 215
Riverdale, MD 20737
301/454-1463

50 members; classical, religious, contemporary, jazz, blues

Senior Citizen's Sitdown Choir
P.O. Box 4416
Ockford Lane
Bowie, MD 20715
301/262-0193

20 members; all kinds of music except rock

Singing Capital Chorus/Barbershop Harmony Society
4516 38th Street, NW
Washington, DC 20016
301/770-4443

65 members; barbershop Harmony

University of Maryland Chorus
2140 Tawes Fine Arts Building
University of Maryland
College Park, MD 20742
Dr. Paul Traver, Director
301/405-5570

125 members (auditioned); classical; performances in Baltimore/Washington area with orchestra

VIRGINIA:

Alexandria Choral Society
P.O. Box 406
Alexandria, VA 22313
301/530-9596

45 members; classical, American, chamber ensemble drawn from membership

Alexandria Harmonizers/Barbershop Chorus & Quartets
P.O. Box 11274
Alexandria, VA 22312
703/836-0969

125 member men's chorus; all types of music in barbershop quartet

Alexandria Singers
P.O. Box 6151
Alexandria, VA 22306
703/941-7464

100 member mixed chorus; show tunes and contemporary music

Arlington Metropolitan Chorus
2700 South Lang Street
Arlington, VA 22206
703/836-4822

100 members; classical, American composers

Arlingtones
2449 North Harrison Street
Arlington, VA 22207
703/536-2025 (hotline)

52 members; barbershop style chorus (9 quartets are part of the group)

Fairfax Choral Society
4028 Hummer Road
Annandale, VA 22003
703/642-0862

85 members; classical, religious, contemporary

Fairfax Choral Society Chorale
4028 Hummer Road
Annandale, VA 22003
703/642-0862

24 members; jazz, classical, religious, showtunes

Fairfax Jubil-aires
4829 Powell Road
Fairfax, VA 22032
703/503-9438

George Chelena Chorale
2826 Kelly Square
Vienna, VA 22181
703/281-1215

A capella mixed chorale; big band music

McLean Choral Society
P.O. Box 6614
McLean, VA 22106
703/356-7464

100 members; classical, religious, American

New Dominion Chorale
P.O. Box 6691
McLean, VA 22106
703/442-9404

150 members; performs choral classics

Potomac Harmony Chorus of Sweet Adelines, Inc.
2700 South Lang Street
Arlington, VA 22206
703/764-3896

76 members, women's barbershop harmony

Reston Chorale
2310 Colts Neck Road
Reston, VA 22091
703/742-9194

120 members; classical to contemporary

Vienna Choral Society
541 Marshall Road
Vienna, VA 22180

4 annual concerts; classical to Broadway show tunes

Vienna-Falls Chorus Chapter
of Sweet Adelines, Inc.
10000 Mosby Road
Fairfax, VA 22032
703/273-9059

125 members; Barbershop harmony for women's voices

Voce
1559 Inlet Court
Reston, VA 22090
703/435-3006

26 singers; smaller ensembles of 4-6; repertoire spans Renaissance to 20th-century music; performances in Reston

Orchestras

The professional level of performance by Washington orchestras is accomplished with primarily amateur musicians. Some of the members in the following groups are paid, but most of the orchestras are composed of dedicated volunteers who love to make music. Rehearsals take place evenings and weekends, enabling those who must work in  other fields a chance to share their musical gifts. Prospective players should attend a few concerts for an objective impression of the repertoire and level of playing. String players are especially sought by area ensembles. Auditions are often held on an on-going basis by arrangement with the conductor. Local orchestras often have active volunteer guilds that sponsor educational and community outreach programs; professional orchestras in the Washington area feature membership organizations that assist in a variety of musical, social, and fundraising activities — see "The Fan Clubs," at the end of the chapter.

DISTRICT OF COLUMBIA

Georgetown Symphony Orchestra
P.O. Box 2284
Hoya Station
Washington, DC 20057
703/866-7106

Professional musicians, semi-pros, dedicated students, and advanced amateur musicians comprise this ensemble, which has performed in Georgetown University's historic Gaston Hall since 1967. Four subscription concerts show imaginative programming of standard orchestral repertoire, and special concerts are presented for students, young people, and senior citizens.

Washington Civic Symphony
1000 16th Street, NW, Suite 505
Washington, DC 20036
202/857-0970

For more than 60 years this volunteer symphony orchestra has been serving the nation's capital. The ensemble prides itself on providing music of the highest quality to music lovers of all economic levels; performances featuring international guest artists are held in the D.A.R. Constitution Hall and free seats are available at every performance. Interested musicians should call conductor Martin Piecuch at 703/765-3701.

MARYLAND

The Jewish Community Center Symphony Orchestra
6125 Montrose Road
Rockville, MD 20852
301/881-0100, ext. 6740

The oldest community orchestra in the area, the JCC Symphony Orchestra presents five concerts each year as well as two celebrated annual children's concerts. The 60 members currently span a 60-year age range, from 15 to 75. This orchestra is perhaps the best place for a volunteer musician to share a stage with the greats: guest artists have included cellist Yo Yo Ma and violinist Daniel Heifitz, and the ensemble has played at the Kennedy Center, Wolf Trap, and for the "Today" show.

The Prince George's Philharmonic Orchestra
P.O. Box 1111
Riverdale, MD 20737
301/454-1462

All of the 85 players in this ensemble are volunteers, but some players are professional musicians and the season of six concerts could easily be that of a professional orchestra. Concerts under conductor Ray Fowler are performed at Northwestern High School and Prince George's Community College. The orchestra presents standard orchestral repertoire with such highly regarded guest soloists as cellist Stephen Kates and pianist Brian Ganz. An active volunteer guild assists with fundraising, production, and benefits.

Takoma Park Symphony Orchestra
8201 Roanoke Avenue
Takoma Park, MD 20912
301/585-4221

Open to "advanced avocational musicians" and professionals, this 70-member orchestra was founded in 1989 under the direction of Nevilla Otteley. The Orchestra performs six annual concerts and a traditional Messiah sing-along. In addition to the major symphonic literature, the Orchestra emphasizes the music of local composers, women, American, and Black composers of all countries. Rehearsals are held on Tuesday evenings for programs performed throughout Prince George's and Montgomery Counties. Auditions are scheduled during the last week of August and by appointment on an ongoing basis (and string players are always especially welcome!).

VIRGINIA
Arlington Symphony
933 North Glebe Road
Arlington, VA 22203
703/528-1817

This symphony is under the direction of former Bolshoi Opera Conductor Ruben Vartanyan. For forty nine years this group of 75 professional and semi-professional musicians have been performing to a large following. A six concert series is planned, including a "Pops" event at Ballston Common.

McLean Orchestra
P.O. Box 760
McLean, VA 22101
703/893-8646

The repertoire of this 87-member, community-based orchestra spans the classics, opera, and popular favorites. Composed of professional musicians and renowned guest artists who range from high-school students to seniors, the orchestra is led by Colonel Arnold D. Gabriel. Orchestra members, patrons, and volunteers have ample opportunity to socialize at benefit dinners, private home concerts, an annual Valentine tea dance and silent auction, and the events of its active Volunteer Guild. A nine-month educational music program offers string players, ages 10 to 17, instruction and performing opportunities with the 55-member Youth Ensemble. Auditions for the McLean Orchestra are scheduled in August and by special arrangement throughout the year.

McLean Symphony
1350 Beverly Road #115-172
McLean, VA 22101
703/448-8088

This orchestra has had three names during its 20-year history, though it has enjoyed the uninterrupted direction of its current conductor, Dingwall Fleary. The 70-member, all-volunteer ensemble performs four concerts each season at McLean's Arden Theater, while a small contingent of players offers a number of programs for chamber orchestra. The symphony is active in community outreach through concerts in retirement centers and nursing homes, and through an apprenticeship program that enables gifted students to rehearse and perform with the orchestra.

Prince William Symphony Orchestra
P.O. Box 2768
Woodbridge, VA 22193
703/680-3344

Community and educational outreach are among the priorities of this orchestra and its principal conductor, Joel Revzen. The ensemble's 54 members are professional musicians. The Orchestra's five concerts present rising young soloists and the standard orchestral repertoire at Christ Chapel in Woodbridge. The Prince William Symphony Orchestra Associates program offers anyone who can "write a press release, type, catalogue music, stuff envelopes, or organize parties" many ways to contribute to the life of the orchestra. Membership begins at $10.

Community Bands

Of all the horn-blowing in this city, the most euphonious is that being performed by local bands. These convivial ensembles draw on all ages, and take their music to many segments of their communities. Most, but not all, audition prospective members. The City of Fairfax Band is a leader in the area (and highly regarded across the country); the other organizations listed below offer similar programs.

City of Fairfax Band
City of Fairfax Department of Parks and Recreation
John C. Wood Municipal Complex 3730 Old Lee Highway
Fairfax, VA 22030
703/385-7858; 703/759-2903

This ensemble of more than 90 players presents more than 20 concerts year-round. Fall, winter, and spring programs take place at Fairfax High School, and weekly summer "Concerts in the Park" fill the City Hall Amphitheater. The repertoire ranges from popular favorites to opera excerpts, and the band has participated in such special events as WMAL Radio's "Christmas at the Kennedy Center." The all-volunteer performers range from university students to seniors, and they rehearse on Wednesdays at Fairfax High School. Small ensembles drawn from the band's membership include a brass ensemble, a Dixieland Band, and the "Alte Kameraden" German Band, which performs the music of Bavaria. Band members pay annual dues of $10.

MARYLAND

Columbia Wind Orchestra
Columbia Union College
Takoma Park, MD 20912
301/585-8317

42-member symphonic wind ensemble; 4 concerts, September to April

The Greenbelt Concert Band of Prince George's County
8405 Margo Road
Lanham, MD 20706
301/552-1444

45-85 members; 20 concerts a year

National Concert Band of America
P.O. Box 10363
Oxon Hill, MD 20745
202/965-1352

Retired armed services musicians

The New Carrollton Band Association
New Carrollton Municipal Building
6016 Princess Garden Parkway
New Carollton, MD 20784
301/577-6426

2 indoor concerts (winter); 6 outdoor concerts (summer)

The Rockville Concert Band
1915 Locust Grove Road
Silver Spring, MD 20910
301/585-8317

65 members; 16 concerts annually (European tour in July of 1994)

VIRGINIA

The Alexandria Citizen's Band
P.O. Box 16861
Alexandria, VA 22302
703/765-8141

50 members; no auditions; Big Band group of 17; 6 summer concerts; over six other concerts at civic events and nursing homes

The Vienna Community Band
1636 Bennington Hollow Lane
Reston, VA 22094
703/787-6828

45 members; 6 to 8 concerts, no formal auditions

The Falls Church Concert Band
1582 Forest Villa Lane
McLean, VA 22101
703/827-9128

25-30 members of all ages; no auditions; monthly concerts at retirement and nursing homes and civic events

Theater

"All the world's a stage" and area residents can choose from more than 80 area theater companies to laugh, cry, and sing with. The range of repertoire and performing  space is vast, but the level of commitment and enthusiasm is common to all. The theater has something for everyone. Singles will meet fellow theater lovers; families can find special productions designed for young people. If you would rather avoid the limelight, backstage crews can always use helping building sets, painting, sewing costumes or selling tickets. We are able to profile only a few of area theater companies, but the following groups will be more than happy to furnish the prospective thespians with further information.

ACTORS' RESOURCES:
Northern Virginia Theater Alliance
2700 South Lang Street
Arlington, VA 22206
703/256-7206

Over 30 community theaters belong to this association, which publishes a useful fact sheet with information on productions, auditions, and performances, as well as a calendar with maps to local theaters.

The Actors' Center
P.O. Box 50180
Washington, DC 20091
202/638-3777

The Actors' Center provides over 600 professional and non-professional actors with access to information concerning all aspects of Washington's theatrical community. A private, non-profit organization operated by members and volunteers, the Center features a hot line with information on auditions, events, and services. The Center also publishes a monthly newsletter and provides a photo/resume file of members for directors and casting agents. Auditions for out-of-town theaters, an annual general audition for local directors, scene nights, and showcase presentations allow members to perform for professional directors and invited audiences. Weekly Saturday morning open houses at the Center's offices bring members together for informal discussions, play readings, and workshops. The membership fee is $45 per year.

The Theatre Lab
202/588-8113

Dedicated to providing affordable services for actors and acting students in the DC area, the Theatre Lab offers classes for beginning through advanced actors in improvisation, scene study, musical theater, audition technique, voice and movement - all taught by professional actors and directors. Professional services include private audition coaching, musical audition coaching and accompaniment, theatrical resume services and head shots.

Adventure Theater

Glen Echo Park
7300 MacArthur Boulevard
Glen Echo, MD 20812
301/320-5331

Adventure Theater offers myriad opportunities for anyone interested in the imaginative world of children's theater. Amateur actors are welcome to audition for the eight annual productions at Glen Echo Park, and behind-the-scenes jobs are seemingly endless. In addition to the regular season productions, Adventure Theater offers in-school productions, theatre arts classes for adults and children, and summer workshops.

Little Theater of Alexandria

600 North Wolfe Street
Alexandria, VA 22314
703/683-5778

This company — one of Washington's most senior and most active — produces seven shows each season in Old Town, Alexandria. Founded in 1934, the Little Theater offers comedy, drama, and musicals, and annually sponsors a national competition for a one-act play that is produced during the regular season. The Little Theater also offers acting, directing, playwriting, voice, dance, and children's classes. Entirely self-supporting, the theater has 800 members and 1,750 subscribers.

St. Mark's Players

Baxter House
118 Third Street, SE
Washington, DC 20003
202/237-9272

More than 300 people participate in the three annual productions of this theatrical ensemble, which provides a lively forum for amateur involvement in all aspects of theater arts. Families are especially welcome and the fall production is usually geared toward young people. St. Mark's Episcopal Church on Capitol Hill provides the rehearsal and performance space, though performances are also given at other locales such as the Children's Hospital. Participants need not be affiliated with the church.

Seasoned Players

1303 Madison Street
Chillum, MD 20872
301/559-4263

This lively group of senior citizens (aged 55 to 85) welcomes enthusiastic dancers and singers. The players perform at the Publix Playhouse in Cheverly and at the Queen Anne Auditorium on the campus of Prince George's Community College. They also perform throughout the year at nursing and convalescent homes, the County's Summer-In-The-Park Program, and at Senior Complexes and Centers.

More Community Theater Groups:

DISTRICT OF COLUMBIA

The British Embassy Players
The British Embassy
3100 Massachusetts Avenue, NW
Washington, DC 20008
703/271-0172

4 productions (some musicals); British
Embassy Rotunda

Capitol Hill Arts Workshop
545 7th Street, SE
Washington, DC 20003
202/547-6839

Instruction in visual arts, drama,
movement, and music for children and
adults; exhibits (see Capitol Hill Art
League); performances, including
community theatre, children's theatre,
faculty work, Summer Dance Festival, and
Capital Hill Chorale

Chevy Chase Players
P.O. Box 42368
Washington, DC 20015
202/328-1961

3 productions; Chevy Chase Community
Center

Foundry Players
Foundry United Methodist Church
1500 16th Street, NW
Washington, DC 20036
202/332-3454

3 productions; Foundry United Methodist
Church

Hexagon
P.O. Box 7519
Washington, DC 20013-5196
703/876-1880

1 production to benefit a different charity
each March; Duke Ellington School for the
Arts (Georgetown)

Trinity Players, Inc.
3513 N Street, NW
Washington, DC 20007
202/965-4680

4 productions (some musicals); Trinity
Theatre (Georgetown)

Washington Savoyards, Ltd.
P.O. Box 34584
Bethesda, MD 20827
703/323-7979

2 productions of Gilbert and Sullivan
operettas; Duke Ellington School for the
Arts (Georgetown)

Washington Shakespeare Company
2700 South Lang Street
Arlington, VA 22206
703/739-9886

5 or more productions of Shakespearean
and classical plays

Washington Storytellers Theater
P.O. Box 5564
Washington, DC 20016
202/625-6496

Storytelling workshops; performances

MARYLAND

Bowie Community Theatre
P.O. Box 604
Bowie, MD 20718
301/464-3088
4 productions; Theatre in the Woods
(Bowie)

Greenbelt Players
P.O. Box 293
Greenbelt, MD 20768-0293
301/441-8770

5 productions & special events at various
sites; children's programs

Hallam Players
Prince George's Community College
301 Largo Road
Largo, MD 20770
301/322-0920

6 productions (some musicals); Prince
George's Community College

Maryland, continued

Montgomery Playhouse
P.O. Box 3490
Gaithersburg, MD 20885
301/977-5751

8 productions (1 musical); Montgomery
Playhouse

Potomac Community Theatre
P.O. Box 59336
Potomac, MD 20859-93364
301/299-6803

4 productions (some musicals) annually,
and Children's Summer Theatre Camp

Prince George's Little Theatre
6016 Princess Garden Parkway
New Carollton, MD 20784
301/577-0357

4 productions (some musicals); Prince
George's Publick Playhouse

Rockville Little Theater
P.O. Box 4466
Rockville, MD 20850
301/340-1417
3 productions (drama, mystery, comedy); F.
Scott Fitzgerald Theatre (Rockville)

Rockville Musical Theatre
P.O. Box 1423
Rockville, MD 20850
301/868-2870

2 productions (musicals); F. Scott Fitzgerald
Theatre (Rockville)

Rosebud Musical Theater Co.
8301 Princess Garden Parkway
New Carrollton, MD 20784
301/982-4812

1 production at various locations

The Side Door Coffee House
Riverdale Presbyterian Church
6513 Queens Chapel Road
University Park, MD 20782
301/927-0477

6 productions; Riverdale Presbyterian
Church

S.T.A.R. Improv Co.
Sylvia Toone Actors Repertory
5520 Oakmont Avenue
Bethesda, MD 20817
301/571-9512

Improvisation workshops

Victorian Lyric Opera Company
P.O. Box 10391
Rockville, MD 20849
301/585-9435

2 productions of Gilbert and Sullivan
operettas; F. Scott Fitzgerald Theater
(Rockville)

VIRGINIA

The Arlington Players
2700 South Lang Street
Arlington, VA 22206
703/549-1063

3 productions (2 musicals); Thomas
Jefferson Community Theater

Ayr Hill Players
Vienna Presbyterian Church
124 Park Street, NE
Vienna, VA 22180
703/560-4884

2 productions; Vienna Presbyterian Church

**The Blue Ridge Alliance of the
Performing Arts (BRAPA)**
P.O. Box 242
Sterling, VA 22170
703/430-9228

3 productions (2 musicals); Sterling Middle
School

Burke Center Players
P.O. Box 287
Burke, VA 22015
703/250-2103

3 productions (1 musical); Landings
Community Center

VIRGINIA, continued

Castaways Repertory Theatre
8817 Portner Avenue
Apartment 6
Manassas, VA 22110
703/330-9814

3 productions; Godwin Middle School
(Dale City)

Children's Theater of Arlington
2700 South Lang Street
Arlington, VA 22206
703/548-1154

4 productions (for and by children);
Gunston Arts Center

Dominion Stage
Gunston Arts Center
2700 South Lang Street
Arlington, VA 22206
703/683-0502

4 productions; Gunston Arts Center
(Arlington)

The Elden Street Players
P.O. Box 5006
Herndon, VA 22070
703/481-5930

5 productions (1 musical); The Industrial
Strength Theatre (Herndon)

Friendship Players
Friendship United Methodist Church
3527 Gallows Road
Falls Church, VA 22042
703/560-5454

2 productions (dessert served); Friendship
United Methodist Church (Annandale)

Great Falls Players
P.O. Box 11
Great Falls, VA 22066
703/759-6224

3 productions; Great Falls Grange and The
Alden Theatre (McLean)

Lewinsville Players
Lewinsville Presbyterian Church
1724 Chain Bridge Road
McLean, VA 22101
703/356-7200

1 production; Lewinsville Presbyterian
Church

Mount Vernon Children's Theater
P.O. Box 372
Mount Vernon, VA 22121
703/768-0703

2 productions (4-5 workshops
productions), theater by and for children,
classes; performances at various locations

Port City Playhouse
P.O. Box 19507
Alexandria, VA 22320
703/838-9303

5 productions; Production locations:
Alexandria Hospital Auditorium, Lee
Center Auditorium, and T.C. Williams
High School Auditorium (all located in
Alexandria)

Prince William Little Theatre
P.O. Box 341
Manassas, VA 22110
703/378-9627

3 productions (some musicals); Linton Hall
School (Manassas)

Reston Community Players
2310 Colts Neck Road
Reston, VA 22091
703/435-2707 - Information
703/476-1111 - Box Office

An all-volunteer, community-based group,
the Players produces 4 mainstage
productions (2 musicals, 2 plays) in the
Reston Community Center Theatre every
season along with numerous travelling
shows, one-acts, play readings, and
workshops.

Springfield Community Theater
St. Christopher's Episcopal Church
6320 Hanover Avenue
Springfield, VA 22150
703/866-6238

4 productions (some musicals); St.
Christopher's Episcopal Church

Trinity Theatre
Trinity United Methodist Church
1205 Dolley Madison Boulevard
McLean, VA 22101
703/356-3322

1 production; Trinity United Methodist
Church (McLean)

The Visual Arts

A stroke of the brush or a spin of the potter's wheel offer a welcome respite from the standard Washington work day. Studio arts programs at museums, art centers, and art leagues throughout the area are popular with both novice and accomplished artists, and include classes, workshops, and demonstrations that foster the creative spirit in all participants. Museums and art centers offer members a chance to discover their talents in every facet of the studio arts, while art leagues such as the Art Deco Society and Kiln Club may focus on a specific art form or craft. Several of these organizations sponsor receptions and exhibition openings, local tours, art history classes, members' special events, and other programs for Washington residents. You'll  also find a comprehensive, affordable curricula of arts classes and programs at local cultural institutions, continuing education programs, and community and recreation centers (see *Education* and *Parks, Recreation, and Community Centers*).

Media Alert!

A Museum Guide to Washington D.C. by Betty Ross (Washington: Americana Press, 1988). This carefully researched and attractively designed book provides information on the history, collections, and programs of 60 area museums.

Washington Art: A Guide to Galleries, Art Consultants, and Museums by Lorraine Arden, Carolyn Blakeslee, and Drew Steis (Great Falls: Art Calendar, 1988). This book is dedicated to "Washington artists... dealers... critics... and collectors." In addition to descriptions of the contemporary galleries in the area, there is information that is particularly useful to professionals in the visual arts.

The Washington Review, the award-winning journal on arts and literature in Washington, features reviews of art, dance, film, literature, theater, and video produced by new and established talent. Poetry, fiction, photography, and feature articles are also included in this bi-monthly publication. Subscribers receive invitations to special events such as openings at dance and musical performances, cast parties, film screenings, readings, and more. Contact the Review offices at P.O. Box 50132, Washington, D.C., 20091, or call 202/638-0515 for further information. Annual subscriptions start at $12.

Museums

Washington has more than 60 museums, most of which offer far more than current exhibitions. Special events for members and the public include concerts, classes, lectures, and films, and help to create a sense of community among the friends and supporters of each institution. Frequent social events allow patrons to meet at receptions, workshops, day trips, and other activities. Described below are some of the museums with the most active membership programs and public events.

Corcoran Gallery of Art
17th Street and New York Avenue, NW
Washington, DC 20006
202/638-1439

The Corcoran Gallery of Art offers a diverse range of educational and social programs to encourage patrons to enjoy the city's finest and oldest private art institution
in Washington. Acclaimed touring exhibitions as well as treasures from the Corcoran's
permanent collection of American and European painting, sculpture, and photography fill the beautiful neoclassic building. Corcoran memberships are available at
various levels to individual and family groups. The 1869 Society, a members group
of 500 young professionals, sponsors exciting annual activities including specially
designed tours, lectures, entertaining receptions and theme parties. The FRIENDS
of the Corcoran holds spectacular annual events including elaborate benefits, special
receptions and unique trips. The Corcoran's Education Department sponsors a scope
of activities, focused on exhibitions and works in the Corcoran's permanent collection, including intimate curator led tours, interesting guest lectures, and interactive
parent/child workshops. Where there's art, there's music, and the Corcoran's got
plenty of it! Every Sunday from 11:00 a.m. until 2:00 p.m., hear the Jazz Gospel
Ensemble perform while enjoying a delicious creole buffet during the Corcoran's
Jazz Gospel Brunch; $15.95 for adults and $8.50 for children under 12. Hear some
of Washington's best musicians during the free noontime jazz series every Wednesday from 12:30 p.m. until 1:30 p.m. in the Frances and Armand Hammer Auditorium. For the classical ear, the Corcoran's Musical Evening Series annually presents
eight concerts notable for their world renowned performers. Artistic talent flour-
ishes at The Corcoran School of Art's Open Program. The Open Program attracts an
enrollment of 2000 Washingtonians annually for classes in ceramics, printmaking,
and sculpture, as well as classes in the humanities and art history. People of all ages
and skill levels are taught by a faculty of nationally acclaimed artists, designers, writers, and scholars.

The National Gallery of Art
Constitution Avenue between 3rd & 7th Streets, NW
Washington, DC 20565
202/842-6353 Calendars
202/737-4215 Information
202/842-6176 TDD

Everyone who is a taxpayer is a member of the National Gallery of Art, which houses
one of the world's most comprehensive collections of Western art. The only membership organization at this museum is the Circle of major donors, who reside throughout
the United States and are invited to several special events each year. Local residents and
visitors, however, enjoy free, daily events that include films, concerts, gallery talks, lectures, and special tours. Weekday and weekend "Reading Art" discussion groups and art
history survey courses are also offered by the museums' education staff members. A
monthly calendar is sent to all who request it through the information office at the
number above.

The Phillips Collection
1600 21st Street, NW
Washington, DC 20009-1090
202/387-2151

Duncan Phillips established the nation's first museum of modern art in 1921, when he opened two rooms of his residence to the Washington community and invited visitors to view the works of Monet, Sisley, Whistler, and others. Today, the entire mansion and adjoining Goh Annex are filled with European and American master-pieces, but the special sense of entering a private home remains. Events sponsored by the museum allow members to participate in even more personalized programs: hands-on parent/child workshops, lectures, symposia, benefits, drawing sessions, and opening receptions enable members to enjoy the wealth of the museum's holdings in the company of fellow art enthusiasts. The Phillips Contemporaries is an organization of young supporters who are invited to a dozen annual events which have included special evening tours of current exhibits, Gallery Walks that explore galleries in the museum's neighborhood, visits to private collections and artists' studios, and "other behind-the-scenes opportunities." The Contemporaries' annual spring benefit raises funds for museum educational programs and contemporary exhibitions. And the weekly Sunday afternoon concert series in the museum's elegant music room has been open to all museum visitors since 1941. Membership at the Phillips starts at $45 (Phillips Contemporaries, $90).

The Smithsonian Institution
Visitor Information Center
Washington, DC 20560
202/357-2700

The Smithsonian is the largest museum complex in the world, with more than 140 million artifacts housed in more than a dozen museums and galleries. The scientific, cultural, and artistic riches could be overwhelming, but the Institution offers a num-ber of programs that help bring this wealth into perspective. The broadest of these is the Associates Program, whose members receive Smithsonian magazine. On the lo-cal level, the most popular programs are sponsored by the Associate's resident pro-gram (see Education) and the Friends of the National Zoo (see Volunteer). In addi-tion, you'll find a number of membership programs to museums such as the National Air and Space Museum, the Renwick Alliance, and the National Museum of the American Indian (scheduled to open on the Mall at the end of the century). The Museum of American History has three membership organizations: The Friends of the First Ladies, the Friends of the National Postal Museum, and the Friends of Music. Members of the latter are supporters of the Institution's numerous resident ensembles, which include the Smithsonian Chamber Players, the Castle Trio, and the Twentieth Century Consort. Membership often includes special invitations to exhibition openings, newsletters, and museum discounts. Questions regarding any of these programs should be directed to the Smithsonian's general information num-ber, listed above.

Visual Arts Centers

These multidisciplinary centers offer much more than exhibit space. Aspiring artists will find the support of their colleagues, and patrons will find many ways to become  involved in the local arts scene, from classes which cater to all ages and skill levels, to fund raising events scheduled throughout the year. There are far more centers in the metropolitan area than profiled below; contact your local arts council listed at the end of the chapter to locate additional facilities in your area.

Arlington Arts Center
3550 Wilson Boulevard
Arlington, VA 22201
703/524-1494

This private, non-profit visual arts center offers both opportunities and encouragement for emerging artists in the metropolitan area. 15 artists have studio space in the Center's historic building, and countless others are served by the lectures, workshops, exhibitions, receptions, tours, and critiques that allow members and non-members alike the opportunity to share ideas and skills. A newsletter provides details of events such as a seminar entitled Examining the Art World Through Its Magazines or a life drawing group open to all interested artists. Membership begins at $20.

The Rock Creek Gallery (formerly The Art Barn)
2401 Tilden Street, NW
Rock Creek Park
Washington, DC 20008
202/244-2482

The tidy exterior of this 19th-century building in the midst of Rock Creek Park gives little indication of the color and creativity to be found inside. Monthly exhibitions, luncheon/lectures, and special programs such as the Summer Children's Art Workshop and Holiday Exhibition and Sale bring together area artists and the 400 members of the Art Barn Association. Membership is open to all. Contribution levels start at $25.

The Art League
105 North Union Street
Alexandria, VA 22314
703/683-1780 (Gallery)
703/683-2323 (School)

Located in the historic Torpedo Factory Art Center, the Art League encourages working and emerging artists and promotes a high standard of art in the Washington area. The League sponsors juried shows of members' works and maintains an art school that enrolls over 1600 students from the beginner to the advanced. The League School, noted for its focus on realism, offers classes in the fine arts (drawing, painting, printmaking, sculpture) and fine crafts (stained glass, pottery, fibers). Classes are held at the Torpedo Factory and several nearby facilities. Fees for eight- to ten-week classes vary according to the subject, but generally range from $90 to $175. The League's gallery is host each year to 16 shows that feature works by the 1200 League members, in addition to seven solo shows by selected artists.

Greater Reston Arts Center (GRACE)
11911 Freedom Drive
Reston, VA 22090
703/471-9242

Exhibits, Youth Art Month, lecture/demonstrations, Summer Art Camp, and art classes are all part of GRACE's efforts to stimulate interest and appreciation for contemporary visual art. Members participate in a variety of ways, and volunteers are active in the "Arts in the Schools" education program, the Reston Fine Arts Festival, the Annual Auction, and Artful Giving, the annual holiday sale. GRACE's arts classes include programs for adults, children, and families. Membership begins at $25.

McLean Project for the Arts
McLean Community Center
1234 Ingleside Avenue
McLean, VA 22101
703/790-0123

The McLean Project for the Arts is a nonprofit visual arts center dedicated to providing education about contemporary art. MPA presents exhibitions by artists from the mid-Atlantic region, gallery talks by curators and exhibiting artists, studio classes and workshops for children and adults, lecture and film series, art tours to area museums, and a children's resource room where an adult and child together explore art concepts using kits developed by artists. The McLean Project for the Arts is located upstairs in the McLean Community Center.

Montpelier Cultural Arts Center
12826 Laurel-Bowie Road
Laurel, MD 20708
301/953-1993

Prince George's County is justly proud of its arts center, located on the grounds of the gracious 18th-century Montpelier Mansion. The Center has three galleries, numerous artists' studios, and a performance schedule that features jazz, recitals, and dance. Classes and workshops put pencils, paint brushes, and palettes into the hands of all, from children to seniors. Beginning to advanced instruction is offered in poetry, creative writing, painting, drawing, sculpture, printmaking, photography, weaving, papermaking, ceramics, and stained glass, to name just a few. Members of the Center pay a small membership fee and receive a 10% discount on all Center events and classes.

Rockville Arts Place
100 East Middle Lane
Rockville, MD 20850
301/309-6900

Founded in 1987, Rockville Arts Place has become the premier visual arts facility in Montgomery County. The facility houses two galleries with 16 exhibitions a year, an education program offering 30 classes a semester, from children through seniors, catering to all levels of interest and skills, and studios for 12 resident artists. Membership ranges from $25 for an individual to $40 for an artist interested in exhibiting in the many juried exhibitions available to members.

Very Special Arts Gallery
1331 F Street, NW
Washington, DC 20004
202/628-0800

Very Special Arts is an international educational affiliate of the Kennedy Center which coordinates arts programs for people with physical and mental disabilities. The Very Special Arts Gallery is one of the first fully mainstreamed art galleries in the country and emphasizes work by professional artists with disabilities. Free receptions are given for each opening, and volunteers with sales and framing/design experience are welcome to assist VSA.

Washington Project for the Arts (WPA)
400 7th Street, NW
Washington, DC 20004
202/347-4813

For 20 years this private, non-profit organization has supported and promoted the contemporary visual arts through exhibitions, workshops, a bookshop, newsletter, and services for local artists. Art of an experimental or controversial nature is the norm here, where the Robert Mapplethorpe exhibition found a home after the Corcoran canceled the event. Facilities include a video lab for media artists, and art residency programs. Special programs include joint exhibitions with the Hirshhorn Museum, workshops sponsored by the National Endowment for the Arts, and an annual "Open Studio" event during which 250 artists open their workspace to visitors. Of the organization's 1500 members, nearly a third are working artists. Membership fees are $25 for artists and $35 for non-artists.

Washington Studio School
3232 P Street, NW
Washington, DC 20007
202/333-2663

Morning, afternoon, and evening classes in painting and drawing are held each week at the Studio School's Georgetown location. An outstanding faculty offers courses at all levels, and special programs feature lectures, workshops, painting and drawing groups, and exhibitions at the School's gallery. Course fees range from $55 for an uninstructed drawing group, to $625 for an advanced painting class.

Other arts centers to consider include:

MARYLAND
Harmony Hall Regional Center
10701 Livingston Road
Fort Washington, MD 20744
301/292-8331
303/292-8203 (TDD)

VIRGINIA
Great Falls Arts Center
P.O. Box 712
Great Falls, VA 22066
703/759-7469

A Place To Paint & Herndon Old Town Gallery
720 Lynn Street
Herndon, VA 22070
703/476-0881

Reston Art Gallery
11400 Washington Plaza West
Reston, VA 22090
703/481-8156

Visual Art Leagues and Organizations

There are scores of local groups that celebrate a specific art form, such as antique art or art deco. In addition, novice and professional artisans have formed local art leagues which specialize in a particular artistic media. Antique associations, watercolor clubs, craft guilds, and multimedia leagues such as the Rockville Art League are profiled below. Since a comprehensive list would be a book in itself, an eclectic sampling is presented below, followed by lists of other organizations in Washington, D.C., Maryland, and Virginia.

Art Deco Society of Washington
P.O. Box 11090
Washington, DC 20008
202/298-1100

Step back into the 1930's with the Art Deco Society, which celebrates the arts, crafts, architecture, design, clothes, music, film, and dance of this period. Members enjoy monthly activities which include tours of historic sites and antique shops, and concerts, dances, and exhibits that toast the  deco days. Annual events include the Expo, a gathering of art deco antique dealers, and the fabulous Art Deco Ball, a 1930s-style event in which swing bands provide the perfect accompaniment for dance and costume contests. The Deco Society also holds monthly board meetings and sponsors continuous historic preservation efforts. A membership fee of $25 includes a periodic newsletter featuring calendars of upcoming events.

Basket Bunch
16000 Croom Airport Road
Upper Marlboro, MD 20772-8395
301/627-6074

Honeysuckle, grapevines, morning glories, poplar bark, and even weeds are the materials gathered and woven by members of this club, which has met monthly for the past 10 years. Day-long sessions (9:30 to 3:00, always on Thursdays) include collecting the natural materials and constructing baskets under the guidance of experienced weavers. Beginners are welcome at all sessions, which rotate between the Patuxent River Park, Harmony Hall Regional Center, and Watkins Nature Center. The $10 annual fee includes a subscription to the club newsletter.

The Bead Society of Greater Washington
P.O. Box 70036
Chevy Chase, MD 20813-0036
301/277-6830

This diverse group meets monthly for slide-illustrated lectures about the history, design and making of beads. Avid collectors and travelers learn of exhibits and reviews of bead shows in the bi-monthly newsletter. A 600 volume lending library is available to members. Annual dues are $25.

The Kiln Club
The Torpedo Factory, Studio 19
Alexandria, VA 22314
703/548-6288

Founded in 1946, this well-established group of area ceramics artists gathers four times a year for regular meetings and an additional three or four times for workshops led by well-known artists. Members are chosen by jury and exhibit at the Scope Gallery of the Torpedo Factory, where you may find out about other local ceramics guilds. The Club's monthly newsletter provides information on ceramics workshops, shows, and classes in the Washington area.

National Enamelists Guild
6511 Callander Drive
Bethesda, MD 20817
301/229-4977

The oldest enamelist guild in the country, this international association includes around 40 local members. The six meetings held each year in the Bethesda area include slide/lectures, demonstrations, and guest speakers. As many as five workshops are offered annually. The Guild publishes a newsletter five to six times a year which features notices of meetings and workshops as well as articles that range from regulation of enameling chemicals to words of wit and wisdom. The annual dues are $15, with a special rate of $5 for students.

Northern Virginia Carvers
6251 Old Dominion Drive, #422
McLean, VA 22101
703/241-1622

You can expect more than idle whittling from the 300 to 400 area woodcarvers who enjoy the many activities of this club. Decoys, relief panels, creches, and other pieces are the creations of members who meet for monthly "show and tells" and demonstrations. The club offers free carving lessons during the summer at Colvin Run Mill in Fairfax County, and maintains an extensive workshop at Oakton High School throughout the year. The group has welcomed carvers of all ages. Monthly membership meetings feature informative programs on a wide array of carving-related subjects. An annual "Artistry in Wood" carving competition, display, sale, and demonstration provides a chance to purchase carved gifts. Woodcarving tools and woods are also available at this event. Annual dues are $12.

Potomac Craftsmen
Sixth Presbyterian Church
16th & Kennedy Streets, NW
Washington, DC
301/498-8019

This group of fiber enthusiasts was founded 50 years ago, and welcomes anyone interested in fiber arts. Instruction is given at the monthly meetings, in addition to lectures, study groups, workshops, public demonstrations and a cooperative gallery. Guild meetings are held the second Saturday of each month, September-June. Annual dues are $18, with discounts for families and seniors.

Pyramid Atlantic
6001 66th Avenue Suite 103
Riverdale, MD 20737
301/459-7154
301/577-3424

Interested book and paper lovers may create handmade paper, prints, and artists' books at this nationally-recognized center. Through exhibits, lectures, workshops, and symposia, artists share their insight and experience and seek to increase appreciation for works of and on paper. Annual events include the Washington Post Book Fair, held at the Corcoran Gallery of Art in November, and the Asian Festival held at Pyramid Atlantic in July. Fees for membership and activities vary.

Quilter's Workshop of Oxon Hill
2204 Piermont Drive
Fort Washington, MD 20744
301/248-9166

It can take more than two years for these quilters to stitch their masterpieces, and the finished products are awarded to one lucky member chosen by lottery. Quilts have also been donated to the American Cancer Society and the American Diabetes Association, and have been featured in national publications which focus on this popular folk art. Several pieced and appliqued quilts, with quilting designs of varying complexity, have been completed since the group was founded in 1973. Membership is $15 per year.

Other local quilting clubs include:

Designing Women
15 Lakeside Drive
Greenbelt, MD 20770
301/345-5957

Quilters Unlimited
P.O. Box 216
Merrifield, VA 22116-0216
703/503-9619

Rockville Art League
P.O. Box 4026
Rockville, MD 20850
or 1019 Brice Road
Rockville, MD 20852-1217
301/424-6193

This more than 250-member league represents all visual arts media except photography and is open to artists of all levels. The League sponsors monthly meetings, open and juried art exhibits, and workshops in varied media by nationally acclaimed artists. A monthly newsletter, which serves as an important resource guide for local artists, features listings of shows, places to exhibit, competitions and other current art-related information. Membership dues are $25 per year.

Sumi-e Society of America, Inc.
7102 Westbury Road
McLean, VA 22101
703/893-5449

This international society celebrates the art of Oriental brush painting. Its larger aims are the strengthening of the cultural bridge between East and West and the creation of an American form of this delicate art. The Washington chapter, with 85 members, is one of nine in the U.S, and meets six times a year for workshops, demonstrations, slide/lectures, and presentations by artists visiting this country on cultural exchanges. The Society participates in the Charles Sumner School Museum program and the Fairfax County Council for the Arts programs. The nationally-published quarterly magazine features articles on Oriental art, events, museums, tours, and other related topics. Classes are offered at several places in the area, and members can guide you to the one best suited to you. The annual membership fee is $30.

Washington Calligraphers' Guild
P.O. Box 3688
Merrifield, VA 22116
301/897-8637

Whether you're a skilled artist or struggling with penmanship, this association of 600 "letter lovers" welcomes you to join them. Monthly meetings feature noted calligraphers who share various aspects of their art through demonstrations, slides, and presentations. An extensive workshop program includes classes for all skill levels, and a growing library of calligraphic slides and publications is housed at Strathmore Hall in Montgomery County. Most programs are held in the Bethesda area. The modest membership fee covers postage of the monthly newsletter and thrice-yearly magazine. Members are active in over two dozen volunteer activities, from archives to workshops.

Other art leagues to consider:

DISTRICT OF COLUMBIA

American Art League
1607 Crittenden Street, NW
Washington, DC 20011
202/291-6404

100 members chosen by jury; speakers, trips, workshops; 2-3 juried exhibits (Arts Club and other sites)

Capitol Hill Art League
545 7th Street, SE
Washington, DC 20003
202/547-6839

300 current members; 8 monthly juried group exhibits; single artist exhibits semi-monthly at 5 other locations; dues are $25; group show submission fee $3 per month.

District of Columbia Art Association
7760 16th Street, NW
Washington, DC 20012
202/882-1849

40 members chosen by jury; trips, exhibitions, workshops.

The Miniature Painters, Sculptors, and Gravers of Washington
5812 Massachusetts Avenue
Bethesda, MD 20816
301/229-2463

35 resident, 150 non-resident members chosen by jury; annual international exhibition at the Arts Club.

The New District of Columbia Collage Society
c/o Bobbie Rydell-Jones
1339 Saratoga Avenue, NE Apt. 3
Washington, DC 20018
202/526-7608

25 members; monthly meetings; exhibitions.

Washington Water Color Association
c/o Concetta Scott
1111 Dead Run Drive
McLean, VA 22101
703/356-5053

125 members chosen by jury; 3 meetings per year (demonstrations, workshops, lectures); 3 annual exhibits (The Arts Club, other sites); this is the oldest arts club in the District.

MARYLAND

Art League of Germantown, Inc.
P.O. Box 855
Germantown, MD 20875
301/924-2497

monthly meetings (speakers,
demonstrations); 2 annual shows)

Gaithersburg Fine Arts Association
P.O. Box 2492
Gaithersburg, MD 20886
301/869-3957

40 members; monthly meetings
(demonstrations, discussions); shows,
retreats.

Laurel Art Guild
10205 Balsamwood Drive
Laurel, MD 20708
301/725-7263

monthly meetings at Montpelier Carriage
House; workshops; juried and open shows.

Montgomery County Art Association
c/o Johanna Lynch
1220 Baltimore-Annapolis
Arnold, MD 21012
410/647-7256
open membership; regular meetings
(demonstrations, lectures, critiques); juried
exhibitions; one-person shows

National Capital Stained Glass Guild
18481 Stone Hollow Drive
Germantown, MD 20874
301/601-0141

50 members; 6-8 meetings (workshops,
demonstrations), public workshops,
exhibitions.

Olney Art Association
17521 Shenandoah Court
Ashton, MD 20861
301/924-5469

50 members chosen by jury; monthly
meetings; exhibitions at Woodlawn
Mansion and Olney Library.

Open Critique
11301 Lux Manor Road
Rockville, MD 20852
301/881-6089
monthly meetings (discussions, peer
critiques)

Potomac Society for the Arts
10121 River Road
Potomac, MD 20854
301/299-6750

50 members; promotes fine and performing
arts, exhibitions, libraries, theater openings

Prince George's Artists Association, Inc.
P.O. Box 2902
Landover Hills, MD 20784
301/262-0841

Monthly meetings; shows, exhibitions,
workshops, demonstrations; juried and
open shows; monthly newsletter.

Southern Maryland Art League
10816 Brookwood Avenue
Upper Marlboro, MD 20772
301/868-6261

45 members (seniors); monthly meetings,
speakers, demonstrations; 2 annual shows of
fine arts and fine crafts.

VIRGINIA

Embroiderers Guild of America
6119 Harmon Place
Springfield, VA 22152
703/451-8593

270 members; workshops, lessons,
certificate program; national magazine,
local newsletter; $36 per year.

Fairfax Art League
3730 Old Lee Highway
Fairfax, VA 22030
703/352-ARTS (2787)

125 members; monthly meetings and
exhibitions in Fairfax City Old Town Hall
and other sites

High Country Basketry Guild
P.O. Box 1109
Fairfax, VA 22030

125 members; classes, workshops, monthly
meetings, tours, demonstrations, newsletter,
annual festival.

Manassas Art Guild
P.O. Box 3565
Manassas, VA 22110
703/620-2936

90 members; monthly meetings (lectures,
demonstrations); Christmas Art and Craft
Mart; juried shows.

VIRGINIA (continued)

Potomac Valley Watercolorists
3510 Wentworth Drive
Falls Church, VA 22044
703/256-1985

membership by jury; 4 annual meetings
(demonstrations, workshops, critiques);
exhibitions throughout the area

Springfield Art Guild, Inc.
P.O. Box 221
Springfield, VA 22150
703/971-0490

150 members; monthly programs (speakers,
demonstrations); workshops; classes for
adults and children; monthly newsletter

Vienna Arts Society
P.O. Box 371
Vienna, VA 22183
703/620-0225

250 members; open membership; monthly
demonstrations; continuous and juried
shows; workshops; newsletter

Waterford Weavers Guild
P.O. Box 111
Waterford, VA 22190

40 members; monthly meetings, members
must help with the annual Waterford Fair

Film

Cinema fans will discover several different genres of film opportunities in the Washington area. In addition to the film clubs profiled below, the Smithsonian Institu-

tion Resident Associate Program (RAP) offers a number of films from around the world in addition to short documentaries relating to current exhibitions. Information on these screenings is published in the Smithsonian calendar printed monthly in the Washington Post Weekend, and in the monthly issues of the Associate magazine, mailed to all RAP members (see Education). The Mary Pickford Theater at the Library of Congress is another rich source of classic film screenings; to be placed on the mailing list, call the Library at 202/707-5677. Finally, many local museums, embassies, universities, and commercial theaters (including the Key and the Biograph) also feature foreign and art films and series.

The American Film Institute (AFI)

The John F. Kennedy Center for the Performing Arts
Washington, DC 20566
202/828-4000

Over 700 films are screened each year in the famous theater of the AFI. Retrospectives feature the work of directors, actors, and others in the film community, and focus on a chosen topic may yield such classics as Casablanca and Lawrence of Arabia, shown during a recent exploration of the desert as it is portrayed in film. The AFI is particularly supportive of foreign films and independent film makers. The more than 3000 local members receive a monthly preview guide, reduced admission, and the opportunity to enjoy special events, such as sneak previews featuring the stars of the films in attendance. Membership is available at several levels, from the basic ($15) to the "Film Club" (major donors), whose members are invited to five or six embassy events each year. The theater at the AFI is but one of the many programs sponsored by the

AFI, which was founded by Congress in 1965 to "bring together leading artists of the film industry, outstanding educators, and young men and women who wish to pursue this 20th-century art form as their life's work."

International Ciné Club
c/o Ilene Photos
The World Bank J 9-017
701 18th Street, NW
Washington, DC 20433
202/473-4660

The Ciné Club offers one of the best (and one of the least known) film series in Washington. The $10 annual fee entitles members to view each of a dozen films at the International Visitors' Center of the International Monetary Fund for just $1. Members also receive a periodic newsletter with background information on each film, invitations to "members-only" events, and the advance reservation for Monday  evening screenings. Films during a recent season included *The Bicycle Thief* (Italy, 1948), *A Clockwork Orange* (USA, 1971) and the rarely seen *Yeelen* (Mali, 1987).

The Fan Clubs

Many of Washington's professional arts organizations sponsor membership programs that bring together patrons and promoters of music, dance, theater, and the visual arts. These organizations often promote fundraising and members-only events that reward the commitment of friends and supporters with champagne and canapé receptions, backstage tours, rehearsals, cast parties, meet-the-artists roundtables, and other special treats. These organizations may also offer volunteer opportunities that range from passing out programs at performances to chairing the benefit ball. Below, we have described especially active programs for patrons of the arts sponsored by local arts organizations and by the many "fan clubs" of the prestigious Kennedy Center.

Bach Backers of the Washington Bach Consort
1690 36th Street, NW
Washington, DC 20007
202/337-1202

The Bach Backers are a spirited group of 200 devoted fans who promote the extraordinary music-making of the Washington Bach Consort. The goal of the Consort is to perform Bach's music — especially the cantatas, passions, motets, and masses — in settings that recall the churches where this music was first heard. Though the ensemble has appeared at the Kennedy Center, its five subscription concerts and regular lunchtime programs are performed in churches in downtown Washington. Founded in 1977 by J. Reilly Lewis, the Consort is considered among the nation's most respected Bach ensembles and was the only North American ensemble invited to Leipzig in 1985 to celebrate the 300th anniversary of Bach's birth. The Bach Backers sponsor several fundraising events such as the annual Bach's Birthday Bash dinner and concert celebration. Members also hold special receptions prior to concerts, accompany the ensemble on tours, usher at performances, assist with subscription renewal, generate publicity, and turn to good use the energy and enthusiasm of the Consort's many supporters.

Bravo!
The Washington Opera
The Kennedy Center for the Performing Arts
Washington, DC 20566-0012
202/416-7838

More than 800 young professionals support opera in Washington while enjoying a number of events especially designed for Bravo! members. Cocktail parties, technical rehearsals, and the annual Valentine's Ball all add to the enjoyment of Washington Opera's superb productions. Members receive both the Bravo! newsletter and the Washington Opera magazine, as well as Green Room privileges and cocktails during intermissions at designated performances. Community outreach programs sponsored by Bravo! have involved students from Gallaudet University and Eastern High School, and have brought performances by young opera singers to senior citizens. Bravo! members are entitled to join the Washington Opera Guild at reduced membership rates. Bravo! membership starts at $25.

Friends Assisting the National Symphony (FANS)
The John F. Kennedy Center for the Performing Arts
Washington, DC 20566-0003
202/416-8310

FANS members promote the Kennedy Center's National Symphony Orchestra (NSO) through cultural, social, educational, and fundraising events. FANS' receive invitations to Working Rehearsals of the NSO, subscriptions to the *NSO News* and the *Kennedy Center News Magazine*, as well as to the annual black-tie fundraising gala. The Women's Committee of the NSO (202/416-8150) also promotes the NSO through its volunteer efforts. FANS works in conjunction with the National Symphony Orchestra Association, page 53.

Friends of the D.C. Youth Orchestra
P.O. Box 56198 Brightwood Station
Washington DC 20011
202/723-1612

These Friends are the guiding force and main financial backers of the one of the most highly regarded orchestras in the nation. They are the parents of the orchestra's 700 young musicians, ages 5 to 18, who participate in one of five orchestras. The orchestras' performances range in difficulty from the simple songs of the youngest string players to Beethoven symphonies performed by the most senior ensemble. In the more than 30 years since the orchestra was founded, the Friends have organized instruction and performances for over 45,000 students from throughout the metropolitan area. A similar program is offered across the Potomac by: **The Northern Virginia Youth Symphony Association**, 4026 Hummer Road, Annandale, VA 22003, 703/642-0862.

Friends of the Kennedy Center

The John F. Kennedy Center for the Performing Arts
Washington, DC 20566-0003
202/416-8300

The 600 Friends of the Kennedy Center support the theater, music, dance, and opera of the nation's cultural center. Friends volunteers serve as tour guides, information aides, and library, gift shop, administrative, and special events staff. Friends' contributions start at $30, which includes Kennedy Center publications and discounts on the Kennedy Center Performance Plus education workshops and programs (see *Education*).

Kennedy Center Stars help the Kennedy Center sustain the spectacular array of artistic and public service programs presented through their membership which starts at $50 per household. Stars receive discounts at the Gift Shops, Olsson's Book and Records, and educational events. They also receive invitations to the National Symphony Orchestra's working rehearsals in addition to advance ticket priority for events at the Kennedy Center.

Friends of the Olney Theatre

2001 Route 108
Olney, MD 20832
301/570-1110

The Olney Theatre is a professional theater in the process of changing from a summer schedule to a year-round program, and this group of over 300 friends and supporters is helping to make it all possible. They have turned the task of major fundraising into an endeavor that mixes fun with funds through a number of special events. The "Sweet Taste of Maryland" appeals to wine connoisseurs, and an art auction and Decorators' Showcase appeals to those with a flair for decor. Four "Mystery Nights" give all attendees a chance to be part of the drama. Volunteers are also welcome to help with office and production needs.

Friends of the Round House Theater

12210 Bushey Drive
Silver Spring, MD 20902
301/933-9530

A corps of 150 volunteers perform as ushers, head ushers, concessionaires, and office assistants. Volunteers have a chance to experience the theatre, to meet others with similar cultural interests, and to be part of a select group helping to make outstanding theatre a reality in the community. Amenities include invitations to special events and volunteer appreciation socials. Round House Theatre, in its 16th season, is celebrating its first season as a private, not-for-profit performing arts organization. For information, call the volunteer coordinator.

The Friends of the Torpedo Factory Art Center
105 North Union Street
Alexandria, VA 22314
703/683-0693

The arts, crafts, and paintings created in this massive brick structure on Alexandria's waterfront are far different from the munitions manufactured here through World War II. Since 1974, the lofty ceilings and large windows have provided space and light for more than 60 studios where artists create, display, and sell their art. Ceramics, fibers, jewelry, painting, photography, printmaking, and sculpture are among the media represented. The Friends of the Torpedo Factory Art Center is an organization of 1200 members who support the Center not only through membership fees, which begin at $30, but by helping to organize educational programs for all audiences and by serving as docents and volunteers. In return, these Friends receive a 10% discount on purchases from many of the Center's artists, free or discounted admission to lectures, tours, and workshops, and invitations to the Center's cultural and social events.

The Summer Opera Guild
1508 Auburn Avenue
Rockville, MD 20850
301/762-5154

This opera guild welcomes members who are interested in supporting the Summer Opera Theater Company at Hartke Theater in Maryland. Although the level of participation varies, opportunities are available for members to assist the Guild in nearly every capacity from fundraising to answering telephones. Membership benefits include trips to other opera companies, a chance to meet the artists and others interested in opera, and cast parties. Single membership is $15, dual membership is $25.

Symphony Orchestra League of Alexandria (SOLA)
P.O. Box 1035
Alexandria, VA 22313
703/548-0045

This professional orchestra had two active membership organizations which merged into SOLA. Frequent events have included the League's Winter Ball, Estate Sale, and a Holiday Medleys event. Membership fees are modest, and individual events vary in price.

National Symphony Orchestra Association (NSOA)
John F. Kennedy Center for the Performing Arts
Washington, DC 20566-0003
202/416-8310

For more than six decades, the NSO has filled Washington with extraordinary music-making from subscription concerts at the Kennedy Center, summer outings at Wolf Trap and Carter Barron Amphitheater, to the traditional Fourth of July performance on the Capitol Lawn. The NSO also brings great music to communities around the country through an American Residencies Project. Because

the National Symphony Orchestra is privately supported, it relies on its members and other contributors to underwrite costs. Members have the opportunity to buy tickets to Kennedy Center events ahead of the general public during special Ticket Priority Purchase Periods and receive invitations to Working Rehearsals of the NSO, subscriptions to the *NSO News* and the *Kennedy Center News Magazine.*

Washington Ballet and Ballet 2000

3515 Wisconsin Avenue, NW
Washington, DC 20016
202/362-3606

The Washington Ballet has two membership organizations: Members of the Washington Ballet, and Ballet 2000. Members of the Washington Ballet, depending upon the level of contribution, enjoy a host of benefits that may include newsletters, ticket priority, and invitations to open rehearsals, galas, and receptions. Contribution levels start at $35. Ballet 2000, comprised of young professionals, is committed to raising scholarship funds for the Washington School of Ballet and to supporting the company's community outreach programs. Members of Ballet 2000 assist in planning fundraising activities, and are invited to special events such as a special members-only reception at the Watergate Hotel. The membership fee is $35.

The Washington Opera Guild

The Kennedy Center for the Performing Arts
Washington, DC 20566
202/416-7800

The Washington Opera is one of the nation's finest operatic companies, and the Washington Opera Guild offers members unique opportunities to enjoy special events before, during, and after performances. Nine membership levels entitle members to varying privileges which include dress rehearsals, pre-performance lectures, backstage tours, cocktail buffets, receptions and round-table discussions with season artists, and invitations to the Opera Ball. Members receive the Washington Opera magazine and advance ticket information, and may join Guild-sponsored trips to other opera companies. Opera fans will discover several volunteer "Operatunities" to organize fundraising events and educational programs, write and edit the Opera Voice, sew costumes for performances at the Kennedy Center's Opera House and Eisenhower Theater, and assist with office work. Volunteers earn dress rehearsal passes based on the number of contributed hours and enjoy a special recognition dinner. Membership fees start at $35 and include Kennedy Center publications and discounts on Kennedy Center Performance Plus education workshops and programs (see *Education*; also see Bravo!, above).

Washington Performing Arts Society (WPAS)
2000 L Street, NW Suite 810
Washington, DC 20036-4907
202/833-9800

The WPAS brings the world's greatest performers to the Kennedy Center, Lisner Auditorium, Warner Theater, Dance Place, and other Washington-area stages and schools. The WPAS also offers a diverse array of membership benefits that include members' and artists' receptions, pre-concert lecture series, and other special events. Depending on the level of contribution, members may receive complimentary tickets and invitations to the annual fundraising Gala Dinner/Dance and Opening Season Party. All members enjoy Museletter subscriptions, discounts on selected performances, and access to the Kennedy Center's elegant Chinese Lounge before WPAS performances and during intermissions. Through the volunteer efforts of its Women's Committee and the Friday Morning Music Club, the WPAS also organizes innovative community projects such as Concerts-in-Schools, the Feder String Competition, Family Programming Initiative, and the Embassy Adoption Program. Other of WPAS' 250 volunteers usher at Dance Place, assist with office work, and staff the volunteer lounge at the Kennedy Center. These activities are supported by the WPAS's 5,000 members whose membership fees start at $25.

Other organizations sponsoring active Fan Clubs (profiled earlier in this chapter):

* Arts Club of Washington
* Friday Morning Music Club
* Levine School of Music
* Prince George's Philharmonic
* Corcoran Gallery of Art
* Phillips Collection
* Smithsonian Institution

We also encourage you to contact your local arts organization and to consult the following profiles in "Volunteering: Culture and the Arts" in *Volunteer.*

* Arena Stage
* Business Volunteers of the Arts
* Folger Shakespeare Library
* Hexagon
* National Building Museum
* Opera Theatre of Northern Virginia
* Smithsonian Behind-the-Scenes Volunteer Program
* The Summer Opera Guild
* Volunteer Lawyers for the Arts
* Wolftrap Farm Park for the Performing Arts

Further Resources

Listed below you'll find arts councils, commissions, and organizations which provide comprehensive information on all kinds of arts programs in the Washington metropolitan area.

District of Columbia

Cultural Alliance of Greater Washington
Stables Art Center
410 8th Street, NW Suite 600
Washington, DC 20004
202/638-2406

This private, non-profit organization publishes a very informative membership directory which describes each of its 300 affiliated arts organizations and lists over 300 individual members. The Alliance seeks to promote the arts throughout the metropolitan area by fostering cooperation between the arts and business communities (through the Business Volunteers for the Arts program) and by making information, resources, and ideas available to its members. Arts Washington, the arts trade paper of Metropolitan Washington, is published ten times a year with a circulation of over 5000. Membership fees vary.

Maryland

Arts Council of Montgomery County
10701 Rockville Pike
Rockville, MD 20852
301/530-6744

Prince George's Arts Council
6611 Kenilworth Avenue, Suite 200
Riverdale, MD 20737
301/454-1455

VIRGINIA

Alexandria Commission for the Arts
1108 Jefferson Street
Alexandria, VA 22314
703/838-6348
703/838-5479 Events line

Arlington County Cultural Affairs Division
2700 South Lang Street
Arlington, VA 22206
703/358-6960

Arts Council of Fairfax County
4022 Hummer Road
Annandale, VA 22003
703/642-0862
⚜

Athletics and Outdoor Adventures
The Sporting Life

Whether you find the idea of gliding down the Potomac River in a kayak exciting, or prefer twirling on the ice at a local rink; if you'd like to join others tossing a frisbee in front of the Washington Monument or listening to the crunch of fall leaves under a horse's hooves, this chapter will help you get out and about in the metropolitan area. Hundreds of opportunities exist for finding new friendships among the active set who enjoy competitive and recreational pursuits. Singles, and families can pick clubs to meet their needs. All levels of experience are accommodated: absolute beginners join Hockey America and the Potomac Polo Club, experienced players compete in lacrosse and volleyball tournaments, and basketball and frisbee players join pickup games at local parks. Hikers can choose from Sunday strolls or more rigorous overnight mountain treks. Sailors,  rock climbers, and archaeologists enjoy programs within and beyond the Beltway. Additional opportunities — especially those in Water Sports and Outdoor Adventures — include a wide variety of classes and workshops, from scuba diving to birdwatching seminars.

Athletic and outdoor organizations span a wide spectrum of interests from rugby teams to rock climbing, skiing, cycling, and flying clubs. You'll find these programs and others profiled in the following categories:

* Sports
* Water Sports
* Outdoor Adventures
* Fitness and Health

Look through this extensive chapter, take a deep breath, and dive into the possibilities. There are activities for every season and hour of the weekend. Have fun !

Media Alert! Watch the following publications for local club activities and announcements for teams seeking players:

Finding Fun & Friends in Washington is a book that is useful in helping all Washingtonians — new or old-timers — get to know their home city. The book has something to offer just about everyone: sports enthusiasts, aspiring actors and singers, hikers, bikers, tropical fish fans, dog lovers, political junkies. If you're looking to get involved in any number of ways, then Finding Fun and Friends is the book for you. Whether you're a recent college graduate, or a retiree looking for more productive ways to spend your time, we have the book for you.

 ✦ The *Washington Post Weekend* "On the Move" (Friday)
 ✦ The *Washington Times Washington Weekend* (Thursday)

Sports

You don't have to be a Redskin, Bullet, or Capital to play competitive sports in this area. Sports programs are more popular than ever in Washington, and include all levels of recreational and competitive league play. From the popular summer softball games on the Mall to the more esoteric winter curling, you're bound to find something of interest in one of the following sections: local departments of parks and recreation; multi-sport networks; sports associations and clubs; aerobics; badminton; baseball; basketball; curling; cycling; fencing; field hockey; football; golf; ice hockey; lacrosse; petanque; polo; rugby; running; skating; soccer; softball; sombo; tennis; ultimate frisbee; volleyball; walking; wrestling.

(For competitive Rowing/Crew, Swimming, and Water Polo, see "Water Sports.")

Departments of Parks and Recreation

Sports coordinators at local departments of parks and recreation fill their fields and courts with leagues and tournaments throughout the year, and encourage you to organize and register your own team. If, however, you are looking for a team to join, there are several approaches: before the season begins, call your local recreation department and ask to speak with the sports coordinator, who may tell you when and where to find teams that are practicing, provide you with a team manager's phone number, pass your name on to a team manager who is seeking players, and/or place you on a waiting list of interested players. Team registration fees may range up to $400. Alternatively, regularly-scheduled pick-up games, clinics, and open-gym nights offer prime time opportunities to meet other players and find potential teammates.

The departments of parks and recreation profiled below organize several sports leagues (if you are interested in aquatic programs, we have listed them under "Watersports").

Some recreation departments also run senior programs and "special population" programs for the disabled. Also see *Parks, Recreation, and Community Centers* for listings of local Young Men's and Women's Christian Associations and Jewish Community Centers, which organize a host of sports activities, leagues, tournaments, and outdoor programs.

WASHINGTON, D.C.

District of Columbia Department of Recreation and Parks
Adult Sports Program
1800 Anacostia Drive, SE
Washington, DC 20020
202/767-7345

Archery: Summer and winter leagues
Basketball: Men's & women's winter leagues
Softball: Men's & women's spring/summer fast-pitch leagues; Lawyer's spring/summer league
Volleyball: Co-ed, men's, & women's winter leagues; Embassy winter league

MARYLAND

Montgomery County Department of Recreation
Adult Sports Leagues and Tournaments
12210 Bushey Drive, Room 306
Silver Spring, MD 20902
301/217-6790

Basketball: Co-ed, men's, & women's summer and winter leagues
Flag Football: Co-ed fall leagues
Soccer: Co-ed spring and fall leagues; Men's open/Men's 35 & over spring and fall leagues; Women's open/Women's Masters spring and fall leagues
Softball: Co-ed, men's, & women's spring/summer/fall leagues
Tennis: Singles, doubles, & mixed-doubles spring/summer/fall leagues; Spring, summer, and fall tournaments
Touch Football: Men's fall league
Volleyball: Co-ed, men's, & women's fall and spring leagues; Winter and summer clinics

Prince George's County
Maryland National Capital Park & Planning Commission
Department of Parks and Recreation; Sports/Permit Division
6600 Kenilworth Avenue
Riverdale, MD 20737
301/699-2400

Basketball: Men's & women's winter leagues
Softball: Co-ed, men's, and women's summer and fall leagues
Touch Football: Men's fall and winter leagues
Volleyball: Co-ed, men's, & women's spring, summer, and fall leagues

VIRGINIA

Alexandria, City of
Recreation, Parks, and Cultural Activities; Adult Sports Programs
1108 Jefferson Street
Alexandria, VA 22314
703/838-4345 (Youth sports)
703/838-5003 (Adult sports)

Basketball: Men's & women's winter leagues
Softball: Coed & men's spring/summer and fall leagues
Soccer: Coed spring and fall leagues
Volleyball: Co-ed fall and spring leagues; Men's and women's winter leagues

Arlington County
Department of Parks, Recreation, and Community Resources
2100 Clarendon Boulevard, Suite 414
Arlington, VA 22210
703/358-4710

Basketball: Co-ed, men's, women's, and master's winter leagues
Flag Football: Co-ed & men's fall leagues
Soccer: Men's & women's fall and spring leagues
Softball: Co-ed, men's, & women's spring/summer, and fall/winter leagues
Tennis: Open and senior's summer tournaments
Volleyball: Co-ed, men's, & women's spring and fall leagues

Fairfax County Department of Recreation and Services
Sports Division
12011 Government Center Parkway, Suite 1050
Fairfax, VA 22035
703/324-5522

Baseball: Men's spring and fall leagues
Basketball: Co-ed, men's, & women's winter leagues; Men's summer league
Flag Football: Co-ed & men's spring and fall leagues
Lacrosse: Men's spring league
Running: Spring races
Soccer: Co-ed, men's, & women's spring and fall leagues
Softball: Co-ed, men's, & women's spring/summer and fall leagues
Tennis: Summer tournaments
Volleyball: Co-ed, men's, & women's spring, fall, and winter leagues

Multi-Sport Networks

The multi-sport network organizations profiled below coordinate athletic events and league competition for team sports which range from badminton to rugby. You may organize and register your own team, or call for information about placement on a team.

Capital Games
Falls Church Medical Center (Sports Offices)
6062 Arlington Boulevard
Falls Church, VA 22042
703/533-0408

The Capital Games are the official "state games" for the District of Columbia, recognized by the U.S. Olympic Committee and the National Congress of States Games. State Games are state level, grassroots Olympic-style multi-sport festivals which include a number of olympic and non-olympic sports, in various age categories for youth (8-20), adult (over 17), and masters (over 30) age groups. The games are held every year, usually in June, and are open to volunteers, coaches, and amateur athletes in the metropolitan Washington area. The Capital Games were originally founded by the Amateur Athletic Union and still work closely with the Potomac AAU in many sports to send local youth athletes on to the national AAU Junior Olympic Games (held annually every July/August), and local "veteran" participants to the World Masters Games (held every four years, 2 years following the Olympics).

Potomac Valley Amateur Athletic Union (AAU)
6062 Arlington Boulevard
Falls Church, VA 22170
703/533-0408

The AAU, the oldest and largest amateur sports organization in the country, includes more than 50 local state-level associations around the country that offer competitive sports for all ages. Nearly 5000 men and women participate as athletes, coaches, and volunteers in over 25 individual and team sports through the local association, the Potomac Valley AAU. The most popular sports programs in the area include aerobics, basketball, wrestling, and track & field. This organization also supports the annual Capital Games (the state games of the District of Columbia), a multi-sport Olympic-style festival held every summer with individual and team competitions and tournaments.

Sports Network
8320 Quarry Road
Manassas, VA 22110
Mr. Bill Turnbull, Director
703/631-5123

Sports Network — a "multipurpose sports center" with more than 20,000 feet of indoor space — welcomes co-ed, men's, women's, over 30, over 35, and youth teams in variety of indoor sports that include indoor soccer, volleyball, box lacrosse, and badminton. This company sponsors divisional tournaments; open, league, ladder, and club play; instruction/coaching for all levels; and player development programs. Individual players "new to the metro area or returning college students who want placement in any sport" should call the Sports Network managers for assistance. Team registration ranges from approximately $200 to $500.

SENIOR SPOTLIGHT:

National Senior Sports Association (NSSA)
10560 Main Street, Suite 205
Fairfax, VA 22030
Mr. Lloyd Wright
703/758-8297

Seniors who can spare the time to putt, drive, and volley with others over 50 will enjoy the benefits of this association, which feature recreational and competitive golf, tennis, and bowling trips. In addition to reasonably priced excursions to events in Georgia, Florida, and Oregon, expect other trips to resorts in Scotland, Spain, or Acapulco. Members receive the newsletter, *Senior Sports News*, with a schedule of events and related news. Membership is $25.

SPECIAL NOTE: While the NSSA provides strictly-senior sports opportunities around the world, seniors are active participants in many of the local organizations profiled throughout this chapter, from the Potomac Valley Seniors running club to the Atlantic Rangers scuba divers. Also contact your department of parks and recreation and/or local community centers for further information on sports leagues and athletic events for seniors (see page 187; also see *Parks, Recreation, and Community Centers*).

Washington Sport and Social Club
124 3rd Street, NE
Washington, DC 20002
202/547-1916

This club is the local arm of the Chicago Social Club, which has extended to fourteen major U.S. cities. The organization plans sporting and social events for busy young professionals and is dedicated to raising money and contributing volunteers to local charities. Co-ed volleyball, softball, football and basketball teams, large holiday theme parties, special sporting events such as golf outings and 5K races, as well as charitable activities are all part of this lively group's agenda. The $30 annual membership includes discounts on all club events and automatic membership into Sport and Social Clubs around the country.

Sports Clubs and Associations

Aerobics

U.S. Amateur Aerobic Sports Federation (Also called USA AEROBICS)
P.O. Box 2342
Falls Church, VA 22042-0342
703/536-9063
703/536-4914 FAX

USA Aerobics conducts local and national competition in aerobic dance for amateurs. Emphasis is on participation and those interested in friendly competition at a

lesser level than the televised "professional" aerobics competitions are encouraged to join. If you can do aerobic dance, you can do this style of
sport aerobics, and amateurs of all ages are welcome. USA-ASF National
Championships have been awarded to Washington in 1986, 1990, and
1994. Open to amateurs of all ages.

Badminton

Shuttlecocks fly at weekly practice in local gyms throughout the area, where badminton enthusiasts enjoy year-round play as members of these specialty clubs. Badminton is especially popular with the international set and draws both beginning
and experienced players.

United States Badminton Association (USBA)
1 Olympic Plaza
Colorado Springs, CO 80909
719/578-4808

Washington Contact:
4547 Grant Road, NW
Washington, DC 20016
202/686-5026

The USBA and its local representative will direct you to Washington area badminton clubs. The following clubs may be found smashing the shuttle regularly:

- Arlington Badminton Club
- Badminton Club of D.C.
- Badminton and Pickleball Club (South Laurel)
- Beltsville Club
- Catonsville Badminton Club
- Columbia Badminton Club
- George Washington University Badminton Club
- Howard University Badminton Club
- Montgomery County Badminton Club
- University of Maryland Badminton Club
- Wednesday Morning Club (Washington, D.C.)

Baseball

Anyone ready to "play ball!' should contact their local
department of recreation (profiled earlier in this chapter) for league information. Teams in search of players
place advertisements in the Thursday *Weekend* section of
the *Washington Post.* Sports activities are listed in "On the Move."

Basketball

Basketball courts throughout the metropolitan area are filled with pick-up and drop-in games, league play for men, women, co-eds, 30-and-overs, and 40-and-overs, open league play, and basketball clinics. For further information, contact the following organizations and resources:

* Local departments of parks and recreation (see page 187)
* Young Men's and Women's Christian Associations and Jewish Community Centers (see *Parks, Recreation, and Community Centers*
* Sports networks (see page 60)
* *Washington Post Weekend* "On the Move"

Curling

This 16th-century Scottish sport has been compared to chess, bowling, and shuffle-board on ice, although the rules are most similar the Italian lawn bowling game boccie. Curling teams of four people take turns bowling 42-pound granite "rocks" down an ice chute toward a circular target, or "house." The object is to have one rock closest to the center, and to have as many rocks both inside the house and closer to the center than your opponents. Enthusiasts of this esoteric sport are quick to point out that curling was included as a demonstration sport in the 1988 Winter Olympics. They also laud the camaraderie developed among fans of an admittedly obscure activity, and often extend invitations to sociable evenings at member's homes after one or two practice sessions.

Potomac Curling Club
Cabin John Regional Park Ice Rink
10610 Westlake Drive
Rockville, MD 20852
Mr. Bob Pelletier
410/715-1655

This club welcomes interested members to stop by the Cabin John Rink on Monday nights from 7:45 p.m. to midnight, November through March, for a first-hand look at a curling practice. Every year the club encourages new members to join. At the start of both eight-week sessions, the Draw Committee assigns all club members to a four-person team of both men and women who may be brand new to the sport or may have up to 40 years experience. The club's 12 to 14 teams participate in in-house playoff competitions during both sessions. Members also get together and carpool to tournaments — also called "bonspiels" — against the Eastern Shore's Chesapeake Curling Club and other clubs throughout the Northeast. Bonspiels are always opened with a handshake and the phrase "Good curling." All you need to play are soft-soled shoes, a broom (the club will also provide a broom), and annual membership dues of $40 and a $190 ice fee, but only $25 dues and a $140 ice fee for new curlers.

Cycling

The abundance of cycling trails in metropolitan Washington are often crowded by the city's large population of avid cyclists, many of whom compete in weekend tournaments throughout the area and the Mid-Atlantic region (for recreational biking, see "Biking/Cycling," page 95).

Armed Forces Cycling Association
120 Cameron Street, #205
Alexandria, VA 22314

Open to members of the U.S. Armed Forces (active, retired, National Guard, Reserves, and D.O.D. Civilians), this local organization sponsors competitive and fitness rides. Membership is $15 per year.

College Park Bicycle Club
4360 Knox Road
College Park, MD 20740
M. Kemal Tuncer
301/779-4848

This is not a touring club for weekend riders. College Park Bicycles sponsors this club for serious bicyclists interested in training, racing, speed, and finish lines. Sunday training continues from November through March until the opening of the racing season. There are over 100 club members and racing opportunities for all age groups. Annual membership dues are $18.

National Capital Velo Club - Team Metropolis
c/o Mike Butler
9036 Saffron Lane
Silver Spring, MD 20901
301/588-2087

Team Metropolis is a member of the U.S. Cycling Federation and has 200 to 250 members, approximately 50 of whom are active racers. Members compete every weekend March through October, and often carpool to out-of-town races. The team meets monthly, publishes a monthly newsletter, *Velo Voice*, and schedules bicycle racing clinics and seminars in the fall. The club also offers cycling training for novices. Membership is open to all metropolitan residents and all age groups (members' ages range from 11 to 65, with many over 30). The team is sponsored by Metropolis Bicycle Shops and requires $30 annual membership dues.

Fencing

For Washingtonians interested in an improved parry or quicker riposte, the Capitol Division of the U.S. Fencing Association publishes a quarterly newsletter with information on local fencing clubs and competitions. Local clubs sponsor workshops and competitive events throughout the area, and encourage prospective members to visit their frequent practices or register for a class. Club dues and floor fees vary, and some clubs provide or rent equipment. The Capitol Division's fencing competitions include the Octoberfest and Champagne Challenge, and men's, women's, and mixed- teams foil, epee, and sabre events (all competitors must be U.S. Fencing Association members). For more information about the Capitol Division clubs and competitions, contact the D.C. Fencer's Club, profiled below, the largest and oldest fencing club in Washington.

D.C. Fencer's Club
205 Baltimore Road
Rockville, MD 20850
Mr. Jack Smith, President
301/294-7852

Everyone from beginning fencers to ex-national champions belongs to the D.C. Fencer's Club, which meets for practice and competition five nights a week, Monday through Friday, at Deal Junior High School on Fort Road and Nebraska Avenue in Washington, D.C. The club coach offers individual and group lessons each night for experienced competitors or for those first picking up the foil, sabre, or epee. Over 80 members of diverse abilities and ages ranging from 11 to 72 belong to this club. Club dues are $110 for six months.

Other fencing clubs that belong to the Capitol Division include:

Chevy Chase Fencing Club (CCFC)
Washington, DC
301/460-3399

The CCFC practices three times per week throughout the year at the Chevy Chase Community Center at Chevy Chase Circle. Beginning and intermediate classes are offered Wednesday evenings. There is a $5 floor fee for visiting fencers.

Fred Appel Club
Arlington, VA
703/536-8538

Formerly the Arlington Fencing Club, this is the only Virginia club associated with the Capitol Division. Practice sessions are scheduled once a week at the Thomas Jefferson Recreational Center, and private and small group lessons are available. There are no floor fees.

Montgomery County Department of Recreation Fencing Club
Potomac, MD
301/217-6880

Club practices and beginning and intermediate classes are held Thursday evenings at the Potomac Community Center on Falls Road. No formal instruction is given.

Ohlson Fencing Club
College Park, MD
301/474-1466; 301/431-0297

This club fences three to four times a week, offers private and group lessons, and sponsors men's, women's, and mixed teams informal bouting. The $100 membership fee includes use of facilities and equipment and free Wednesday night group sessions.

Southern Maryland Fencing Club (SMFC)
Lusby, MD
301/862-3279

The SMFC meets at the Southern Community Center in Lusby on Monday and Thursday evenings. Classes and limited equipment are available.

Field Hockey

United States Field Hockey Association (USFHA)
1750 East Boulder Street
Colorado Springs, CO 80909
719/578-4567

Ms. Karen Robinson
1730 16th Street, NW, #7
Washington, DC 20009
202/265-3703

Field hockey players will find two USFHA-sanctioned clubs in the D.C. area: the Washington Club, which is comprised of four teams, and Northern Virginia's Mulberry Club. From September through November, these teams play against each other and against other teams in Maryland, Virginia, and Pennsylvania. Women, and occasionally men, participate on teams of varied skill levels. To locate a local team/club or to start your own team, contact the USFHA number listed above, or the current local representative.

Football

Capitol Hill Touch and Flag Football League

P.O. Box 1399
Longworth House Office Building
Washington, DC 20515
Ms. Cathi Kaliniak
202/547-3721

In over 20 years of play, this co-ed league has grown to include 75 teams of 20- to 50-year-old Washington residents who compete in refereed games Saturdays and Sundays on Anacostia Park fields. The spring and fall seasons are bridged by a between-season warm-up, which includes a two weekend tournament. If you have organized your own team, you are welcome to join the league. If you wish to locate a team, contact the league commissioner at the above number.

Golf

The courses and clubhouses of local private country clubs provide the traditional milieu for Washington golfers; however, groups of golfers occasionally establish informal 'clubs' at specific public courses. Inquire at your local public golf course for more information, or try the Rock Creek Golf Club, below.

Rock Creek Golf Club

c/o Rock Creek Park Golf Course
16th and Rittenhouse Streets, NW
Washington, DC 20011
Ms. Priscilla McClain
202/882-7332 Golf Course
202/955-1549 Club (evening)
202/462-3238 Club (day)

The Rock Creek Golf Club is an affordable way to play competitive golf, improve your game, and meet fine golfing companions. Established in 1951, the club still retains a corps of original members, and new enrollments are always welcome. The only requirement is your love of the game. The season lasts from April through October, and features both local and Mid-Atlantic tournaments. All members are automatically invited to the Awards Dinner held free of charge at one of the local clubs in the Washington metropolitan area. Applications are accepted at the Club House, where you may also register for an upcoming tournament. Membership is $40 annually.

Ice Hockey

Hockey North America (HNA)
11501 Sunset Hills Road
Reston, VA 22090
703/471-0400

HNA offers beginner, intermediate, and advanced league play at eight rinks in the D.C. area. After beginners graduate from an eight-session hockey school, they compete in eight games and local playoffs (this program costs $399 and runs from late November through March). More experienced players compete in Mid-Atlantic tournaments and the North American Playoffs. The true hockey die-hards will appreciate HNA's Summer League or "Summer School," for lower intermediate to advanced players.

Lacrosse

The Lacrosse Foundation
113 West University Parkway
Baltimore, MD 21210
410/235-6882

Mr. Thomas R. Sheckells
6011 Osceola Road
Bethesda, MD 20816
301/229-5811

The Lacrosse Foundation is your key to competitive lacrosse in the metropolitan area. This Foundation publishes a list of local lacrosse clubs, the *Lacrosse* magazine, and quarterly newsletters. Membership dues start at $25 and include free admission to Baltimore's Lacrosse Hall of Fame Museum. The Foundation's 29 chapters nationwide include two Maryland and two Virginia chapters. Local membership is about $10. Call the Foundation directly or a current regional chapter representative, listed above. A few of the local lacrosse clubs include:

Northern Virginia Club
Mr. Doug Foster
703/683-7605

T-Bones Lacrosse Club
Mr. Tristan Zaia
4429 River Road
Washington, DC 20016
703/602-6126
703/362-1143 (Press 3 on the Voice Mail system)

Severn River Lacrosse Club
Mr. Mike Rupert
219 Holland Road
Severna Park, MD 21146
410/544-3320

Washington Lacrosse Club
Mr. Chip Veise
4612 Creek Shore Drive
Rockville, MD 20852
301/984-0843

Orienteering

A game of land navigation, orienteering combines the use of wits, legs, a map, and a compass. This sport can be competitive, or a means for people of all ages and fitness levels to enjoy the outdoors.

Quantico Orienteering Club
6212 Thomas Drive
Springfield, VA 22150
703/471-5854

This organization began at the marine base in 1970, but is now almost entirely civilian. An assorted group of 250 people who enjoy maps, walking and running outdoors comprise the membership of this organization. Usually two events are held each month in various MD, VA, and D.C. parks. All ages and ability levels are welcome, and events are open to non-members as well. Fees are $12 for individual membership and $15 for families.

Pétanque (Lawn Bowling)

The French motto: "Liberté, Égalité, Fraternité" applies perfectly to the game of Pétanque. It is inexpensive, so the game is accessible to everyone (Liberté), the same equipment is used by all players from eight to 80 years old (Égalité), and according to the International Federation of Pétanque, up to 17 million people play the game annually - hence the Fraternité. Both of the groups below welcome new players; La Joyeuse Boule also offers an excellent opportunity for French speakers to practice their language skills.

La Joyeuse Boule
Mr. Gilles Gouin
301/933-4123

This group gathers to play in friendly competition on Sundays from noon until 5 p.m. at Carderock Park, in Maryland. Members contribute picnic-type food which is shared by everyone in the afternoon. La Joyeuse Boule encourages anyone interested in enjoying casual exercise while learning more about the French culture to join them. Annual membership is $30, which also includes membership in the International Federation.

National Capital Club de Pétanque
208 N. Royal Street
Alexandria, VA 22314
703/548-6550

Virginia Highlands Park is the site of the National Capital Club's outdoor lawn bowling. They meet on Saturdays from 1-6:00 p.m. and have monthly competitions. All ages of interested players who are willing to abide by the rules of the organization are welcome to join. Picnics are held at local competitions. Annual membership is $30 and loaner boules are available.

Polo

Middleburg Polo Club
P.O. Box 908
Leesburg, VA 22075
Mr. Dick Riemenschneider
703/777-0775

This small club of experienced players meets every Sunday from June through September on the polo fields at Crenshaw Road and Route 50 in Middleburg, Virginia. While only 10 members actually play teams from throughout Virginia, Maryland, and Pennsylvania, about 50 join as "subscribers," and enjoy the summer polo matches and occasional social events. Interested players — or subscribers — should call or stop by a Sunday match for more information. General admission to the matches is $5.

Potomac Polo Club and School
5101 Wisconsin Avenue, NW Suite 508
Washington, DC 20016
202/362-0840
301/972-7303

Even if you've never ridden a horse, you can still take polo lessons and compete in league play with the Potomac Polo Club and School. All you need is a hard hat, heeled boots, and a determination to learn. Experienced players may try out for the more competitive league which competes in 12 summer tournaments. Practice and games are scheduled year-round at the Club's eight fields located at Hughes and River Road in Poolesville, Maryland. During the summer, three to four games are scheduled every day except Monday. The Potomac Club also offers trail rides and riding lessons. Group polo lessons start at $50, and may include discounts for series purchases. Admission to summer tournaments is $3.

Rugby

The Potomac Rugby Union
P.O. Box 15057
Washington, DC 20003
202/543-6862

The men's and women's Potomac Rugby Union clubs practice and compete in the spring and fall. Special events include the women's summer tournament, Rugeramma, the Cherry Blossom tournament on the mall in conjunction with the Cherry Blossom Festival, and a fall Halloween tournament. Divisional leagues enable players of all levels to join in the games. Selected players chosen from regional and national championships may compete in international tournaments.

Local teams in the Union include:

Columbia Club
Maryland Exiles Club

Severn River Club
Washington Club

Maryland Women's Club
Northern Virginia Women's Club
Potomac A.C.
Rocky Gorge Club

Washington Irish Club
Washington Women's Club
West Potomac Club
Western Suburbs Club

Rollerblading

Caravan Inline Association
Caravan Skate Shop
10766 Tucker Street
Beltsville, MD 20705
301/937-0066

On the ice or on the asphalt, the Caravan Inline Association offers something for every speedskating enthusiast. Beginners can hone their skills at clinics indoors and outdoors, and two race teams practice on Tuesday and Thursday nights. Adventure Fun Skates are held during the week and on weekends. Annual fees are $25 for families and $15 for individuals.

Running

Washington metropolitan runners work out and train with the area's running clubs. Club activities include training runs, track workouts, distance and marathon training, races, coaching, clinics, team participation programs, running partner finder services, meetings, postrun gatherings, outings, parties and other special events. Membership is generally $10 to $15 annually.

 Media Alert! **Washington Running Report**
3409 Haines Way, Suite 102
Falls Church, VA 22041
703/671-1003

This publication appears six times annually and includes local race results, race calendars, entry forms, and articles of interest to Washington area runners. You'll find the Report at selected local sporting stores. And, as always, the *Washington Post* "Weekend" lists information on training meetings for distance and marathon events, "fun" and group runs, and running club activities.

Road Runners Club of America (RRCA)
1150 South Washington Street
Alexandria, VA 22314
703/836-0558

The largest running organization in the country, the RRCA includes more than 160,000 runners in 460 nationwide clubs. If those statistics don't impress you, this one should: there are 16 clubs in the Washington metropolitan area alone. The clubs are all different, and may sponsor group runs, races, training, weekly workouts, and social events. Below are listings of a just a few of RRCA's local chapters; call the number above for more information on RRCA's programs and other metropolitan area clubs.

D.C. Roadrunners
P.O. Box 1352
Arlington, VA 22210
Mr. Roger Peet
703/765-1837

Prince George's Running Club
14817 Bell Ami Drive
Laurel, MD 20707
Mr. Rich Fulton
301/498-3672

Montgomery County Road Runners Club (MCRCC)
P.O. Box 1703
Rockville, MD 20849
Mr. Don Carter
301/353-0200

Washington Runhers, Unlimited (women only)
1206 16th Street, NW #701
Washington, DC 20036
Ms. Carol Mitten
202/347-4176

Northern Virginia Runners Club

Potomac Valley Track Club
5302 Easton Drive
North Springfield, VA 22151
703/941-4317

The Potomac Valley Track Club welcomes athletes of all ages and abilities. Track and field, long distance running and racewalking are its focus. Races and competitions are held throughout the year. The racewalk division (Potomac Valley Walkers) hosts a number of well organized races each year, including the National Invitational Racewalk in March. The Walkers also offer expert instruction through ongoing clinics, and all running races include a racewalk division.

Skating

From bumbling beginners to graceful gliders, a variety of speed skating, figure skating, and rollerskating clubs offer opportunities to learn and skate with a small group of other devotees.

National Capital Short Track Speed Skaters
H.G. Wells Rink
5211 Calvert Road
College Park, MD
301/445-3508

Potential Bonnie Blairs and Dan Jansens and other blade runners meet every Tuesday evening, November through March, at the H.G. Wells Rink for speed skating practices. These skaters also meet for dry land winter training sessions in Bethesda, and ten-week summer sessions beginning in late June in Alexandria. Monthly races are held in Baltimore. The club recommends some experience, although it is not required. Annual dues are $250, and skates may cost you around $300.

Washington Area Rollerskaters (W.A.R.)

P.O. Box 2963
Reston, VA 22090
703/450-9420

Weeknight and weekend skates, hockey games, races, and monthly club committee meetings can fill a skater's calendar throughout the year. W.A.R. members glide together Wednesday evenings at 6:30, and Sunday mornings and afternoons at locales throughout the metropolitan area. These events feature recreational skating as well as clinics, workshops, coning, and ramping. Sunday skates are often scheduled at the scenic Baltimore and Annapolis Trail or the Great Seneca Highway. W.A.R. rates all of their skating trips by ability and speed/distance, and the calendar has something for everyone's skill and endurance level. Membership is $24, and includes a periodic newsletter that includes a skate event schedule, a t-shirt, and invitations to special events.

Washington Figure Skating Club

Mount Vernon Ice Arena/Recreation Center
2017 Belle View Boulevard
Alexandria, VA 22307
Ms. Florence Sifferd
703/768-3224

Strong on dance and competitive figure skating, this club holds occasional seminars and competitions at its three home rinks, Cabin John, Fort Dupont, and Mount Vernon. The Club also blocks out specific skating times for members and guests. The club is one-third adults and one of the few in the area which uses United States Figure Skating Association approved-officials in its competitions. Other figure skating clubs based at rinks throughout the area are listed below. Keep in mind that some clubs skate only in the winter, others skate year round; some are quite social and others oriented toward the competitive skater. For the novice skater, most rinks offer group and individual lessons which may cost from $7 to $25 per half hour.

Bowie Figure Skating Club
Bowie Ice Rink
3330 Northview Drive
Bowie, MD 20716
Mr. Tom Jerrick
301/249-2088

Columbia Skating Club
Columbia Ice Rink
5876 Thunderhill Road
Columbia, MD 21040
410/730-0321

Skating Club of Northern Virginia
Fairfax Ice Arena
3779 Pickett Road
Fairfax, VA 22031
Mrs. Clair Chinn, President
703/644-1944

Suburban Skating Club
Wells Ice Rink
5211 Calvert Road
College Park, MD 20740
Ms. Dorothy Zukor
301/277-3717

Media Alert! For further information on skating clubs and opportunities, contact *Skater's Edge*, an international illustrated how-to publication written for people who love to skate, with articles by the world's top skating coaches and pros, at Box 500, Kensington, MD 20895 (301/946-1971). Subscriptions of five issues per year are $18.

FUN FACTS: After-hours during the winter months you'll find a host of Washingtonians at the National Sculpture Garden's Ice Rink on Constitution Avenue and Seventh Street (202/371-5340).

Soccer

U.S. Soccer Federation (USSF)
U.S. Soccer House
1801-1811 South Prairie Avenue
Chicago, IL 60616
313/808-1300

Metropolitan D.C./Virginia Soccer Association
5201 Queensberry Avenue
Springfield, VA 22151
Mr. Wallace R. Watson, President
703/321-7254

Maryland State Soccer Association
Ms. Anna Steffen
1 Maple Avenue
Baltimore, MD 21228-5522
410/744-5864

Contacting the USSF will put you in touch with several area soccer leagues. Each league may include one to four divisions separated by skill level, as well as "Over-30" leagues. Representatives stress everyone from the beginning player to the professional is welcome to join. Call the USSF number or contact your local association's current representative, who can assist in placing you with a team.

Washington Area Women's Soccer
Ms. Janet Hughes
703/827-7907

This is a competitive league of experienced women soccer players who are likely to own several pairs of well-worn cleats. The league is organized into two divisions of more than 15 teams that play during the fall and spring. Both divisions play in local and state tournaments. The competition is intense: three women in Division I played on the U.S. Women's Team, which won the 1991 Women's World Soccer Cup. Individual fees are usually $30 to $35 per season.

Media Alert!	**Soccer America**
Finding Fun & Friends in Washington is a book that is useful in helping all Washingtonians — new or old-timers — get to know their home city. The book has something to offer just about everyone: sports enthusiasts, aspiring actors and singers, hikers, bikers, tropical fish fans, dog lovers, political junkies. If you're looking to get involved in any number of ways, then Finding Fun and Friends is the book for you. Whether you're a recent college graduate, or a retiree looking for more productive ways to spend your time, we have the book for you.	P.O. Box 23704 Oakland, CA 94623 510/528-5000

Soccer America, a weekly national soccer newspaper, includes coverage of soccer teams around the world as well as valuable information on soccer clinics, tournaments, and other events. Annual subscriptions start at $45.

Softball

During the summer, the Monument grounds and other fields of dreams are crowded with amateur softball teams from Capitol Hill, government agencies, private firms, non-profit associations, and other organizations which keep the Washington wheels spinning. Call your local department of parks and recreation about softball leagues in your area (see page 187). Or join your nearest YMCA, YWCA, or JCC (consult the resources in *Parks, Recreation, and Community Centers*). And, as always, you may consult the *Washington Post Weekend* for teams and leagues needing players.

Sombo

United State Sombo Association
P.O. Box 2196
Falls Church, VA 22042-0196
301/530-4140
301/530-4106 Fax

Sombo is a Russian sport that combines elements of both wrestling and judo, often described as Russian self-defense jacket wrestling. (the term sombo is an acronym derived from the Russian phrase "self-defense without weapons"). Instruction for both men and women is available at local clubs in the metropolitan area. The U.S. Sombo Association is the National governing body for sombo recognized by the International Amateur Sombo Federation. Many local athletes have participated in international sombo competition over the years, including the Pan American Games and the World Games (each held every four years in the years preceding and following the Olympics, respectively).

Tennis

While the area's private tennis clubs are the most traditional places to shake hands across the net, the Mid-Atlantic Tennis Association profiled below offers alternative competitive tennis opportunities. YMCAs, YWCAs, and JCCs are also ideal places to find tennis players and companions for singles, doubles, and mixed-doubles leagues and tournaments (consult the resources in *Parks, Recreation, and Community Centers*).

United States Tennis Association (USTA)/Mid-Atlantic Section
2230 George C. Marshall Drive, Suite E
Falls Church, VA 22043
703/560-9480

Meet and compete against new tennis players with MATA, a non-profit, volunteer organization of over 22,000 members in the Mid-Atlantic region. Enjoy competitive tennis through MATA's Adult and Senior Divisions of six ability levels that range from advanced beginner through advanced. Over 150 tournaments throughout the year include singles, doubles, mixed-doubles, and family competition; categories of play extend from the Adult Open Division to Senior Men's and Women's and Junior's Divisions. In addition, USTA Play Tennis America "combines instruction and player while emphasizing the fun and social aspects of tennis" through recreational play at a reasonable cost.

Ultimate Frisbee

Washington Area Frisbee Club (WAFC)
6017 North 26th Street
Arlington, VA 22207
301/588-2629

An outbreak of Ultimate Frisbee fever has hit the Washington area in recent years, making the WAFC the largest frisbee club in the world. The 1300-member organization encourages both beginning and advanced frisbee players to join one of four leagues: Amateur (beginner to intermediate level), Pro (more experienced), Corporate (government agencies and corporations), and Ecumenical (local churches). In summer, 80 co-ed teams play week nights on the Mall near the Reflecting Pool and at Sligo Middle School. Spring and fall leagues play weekends at Anacostia Park. Frisbees also fly at seasonal tournaments and parties, such as the April Fools Tournament and the Annual Gender Blender.

WAFC's weekend scrimmages are also exceptionally popular: call them for pick-up game locations in the winter. The club welcomes interested players to stop by and join in the fun. In addition to Ultimate, the club also sponsors frisbee golf at seven local courses in the metropolitan area. WAFC membership costs $5, which includes a subscription to the club newsletter, *Disc News*, featuring information on league play and registration forms. League play generally starts at $5.

Volleyball

Open gyms and clinics, drop-in play, and men's, women's, and co-ed leagues are among the host of offerings for local volleyball fans. The best way to join a Washington volleyball team or register for an upcoming clinic is to call the organization profiled below, which acts as a clearinghouse on volleyball tournaments and events throughout the city (including those sponsored by your local community centers and department of parks and recreation).

Mid-Atlantic Volleyball Association (MAV) and
Federation of Outdoor Volleyball Associations (FOVA)
c/o Off the Net
5504 Wilkins Court
Rockville, MD 20852
301/881-7795

MAV is the place to contact if volleyball is your sport. The MAV Metro League plays on the Mall in June and July, and in local indoor and outdoor tournaments throughout the year. If summer weekends find you at Rehobeth Beach, drop by the Night Beach Recreation Area where MAV teams meet at the nets for Beach Volleyball Tournaments. Local MAV teams also play in national tournaments such as the FOVA

Grass and Sand Championships. The MAV is skilled at matching volleyball players and teams, and also posts a bulletin board at Off the Net, listed above, which features notices of players seeking teams and teams seeking players.

In addition to league and tournament play, the MAV offers over 70 volleyball clinics during the year in conjunction with private health clubs and local departments of park and recreation. These clinics are ideal locales for finding future teammates. MAV annual membership is $25 and includes a subscription to *Service Line*, an up-to-the-minute reporting on volleyball news. The annual dues also include FOVA membership and discounts on tournaments. Clinics usually start at $50 and tournaments start at $5 per player.

Walking

Millions of Americans walk for their exercise. Whether you are seeking competitive or contemplative routes, groups in the metropolitan area offer activities ranging from races to bird watching. The organization profiled next has more than 600 clubs in the U.S. and groups in 25 different countries. For additional information on walking-related groups, refer to "Hiking" and "Running" segments of this chapter.

American Volkssport Association/Atlantic Region
5605 Asbury Court
Alexandria, VA 22312-1735
703/354-1735

Providing fun-filled, safe exercise in a stress-free environment is the hallmark of Volkssporting, translated from German as "the sport of the people". Walking is the most popular of all volkssporting activities; but biking, swimming, cross-country skiing, snowshoeing, rollerskating and ice skating are also Volkssporting possibilities. All events are non-competitive, the volkssporter chooses the sport, the distance, and the pace. Activities take place year-round, across the country. Historic and scenic sites are chosen for the enjoyment of the Volkssporters. These local Volkssporting Clubs can provide additional information about the club nearest you:

DISTRICT OF COLUMBIA:
Walter Reed Wandervogel Club
P.O. Box 59652
Washington, DC 20012-0652
301/681-9084

MARYLAND:
Great Greenbelt Volksmarchers, Inc.
4-D Crescent Road
Greenbelt, MD 20770
301/345-3203

VIRGINIA:
Potomac River Volksmarching Club
P.O. Box 19524
Alexandria, VA 22320-0524
202/483-1925

Wrestling

Potomac Valley Wrestling Association (PVWA)
P.O. Box 2196
Falls Church, VA 22042-0196
301/530-4140
301/530-4106

The Potomac Valley Wrestling Association was established in 1983 to run wrestling tournaments and coordinate wrestling programs in the Metropolitan Washington area, including local folkstyle leagues and independent Olympic style wrestling competitions run under the auspices of USA Wrestling and the AAU. The organization runs events and serves as an information clearinghouse for wrestling in the national capitol area.

Washington Wrestling Club
P.O. Box 2196
Falls Church, VA 22042-0196
202/537-5754
301/530-4140

The Washington Wrestling Club provides instruction and opportunities to work out in all four styles of wrestling (American high school and collegiate style, Olympic freestyle, Olympic Greco-Roman, and International Sombo). The club meets weekly for practice sessions and some members participate in local and national competitions sanctioned by both USA Wrestling and the AAU. Membership is made up mostly of former wrestlers out of college, although it includes wrestlers of all ages and experience levels. Beginners welcome. Established in 1967, the club is the oldest continuous wrestling club in the area. Although it is primarily for adult wrestlers interested in friendly workouts, over the years the club has produced national champions in all styles of wrestling and all age categories.

Water Sports

Swimmers and divers, Chesapeake Bay mariners, and Potomac River paddlers will have limitless opportunities to find crewmates and teammates both in and out of the water at sports clubs and programs that include:

* Boardsailing
* Canoeing/Kayaking
* Fishing
* Rowing/Crew
* Sailing
* Scuba Diving
* Swimming
* Water Polo

For further information on scuba diving, swimming, and water polo, consult the local aquatics departments in Washington, D.C., Maryland, and Virginia listed at the end of this chapter.

For further information on boardsailing, canoeing/kayaking, rowing/crew, and sailing lessons in the area, contact the following organizations:

Thompson's Boat Center
Virginia Avenue and Rock Creek
Parkway, NW
Washington, DC
202/333-4861

Washington Sailing Marina
George Washington Parkway
(south of National Airport)
703/548-9027

Fletcher's Boat House
4940 Canal Road, NW
Washington, DC
202/244-0461

Boardsailing

Washington Boardsailing Club
c/o Windsurfing Unlimited
4913 Cordell Avenue
Bethesda, MD 20814
301/951-0705

The surf's up at the Washington Boardsailing Club, which meets monthly at the Washington Sailing Marina on George Washington Parkway. During the summer, this club organizes boardsailing day trips across the Chesapeake Bay at Sandy Point, and occasional weekend trips to the Atlantic Ocean. Regattas, meets, clinics, and picnics round out the agenda for the over 100 members of this active club, which welcomes all levels of boardsailors. Membership dues are $15, and include a quarterly newsletter with a calendar of upcoming events.

Canoeing/Kayaking

On most weekends during the spring, summer, and fall, you'll find Washington canoers and kayakers at Violettes Lock and Anglers Inn preparing to challenge the swift white waters of the nearby Potomac River. However, whether you choose to paddle the quiet Potomac near Roosevelt Island or shoot the roaring rapids of the Cheat River, you'll find plenty of opportunities for canoeing and kayaking adventures in the Washington area.

Canoe Cruisers Association of Greater Washington, DC (CCA)
P.O. Box 15747
Chevy Chase, MD 20825
Mr. Gus Anderson
301/656-2586

The CCA, the nation's largest canoe club, brings together dedicated paddlers through canoeing excursions and training programs. From paddling lessons at a local swimming pool to outdoor adventures in Wyoming, CCA integrates a variety of classes and trips for all canoers and kayakers. CCA trips are planned for all skill levels — from beginner to experienced — on the tranquil Potomac and on white water mountain rivers such as the Lower Youghegheny and the Savage Rivers. CCA's monthly meetings feature guest speakers who share stories of their canoeing and kayaking odysseys in South America, Russia, Idaho, and the Grand Canyon. The CCA's Slalom Division is the local club for members of the U.S. Whitewater Slalom Team. CCA members range in age from the teens to the seventies, and include paddlers who joined when the club first formed in 1956. Call the number listed above for a recording of upcoming events.

Washington Canoe Club (WCC)
3700 K Street, NW
Washington, DC 20007
202/333-9749

This flat water canoe club, located just upstream (north) of the Key Bridge, is for experienced canoeists and kayakers. Over 80 years old, the WCC is the last private canoe club in the nation's capital. The 200-member club often sends members to the Olympic games. Initiation dues are $100, and annual dues of $150 include boat storage.

If you'd rather test the waters with a few classes in canoeing and kayaking, join the host of other beginning navigators who have participated in the white water canoeing and kayaking programs listed below. Classes are generally held on the Potomac River weekends May through October, and teach the fundamentals of white water paddling. In one and two-day co-ed river courses, you and fellow paddlers will learn basic river maneuvering skills and effective techniques to maximize the enjoyment of river paddling. More advanced courses teach skills such as the up-stream ferry, peeling-out into fast currents, the Eskimo roll, and other white water challenges.

Adventure Sport
13521 Straw Bale Lane
Gaithersburg, MD 20878
301/258-0187

Canoeing Adventures Whitewater School
2706 Chain Bridge Road
Vienna, VA 22181
Mr. David Brown
703/281-4380

For additional canoeing/kayaking information, contact:

American Canoe Association
7432 Alban Station Boulevard Suite B-226
Springfield, VA 22150
703/451-0141

Fishing

The organizations profiled below feature fishing excursions, tournaments, and other activities to suit especially ardent anglers.

Media Alert!

Finding Fun & Friends in Washington is a book that is useful in helping all Washingtonians — new or old-timers — get to know their home city. The book has something to offer just about everyone: sports enthusiasts, aspiring actors and singers, bikers, hikers, tropical fish

fans, dog lovers, political junkies. If you're looking to get involved in any number of ways, then Finding Fun and Friends is the book for you. Whether you're a recent college graduate, or a retiree looking for more productive ways to spend your time, we have the book for you.

The Fishing Line, at $5 for seven issues, offers a wealth of information on fishing events and fishing lore. Contact 5008 Roslyn Road, Annandale VA, 22003, 703/941-3306 for a subscription. *The Washington Post Weekend* advertises fishing shows scheduled throughout the year and also publishes "Fish Lines," featuring reports on the latest catches in D.C. and the vicinity, the Chesapeake Bay, and the Atlantic Coast.

Fishbusters Fishing Club
P.O. Box 44444
Fort Washington, MD 20749-4444
Mr. Lamar Sessoms
301/292-8377

Chart the Mid-Atlantic coast with Fishbuster Fishing Club trips to Maryland, Delaware, Virginia, New Jersey, and North Carolina. Join six to 12 other men and women on weekly, year-round excursions in search of rockfish, tuna, and flounder. Members carpool to area fishing sites and compete in occasional tournaments. Call for a trip schedule, newsletter, and registration form. Trips start at $55. Membership entitles you to trip discounts and is free when you register for a trip.

Fly Fishing Schools
Mark Kovach Fishing Services
737 Thayer Avenue
Silver Spring, MD 20910
301/588-8742

Neophyte fishermen and women may first want to explore the basic and intermediate classes offered by this fishing school. Spend a full day of instruction and fishing — from 8:30 a.m. to nightfall — with a small group of fishing enthusiasts along the banks of Big Hunting Creek or the Potomac River. Join other aspiring anglers during the spring and summer and learn to fly-cast for trout and smallmouth bass, read water, and recognize fish habitats. The class is $120, with a $5 fee for fishing gear.

Potomac Bassmasters of Virginia
9705 Kisconko Road
Fort Washington, MD 20744
Mr. Arnold Aspelin, President
301/567-3030

This specialized fishing club sponsors tournaments, outings, seminars, youth programs, and social activities. In nine club tournaments and outings scheduled from March through November, individual club members compete for the "Mr. Bass" honor and other awards. Teams of Bassmasters compete in the club's Potomac Team Tournaments, and top Bassmasters may qualify for state and other regional competitions. The 30 or so thirtysomething members are mostly men, although the club also sponsors recreational "his and her" fishing tournaments. This club meets on the first Monday of the month at 7:00 p.m. at the John Marshall Community Library in Franconia, Virginia. Potential members must submit an application, attend meetings, participate in at least three club activities, and be voted in as a member by unanimous blind ballot. Members pay $35 annually and an additional $15 per year to the National Bass Anglers Sportsman's Society, with which the club is affiliated. Tournament costs vary.

Rowing/Crew

Capital Rowing Club
P.O. Box 66211
Washington, DC 20035
Mr. Kevin Harris
301/248-0275

Both novice and advanced oarsmen and women may row in doubles or larger boats at Thompson's Boat Center (beginners may take lessons at Thompson's May 30 through Labor Day; call 202/333-4861). Fees are $110 a quarter for club members, and $10 a month for recreational rowers.

Community Rowing Program of Alexandria Crew Boosters Club
P.O. Box 3202
Alexandria, VA 22302
703/379-8330

This program, held at the boat house on Madison Street in Alexandria, offers novice sculling and intermediate sweep and sculling programs year-round, as well as novice sweep programs during the summer. This club offers classes and participates in local regattas. The 100 or so members pay $200 in annual membership dues.

Occoquan Boat Club
9527 Blackburn Drive
Burke, VA 22015
Mr. Jay Tennent
703/751-3677

This club sponsors recreational and competitive sculling and sweep rowing on the Occoquan River at the boat house at Sandy Run Regional Park in Lorton, Virginia. There are opportunities for both novice and advanced rowers during the summer. Membership is open to all interested rowers, and includes a $100 annual membership fee with $150 initiation fee.

Potomac Boat Club
3530 Water Street, NW
Washington, DC 20007
202/333-9737

The Potomac Boat Club was established in 1898 and is the oldest boat club in the area. It houses a U.S. Development Center for men's heavyweight sweep rowing, a lightweight women's and men's sweep program, and members' competitive sculling and recreational activities. Members must apply and pay quarterly dues of $100; there is a dues structure for non-members who participate in the competitive program.

Sailing

Nearby Annapolis, famous for its cobblestone streets and colonial charm, is also renowned for the elegant yachts and high-masted boats which grace its harbors. Amid the throngs of tourists here in "Boat Town, U.S.A." are scores of sailors and a host of marine activities. Whether you're a novice or accomplished mariner, you'll find plenty of opportunities to enjoy the Chesapeake Bay and other nearby waters surrounding metropolitan Washington.

Sailing Club of Washington (SCOW)
P.O Box 14138 Ben Franklin Station
Washington, DC 20044
703/361-2720

During sailing season, SCOW welcomes metropolitan residents to join its Thursday night "social sails" on the Club's 19-foot Flying Scots and 24-foot cruising boats. These events, free and open to the public, are surely one of Washington's best kept secrets. SCOW members enjoy weekend raft trips, day cruises, crab feasts, brunches, dinner dances, and other special events. Members may also enroll in SCOW's sailing courses, which have included a piloting course of six evening sessions concluded with a day on the river. Interested sailors are welcome at the SCOW monthly meetings. The Club's newsletter is published and posted at Washington Sailing Marina. Membership is $30 annually.

Tiller Club
c/o Chesapeake Sailing School
7074 Bembe Beach Road
Annapolis, MD 21403
Mr. Winston Kinard
410/269-1594
301/261-2810
800/966-0032

You don't have to be rich and famous to sail: Chesapeake Sailing School Tiller Club touts sailing for the masses. However, you still have to afford membership fees which range from $400 to $600 per year. Membership offers access to the Sailing School's facilities and charter fleet (including a fleet of Tanzer 22s), social events, and discounts on services at the school, but options vary according to your preference for a Racing, Cruising, or Yachtsman membership. For instance, Cruising members relax on Weekday Sails, while Racing and Yachtsman members compete in Frostbite Races, Thursday Night Races, and the Annual Fall Regatta. No matter what your sailing style, all members may join the Launching Parties, Saturday Evening Happy Hour Sails, the Summer Crab Feasts, and receive the *Quarterly Seabag* newsletter. For beginning sailors, the Chesapeake Sailing School offers classes which include Two-Day Basic Weekend ($180), Weekend Basic Coastal Cruising ($360), and a Piloting minicourse ($95-125).

Womanship

The Boat House 410 Severn Avenue
Annapolis, MD 21403
Ms. Suzanne Pogell, President
410/269-0784 (from Annapolis or Baltimore)
800/342-9295 (from other locations)

This sailing program provides an excellent opportunity for women to learn the art of sailing with other women. Womanship offers courses and clinics in Annapolis and the Chesapeake Bay from mid-March through mid-November, and adventure vacations throughout the year in New England, Florida, Pacific Northwest, and the Virgin Islands. Course options include Live Aboard 2 to 14 Days, Wanna Be a Skipper Weekends, Sail Yourself Safely Home Clinics, Daytime Cruise Courses, Racing Clinics, and Offshore Programs (for the more advanced sailor). Completing a program with Womanship entitles you to free membership. Womanship's Foreign Travel program includes sailing and sightseeing trips to Greece and New Zealand. Call for placement on the mailing list. Womanship also customizes courses for couples, families, and groups. Course fees vary.

Scuba Diving

Many swimmers are taking the plunge and joining scuba diving clubs. Scuba (an acronym for Self-Contained Underwater Breathing Apparatus) is a sport enjoyed by scores of underwater explorers, and finding underwater companions is a fringe benefit of joining a scuba club. Each club has its own personality, and  often includes varied levels of new and experienced divers interested in an array of diving activities. Club members range in age from 12 years old and up, and may join as families, couples, and individuals. Though club membership is inexpensive, proper equipment is necessary and getting serious is a costly commitment.

The clubs profiled below will give you a head start on the diverse selection of scuba diving clubs and activities in the Washington area. Many scuba clubs focus on wreck-diving. Maryland, Virginia, and Pennsylvania diving quarries are filled with sunken cars, trucks, and planes, and are surprisingly busy places overflowing with weekend diving trainees. Less experienced divers may take advantage of club classes and workshops (offered at local recreation departments and area dive shops). An ambitious initiate can go from classroom, to pool, to diving quarry within a month, and later out to the ocean in search of submerged treasures and wreck photography.

Atlantis Rangers

P.O. Box 210
College Park, MD 20740
Mr. Tom Allen
301/258-0786

These wreck divers are anything but reckless: the majority of the club's experienced members welcome recently-certified beginner divers into the "Buddy-up" program, which teams less experienced divers with experienced partners. In addition to frequent diving trips, Atlantis Rangers organizes social activities, such as rollerskating and rollerblading get-togethers, baseball games, rafting trips, and monthly meetings. The newsletter, *Ranger Reporter*, with its scattered comics and activities schedule, keeps members well informed on upcoming scuba diving events. Membership fees start at $25, with an initiation fee of $7.50.

Capital Divers Association

14017 Mathews Drive
Woodbridge, VA 22191
Mr. James Gallagher, President
703/490-5363

Capital Divers, a club of over 150 experienced and new divers, offers a variety of diving opportunities which include a Divemaster training program and occasional social events, such as weekend camping trips and an annual crab feast at a diving quarry. A Polar Bear Dive opens the new year, followed by a special benefit Treasure Dive and an unusual Fall Underwater Pumpkin Carving Contest. This association also sponsors monthly quarry dives, wreck dives, and meetings, as well as annual Caribbean Island trips.

National Diving Center

4932 Wisconsin Avenue, NW
Washington, DC 20016
202/363-6123

Riding the Waves with National Diving Center, this store's monthly newsletter, provides updates on the Center's diving classes and trips. On Saturdays April through

October, the Center sponsors wreck diving trips aboard the *Leanna Katherine* off Chincoteague Island, explorations of local quarries and lakes, artifact collecting, and observing and collecting marine life. The Center also offers Open Water Diver Training Programs, which include classroom instruction, pool training, and four open water training dives. Other programs feature special trips to Bermuda, Florida, and Mexico and specialty courses in photography and ice diving.

Swimming

U.S. Masters Swimming

2 Peter Avenue
Rutland, MA 01543
508/886-6631

Local aquatics programs sponsor U.S. Masters Swimming teams and other competitive teams for individuals who want to work out on a regular basis and/or swim competitively on a local, national, and/or international level. Three divisions allow competition on varying levels from relaxed to die-hard, and swimmers range in age from 19 to 90-plus. Individuals may practice up to six days a week, usually on weekday evenings and weekend mornings, and often compete monthly in local meets. The teams encourage interested swimmers to drop by the pool and speak with the coaches for further information (call first for team practice schedules). Dues vary in each program — from $8 a practice to $100 for a season — and are often less expensive if you are a resident of the district where the pool is located. In addition to the pools listed below, several local YMCAs and YWCAs also offer Masters Swimming programs; consult the resources in *Parks, Recreation, and Community Centers*. You can also contact Joann Leilich, the Washington area contact person for *U.S. Masters Swimming*, at 7209 Hansford Court, Springfield, VA 22151, 703/354-2130.

WASHINGTON, D.C.

Capitol East Natatorium
635 North Carolina Avenue, SE
Washington, DC 20003
202/724-4495

Woodrow Wilson Senior High School
Nebraska Avenue and Chesapeake Street
Washington, DC 20016
202/282-2216

MARYLAND

Montgomery County
Montgomery County Aquatic Center
5900 Executive Boulevard
Bethesda, MD 20852
301/468-4211

Martin Luther King Swim Center
1201 Jackson Road
Silver Spring, MD 20904
301/989-1206

Prince George's County
Fairland Aquatic Center
13820 Old Gunpowder Road
Laurel, MD 20707
Mr. Joe Hampton; Ms. Mary Lou Obershmit
301/206-2359

VIRGINIA:

Alexandria
Chinquapin Recreation Center
3210 King Street
Alexandria, VA 22302
703/931-1127

Arlington County:
Yorktown Pool
5201 North 28th Street
Arlington, VA 22207
703/536-9739

Fairfax County:
Oak Marr Recreation Center (Monday & Wednesday evenings)
3200 Jermantown Road
Oakton, VA
703/281-6501

Providence Recreation Center (Saturday mornings)
7525 Marc Drive
Falls Church, VA
703/698-1351

Wakefield Park (Tuesday & Thursday evenings)
8100 Braddock Road
Annandale, VA
703/321-7081

Water Polo

For strong swimmers interested in another approach to their swimming experience, the Eastern Water Polo League and local departments of parks and recreation often organize competitive polo teams. Generally sponsored by the U.S. Water Polo Association, these teams are a growing facet of several local aquatics programs.

Rockville-Montgomery Water Polo Club
Montgomery County Aquatic Center
5900 Executive Boulevard
Bethesda, MD 20852
Mr. Larry Marcus
301/424-3278; 301/468-4211

These skilled swimmers and water polo players join co-ed Open Age Development Teams for competitive league play at the Montgomery County Aquatic Center. They also play with regional traveling teams, which compete in nationwide tournaments.

Northern Virginia Water Polo Club
4016 Travis Parkway
Annandale, VA 22003
Mr. Mark Sommerfield
703/256-0459

This competitive club, which started nearly 30 years ago and is a member of the Eastern Water Polo League, holds practices, scrimmages, and tournaments at Fairfax County's Highland Pool. The club encourages new members, and two divisions allow both experienced and beginning players to compete. Practice is twice a week, and members are men and women generally around age 25. Club fees are reasonable.

Aquatic Departments

For further information on scuba diving, swimming, water polo, water aerobics, and other aquatic programs in the metropolitan area, contact the aquatic division of your local department of parks and recreation listed below (also contact your local YMCA, YWCA, or JCC listed in *Parks, Recreation, and Community Centers*).

WASHINGTON, D.C.

D.C. Department of Recreation and Parks, Aquatic Division
1230 Taylor Street, NW #203
Washington, DC 20011
202/576-6436

MARYLAND

Montgomery County Department of Recreation, Aquatic Section
12210 Bushey Drive
Silver Spring, MD 20902
301/217-6840

Prince George's County/Maryland National Capital Park and Planning Commission
Enterprise Division Headquarters
2904 Enterprise Road
Mitchelville, MD 20721
301/249-7200

VIRGINIA

Alexandria:
Aquatics, Indoor Programs
Chinquapin Recreation Center
3210 King Street
Alexandria, VA 22302
703/931-1127

Aquatics, Outdoor Programs
1108 Jefferson Drive
Alexandria, VA 22314
703/931-1127

Arlington County: Washington Lee Center
1300 North Quincy Street
Arlington, VA 22201
703/358-6262

Fairfax County Park Authority, Aquatic Section
3701 Pender Drive
Fairfax, VA 22030
703/246-5601

Outdoor Adventures

The vast array of local organizations that answer the call of the great outdoors provides wonderful opportunities to enjoy wilderness adventures. These organizations offer a host of hiking, canoeing, rock climbing, and other challenges such as trail and cabin maintenance, cave excursions, and conservation and natural resource preservation. Opportunities include:

* Comprehensive Outdoor Programs
* Archaeology
* Biking/Cycling
* Birdwatching
* Flying
* Hiking
* Horseback Riding
* Motorcycling
* Rockclimbing
* Skiing

Many clubs extend invitations to non-members by publicizing scheduled activities in local newspapers and outdoor store bulletin boards. You may also call to request placement on mailing lists and for copies of recent newsletters.

American Youth Hostels (AYH)
Potomac Area Council
P.O. Box 28607 Central Station
Washington, DC 20038
202/783-0717

With members hailing from all parts of the globe, a local rafting trip with AYH may turn into an international affair. The local Potomac Area Council sponsors an impressive array of day trips and overnight excursions that feature nearby hiking, biking, canoeing, cross-country skiing, rafting, sailing, and horseback riding opportunities. AYH members may also participate in AYH's numerous sports leagues and tournaments.

AYH cultural and social activities have included a "Discover America" lecture series, a Whole World Adventure program, theater outings, and other special events with hostelers from around the world that have featured Oriole's baseball games, language roundtables, film nights, a Bastille Day Celebration, and a tour and dinner in Washington's Chinatown. AYH members receive a *Calendar of Events* and other publications that list local AYH activities, global travel opportunities, and travel services. Membership also opens doors to more than 5000 AYH hostels worldwide, including several hostels in metropolitan Washington. Membership starts at $25, is open to all ages, and includes discounts on international travel. While some AYH programs are free, others vary considerably in cost.

Audubon Naturalist Society (ANS)
8940 Jones Mill Road
Chevy Chase, MD 20815
301/652-9188

Established in 1897, the ANS has deeply embedded roots in local natural resource renewal and preservation. The ANS offers extensive opportunities to explore and protect our region's habitats and wildlife through visits to the Chesapeake Bay, nearby rivers, beaches, streams, and terra firma. Membership yields a bountiful selection of free and discounted field trips, classes, workshops, lectures, and natural history tours led by expert naturalists. Added benefits include a subscription to the monthly *Naturalist News*, invitations to special events and exhibits, volunteer programs, and a forum to lend your voice to local conservation efforts. ANS members have also enjoyed local cave excursions, a Sugarloaf country farm visit, photography workshops, spring wildflower walks on the C&O Canal towpath, twilight canoeing through a Patuxent River marsh, and hikes with an urban geologist through Civil War forts. More adventurous members have explored the Olympic Peninsula and other exotic locales including Madagascar and Costa Rica. ANS volunteers are welcome to tend the greenhouse and gardens, staff the bookshops, and join the Annual Assateague Beach Clean-up. ANS volunteers also help to manage a 40-acre historic estate, Woodend, in Chevy Chase, Maryland. A wandering visitor may also explore Woodend's forests, woods, fields, ponds, and thickets which are free and open to the public. Membership starts at $18.

Expanding Horizons
P.O. Box 3753
Arlington, VA 22203
703/525-4724

Women who are interested in fun, personal growth, and skill attainment will find comrades at Expanding Horizons. Backpacking, canoeing, caving, cycling, orienteering, rock climbing, and sailing are all offered by this group. There is no membership fee; each activity is paid for and discounts are offered to seniors and students. Nationally certified American Sign Language interpreters are available for all programs.

Inner Quest, Inc.
Route 1, Box 271C
Purcellville, VA 22132
703/478-1078 (Fairfax)
703/771-4800 (Leesburg)

This multi-adventure company offers classes in canoeing, kayaking, and rock climbing in and along the banks of the Potomac River. In association with REI, a popular outdoor equipment store, Inner Quest also offers indoor rock climbing in three, two-hour evening sessions (call the REI store at Bailey's Crossroads, 703/379-9400). And Washington's spelunkers will enjoy Inner Quest's caving classes, which explore the ecology, geology, and biology of the underground around Harper's Ferry. Most classes are scheduled May through November and accommodate all levels. Class fees generally start at $50.

Outdoor Excursions
P.O. Box 24
Boonsboro, MD 21713
703/821-5220

"White Water... no sport compares for thrills and adventure," proclaims this company, which operates local river kayaking and rafting trips on day and overnight expeditions. Outdoor Excursions also organizes national and international water adventures from the islands of southeastern Alaska to the tropical rain forests of South America. If you prefer land adventures, you may opt for Outdoor Excursion's trips for hikers, backpackers, and rock climbers who challenge the trails and cliffs throughout the area.

Potomac Appalachian Trail Club (PATC)
118 Park Street SE
Vienna, VA 22180
703/242-0965
703/242-0315

If hiking, backpacking, cross-country skiing, and rock climbing along this historic trail are on your agenda, you'll be delighted to discover the PATC. Originally established to maintain a 240-mile section of the Appalachian Trail and over 600 miles of additional trails, the PATC offers purposeful outdoor activity for those who share an interest in the Appalachian Trail. Nearly 5000 members lend a hand in trail and trail-side shelter maintenance and construction, cabin maintenance and restoration, and other PATC "worktrips" (see *Volunteer*). PATC also sponsors several monthly outings that have included Sunday Strolls and Circuit Hikes in Shenandoah National Park, Natural Sciences Trips, Civil War Hikes, Backpack Trips Beyond the Shenandoahs, hiking trips to the New York Adirondacks, and weekend cycling excursions through the Blackwater Wildlife Refuge. Cross-country skiers should check out the PATC's Cross Country Ski Touring Section, profiled under "Outdoors Adventures, Skiing," and local climbers will want to explore the club's Mountaineering Section, profiled under "Outdoor Adventures, Rock Climbing."

New PATC members must be sponsored by a current member with at least one year's standing (Prospective members are encouraged to get to know a PATC member/sponsor by visiting headquarters or joining an activity). Membership starts at $25, and includes a monthly newsletter, *Potomac Appalachian*, with updates on trail news and volunteer and outings schedules. Some events include a fee, and volunteer worktrips are free.

Potomac Backpackers Association (PBA)
P.O. Box 403
Merrifield, VA 22116
703/524-1185

PBA sponsors weekend backpacking trips within a two- to four-hour drive from Washington. For a change of pace, the organization also sponsors cross-country skiing, bicycling, and whitewater rafting excursions. Members gather at pot-luck parties, attend backpacking clinics, and explore the Grand Canyon and other far away places. To find out more about this adventurous group, attend the monthly meetings at Arlington's Aurora Hills Recreation Center (703/358-5722); or leave your name and address on the club hotline listed above to receive a sample newsletter. Membership is $12 per year.

Sierra Club
404 C Street, NE
Washington, DC
202/547-2326 Activities Hotline
202/298-6716 Membership Information in D.C.
703/960-7687 Membership Information in VA
301/977-5784 Membership Information in MD

If you have prematurely recycled your Sierra Club newsletter and want to take a hike, simply call DIAL-A-HIKE (202/547-2326), the local Sierra Club's recorded announcement of events. Trip opportunities range from Sunday walks in Rock Creek Park, to hikes or backpack trips in the Shenandoahs. During the week, members often gather for evening seminars and informal luncheons. Additionally, the local clubs run service trips to maintain and restore nearby trails. The Sierra Club also plays a critical national role in an environmental advocacy program dedicated to clean air and water, toxic waste control, protection of forests, parks, and wildlife habitats (see *Volunteer*). Membership generally starts at $35, and benefits include subscriptions to the *Sierra Magazine* and chapter newsletters that provide information about local meetings and outing schedules. Call the Membership Information number listed above for information about the chapter in your area.

Ski Club of Washington, D.C. (SCWDC)
5309 Lee Highway
Arlington, VA 22207
703/536-TAPE (Weekly activities recording)
703/532-7776 (Main office)

The largest, year-round ski club in the nation, this 6000-member organization sponsors one-day, weekend, and week-long ski trips throughout the winter. Newcomers to the slopes will appreciate the Club's free instruction program. The Club's off-ski season line-up includes softball, volleyball, tennis, hiking, bicycling, white water rafting, and sailing. Social and cultural events have featured picnics, wine festivals, happy hours, beach weekends, Octoberfest, and evenings at local performing arts events. Always on the agenda during the fall and spring are monthly meetings in Arlington. We have been told that since SCWDC's inception in 1936, single ski lovers have especially enjoyed the Club's activities both on and off the slopes, and many marriages have resulted from friendships formed here. Membership is $35 and includes a subscription to the Club magazine. For information on other ski clubs in the area, see page 105.

Washington Women Outdoors, Inc.
P.O. Box 345
Riverdale, MD 20738
301/864-3070

Answer the call of the wild as part of a group of 300 to 400 women who love bicycling, cross-country skiing, backpacking, hiking, rock climbing, kayaking, and canoeing. Excursions range from a few hours to three days in length, and run the gamut from tranquil sojourns on park bike trails, rolling back-country roads, and local hiking paths, to challenging circuit hikes in the heart of the Shenandoahs or challenging climbs on rock faces overlooking the Potomac River. Day trip fees start at $5 for members and $7 for non-members, though fees vary depending on the activity. Membership, starting at $30, entitles women to trip discounts, local events, quarterly brochures/newsletters, and the members-only first-aid and leadership training program.

Archaeology

The Washington area is filled with opportunities for the amateur archaeologist to excavate sites, catalogue artifacts, and find out about our local history. This is one activity in which the thrill of discovery is part of the learning process.

Media Alert!

National Museum of Natural History
Anthropology Outreach and Public Information Office
NHB-363MRC 112 Smithsonian Instutition
Washington, DC 20560
202/357-1592

This Office distributes information on archaeological fieldwork opportunities in publications which include *A Guide to Resources on the Local Archaeology and Indian History of the Washington D.C. Area* and *Local Archaeology Resource Guide for the District of Columbia, Maryland, and Virginia.*

Alexandria Archaeology
Torpedo Factory Art Center
105 North Union Street #327
Alexandria, VA 22314
703/838-4399

Friends of Alexandria Archaeology
P.O. Box 21475
Alexandria, VA 22320
703/838-9304

Anyone with an interest in history and archaeology is invited to join the Alexandria Archaeology and Friends of Alexandria Archaeology volunteers, who dig on site, research in the lab, and catalogue artifacts at the Torpedo Factory Art Center. Joining the Friends of Alexandria Archaeology allows you to participate in rescuing archaeological sites and to enjoy site visits, seminars, field trips, tours, and parties. These club members receive a newsletter and pay annual dues of $20 to develop educational materials and to help further archaeological research.

Archaeological Society of Maryland
17 East Branch Lane
Baltimore, MD 21202-2301
Ms. Iris McGillivray, Membership Chair
410/727-6417

This Society, which includes ten chapters in the state of Maryland, is comprised primarily of amateur archaeologists devoted to excavating, researching, and curating archaeological finds in Maryland. Membership includes a monthly newsletter, biannual bulletin, and invitations to an annual meeting, spring symposium, and a ten-day spring field session at selected historic and pre-historic sites in Maryland. For information on the chapter nearest you, call the number listed above.

Archaeological Society of Virginia, Northern Virginia Chapter
c/o Fairfax County Heritage Resources
2855 Annandale Road
Falls Church, VA 22042
703/237-4881

This volunteer group was formed in 1966 to research, locate, survey, excavate, and document archaeological sites in Northern Virginia. Today, metropolitan residents interested in digging up facts on our local origins may join professional archaeologists to retrieve, identify, and catalogue artifacts. Besides the on-site camaraderie, members enjoy field trips, monthly meetings with guest lecturers, and newsletters filled with information on current and future Chapter activities. Members may also become certified as para-professional archaeologists. Annual dues are $10 for individuals, $12 for families, and $5 for students. Some events are open to the public.

Archaeology in Annapolis
194 Prince George Street
Annapolis, MD 21401
Ms. Marion Creveling
410/268-7770

This joint project of the Historic Annapolis Foundation and the University of Maryland conducts an archaeology summer field school, a six-week basic archaeology course in excavation and lab techniques. You'll also find opportunities for lab work throughout the year at the Victualling Warehouse Maritime Museum on 99 Main Street in Annapolis, Maryland. Over two dozen 18th and 19th-century sites have been excavated, including the town's Charles Caroll House.

Environmental and Heritage Resources Branch
Fairfax County Office of Comprehensive Planning
2855 Annandale Road
Falls Church, VA 22042
Manager of Volunteer Programs
703/237-4881

Archaeologists have discovered evidence of 11,000 years of human settlement in Northern Virginia, and they welcome current metropolitan residents to work in the lab, to clean and process artifacts, and to participate in the organization's ongoing archaeological and historical research. Amateur archaeologists young and old also join excavation teams at Fairfax County archaeological sites, which have included an early 19th-century house and an American Indian village in the Mason Neck area.

Regional Archaeology
National Capital Region, National Park Service
1100 Ohio Drive, SW Room 218
Washington, DC 20242
Mr. Bob Sonderman
301/344-3385

This office of the National Park Service accepts volunteers interested in assisting in its various projects, which include excavating and processing artifacts at various sites in the Washington metropolitan area.

Other organizations which offer information on amateur fieldwork opportunities in local archaeology include:

American Anthropological Association
4350 North Fairfax Drive, Suite 640
Arlington, VA 22203
703/528-1902

Maryland Historical Trust
21 State Circle
Annapolis, MD 21401
301/974-5004

Biking/Cycling
Rock Creek Park, Mount Vernon Trail, and other scenic biking locales are often crowded with all varieties of cyclists, from occasional cruisers to impassioned racers. Biking/cycling clubs provide options to accommodate a host of individual styles, and include mountain bike clubs, community-based touring clubs, and the large, all-encompassing Potomac Pedalers Touring Club, Inc. Membership fees in most clubs are generally under $20. (Those interested in competitive cycling should see "Cycling" on page 65).

Media Alert!

Finding Fun & Friends in Washington is a book that is useful in helping all Washingtonians — new or old-timers — get to know their home city. The book has something to offer just about everyone: sports enthusiasts, aspiring actors and singers, hikers, bikers, tropical fish fans, dog lovers, political junkies. If you're looking to get involved in any number of ways, then Finding Fun and Friends is the book for you. Whether you're a recent college graduate, or a retiree looking for more productive ways to spend your time, we have the book for you.

Washington Area Bicyclist Association (WABA)
1819 H Street, NW Suite 640
Washington, DC 20006
202/872-9830

Send a self-addressed, stamped envelope to WABA for a listing of current bicycle clubs, information for bicycle commuters, and maps of local bicycle trails.

Arlington Bike and Hike Club
3501 South 2nd Street
Arlington, VA 22204
Mr. Michael McDonald
703/521-4331

You won't see this group joining the rigorous Tour de France race or a current expedition through the Amazon jungles. Instead, the Arlington Bike and Hike Club cycles and hikes along scenic trails throughout the metropolitan area. Members enjoy day rides and hikes on area trails; occasional day hikes in the Shenandoahs; and biking and hiking excursions through the countryside and historic towns. The club's pot luck dinners — veritable "moveable feasts" — are also very popular. The bimonthly newsletters keep you up-to-date on this network of easygoing outdoor enthusiasts.

Oxon Hill Bicycle and Trail Club
P.O. Box 81
Oxon Hill, MD 20750
Mr. Bob McMaster
301/839-4270; 301/567-6760

Bikers in this 150-member club pedal at all paces on weekday and weekend day rides. The club schedules rides for varying levels, from AA (fast touring) to E (slow, short, and easy). In addition to biking excursions, this club holds meetings, annual dinners, and picnics. The club's newsletter, *The Spoke 'n' Word*, announces club activities, bicycling news, and bicycling events and races scheduled in D.C., Maryland, Virginia, West Virginia, and Pennsylvania. Annual membership starts at $10.

Potomac Pedalers Touring Club, Inc. (PPTC)
6729 Curran Street
McLean, VA 22101
Mr. Jack Ramsey
202/363-TOUR

Whether you're Greg LeMond or a turtle on wheels, PPTC has a ride to match your cycling style. This club has approximately 5000 members throughout the area. Each weekend during the spring and fall, the PPTC organizes 25 to 30 rides which begin from various points throughout the area, and range in difficulty from easy to racing or training rides. The PPTC also offers occasional All Terrain Bicycle Rides, after-work rides, multi-day tours, and occasional weekend events such as September's

Club Century ("the test of cycling endurance") and October's Frederick Fall Foliage Frolic. Individual and family memberships entitle bikers to *Pedal Patter*, the monthly newsletter with complete schedules of rides and events. PPTC invites interested bikers to call the number listed above for more information, or to check out local bike shop bulletin boards for current schedules of PPTC events.

Birdwatching

Bird lovers will find a host of Washington societies and clubs which offer field trips, tours, classes, and other birding activities. According to the Audubon Naturalist Society's "Voice of the Naturalist" recording (301/652-1088), recent sightings have included lagerhead shrikes, razorbills, merlins, and cormorants. More unusual sightings have included a peregrine falcon hovering near the Pavilion at the Post Office, and a bald eagle soaring high above the Blackwater Wildlife Refuge. Whether you're a backyard birdwatcher or an adventurous expeditioner, you're bound to discover Washington's fine feathered friends by exploring the activities profiled below.

American Wild Bird Company Showroom
591 Hungerford Drive
Rockville, MD 20850
Ms. Heidi Hughes
301/279-0079

If you wish to know more about those avian residents who share your backyard, you may want to attend the American Wild Bird Company's free seminars. These seminars feature topics such as birding by ear and how to attract bats, owls, and hummingbirds to your yard. This company also sponsors Sunday morning field trips to sites throughout the Washington area. In addition, the company operates a retail store which offers products and advice for backyard birdwatchers.

Maryland Ornithological Society, Montgomery County Chapter
P.O. Box 59639
Potomac, MD 20859
Mr. Byron Swift
202/333-6890

Area bird lovers are welcome to eye aerie eagles and other rare birds on exploratory field trips in Washington, D.C., Maryland, Virginia, Delaware, Pennsylvania, and North Carolina. Trips scheduled on weekdays and weekends may include outings to the Potomac River, Violette's Lock, and Georgetown Reservoir. Longer excursions may lead to migratory hot spots on the Chesapeake Bay or the Outer Banks. Membership starts at $18 and includes access to frequent field trips, monthly meetings from September through May, a Spring Social, and several publications from the local chapter and the state organization.

National Audubon Society (NAS)
The NAS, which adopted the name of the famous artist and naturalist John James Audubon, was founded at the turn of the century by a group of bird preservation

clubs. Today, the NAS includes 550,000 members nationwide who have expanded the scope of their movement to include wildlife conservation, pollution control, and land and water management. For Washington's bird lovers, the NAS' local chapters continue to offer bird watching and other aviary activities. Annual NAS membership starts at $20 and includes membership in the local chapters profiled below. Also see *Volunteer*.

Fairfax Audubon Society (FAS)
P.O. Box 82
Vienna, VA 22183
703/256-6895 Ms. Meredith Compton, Volunteer Coordinator
703/642-0862 Packard Center, Annandale Community Park

The FAS gets its feet wet in an assortment of conservation and ecological pursuits, which include birdwatching, wetland reclamation, recycling, and conservation education. This chapter taps its 4000 members from the entire Washington metropolitan area. A member may join the FAS flock for Owl Prowls, Bald Eagle Field Trips, and other monthly birding events in diverse habitats at various locations in Northern Virginia. Members may also build and monitor wood duck nest boxes, assist the annual great blue heron count, coordinate the bald eagle survey, and participate in an annual Christmas bird count and chili feast. You may find out more about the FAS aviary activities, special events, and volunteer opportunities by attending the monthly meetings or calling for a copy of the *Potomac Flier*, the FAS newsletter.

Prince George's Audubon Society (PGAS)
P.O. Box 683
Bowie, MD 20718
Mr. Tom Loomis
301/937-2257

Count on heavy binocular use during frequent birdwatching field trips with the PGAS. In between sightings, PGAS schedules monthly meetings attended by up to 50 people, lectures by expert naturalists, and other special events. The club also organizes volunteer activities at the Fran Uhlur Natural Area, a wooded, wetland area with nature trails and bluebird houses. The club's 1000 members receive nine issues of the PGAS newsletter, *Bluebird.*

Virginia Society of Ornithology (VSO), Northern Virginia Chapter
P.O. Box 5424
Arlington, VA 22205
703/847-9368

By joining this chapter of the VSO you can embark on field trips to observe birds in a variety of habitats throughout Northern Virginia. Everyone from beginners to professional ornithologists are welcome on weekday walks and outings, Saturday field trips, and occasional excursions beyond local parks and preserves. During the peak of shorebird migration on the Virginia coast, the group organizes its annual spring Chincoteague weekend. Membership, which costs $5 for families and $3 for individuals, includes field trips, evening programs, and a quarterly newsletter, *Siskin*, which features information on trips, meetings, and current VSO programs.

Wild Bird Center
7687 MacArthur Boulevard
Cabin John, MD 20818
Mr. George Petrides
301/229-3141

Did you know that water sounds can attract birds to your yard? Or that the Woodpecker's chisel-shaped skull, reinforced to withstand continual shocks and vibrations, has influenced motorcycle helmet construction? The Wild Bird Center presents these and other interesting facts on weekly walks led by wild bird experts. Interested birdwatchers meet at the Center on Saturday mornings at 8:00 a.m. and head out to Great Falls or other birdwatching locales. The Center's monthly seminars have featured topics such as attracting and helping bluebirds in the winter, and identifying and attracting migratory sparrows. The Center's free newsletter, *Wild Bird News*, includes a complete schedule of special events. Events are open to the public.

Flying

FAA Flying Club of Washington, DC
P.O. Box 2098
Springfield, VA 22152
301/292-2825

This organization aims to introduce the fun of flying to those who have only dreamed of sitting in the pilot's seat. Members develop aeronautical skills and knowledge to enable them to begin the necessary licensing process. Two Wash & Wax parties are held annually, at which time demonstration flights are available. Members are required to pay an initial membership fee, deposits on aircraft flown, and an hourly rate for use of the planes.

Fun Flight Flying Club, Inc.
4105 Duke Street
Alexandria, VA 22304
Mr. Bruce Peters
703/751-5445

If sunsets over the Potomac, fall foliage, and the wind whipping across your face — all from nearly 200 feet above the ground — appeal to your sense of adventure, join the growing number of open-cockpit, ultralight aircraft flyers. Bruce Peters of Fun Flight Club, Inc. calls the ultralight a "motorcycle of the sky." This club is a chapter of the United States Ultralight Association (USUA), and provides "sport aviation enthusiasts with an affordable alternative to the high cost of aircraft rental or ownership for both licensed pilots and first time flyers" by selling shares of aircraft to its members. The Club's requirements vary for the two-seat and single-seat aircraft, and may include a successful completion of the Fun Flight solo training program or comparable USUA course. Members pay $45 a month in dues and $49 per month to purchase a share of an aircraft.

Hiking Clubs

Washington has a variety of hiking clubs, and each club provides hikes to suit the speed and interests of their members. Weekday, weekend, and overnight hikes along local towpaths and rocky Shenandoah trails can be a brisk workout or a leisurely stroll to observe nature upclose. Volunteers are always needed to help with trail maintenance. Some clubs also offer canoeing and horseback riding. Non-members are usually welcome on club excursions. Nominal membership fees include newsletters with information on upcoming trips, special events, and advance registration. Hikers often carpool to destinations, and trip fees vary.

In addition to the hiking clubs profiled below, you'll also want to consult the following organizations that offer hiking trips and opportunities (starting on page 89):

* American Youth Hostels (Potomac Area Council)
* Audubon Naturalist Society
* National Audubon Society
* Potomac Appalachian Trail Club
* Potomac Backpackers Association
* Sierra Club
* Ski Club of Washington, D.C.
* Washington Women Outdoors

Arlington Bike and Hike Club
3501 South 2nd Street
Arlington, VA 22204
703/521-4331

See Biking/Cycling Clubs, page 95.

Capital Hiking Club
3324 Glenmore Drive
Falls Church, VA 22041
Mr. John Restall
703/578-1942

The Capital Hiking Club, one of the oldest clubs in Washington, has left its collective shoe leather on virtually every mountain in the area. On Sunday mornings, up to 49 Capital Club hikers and hike leaders travel by bus to Old Rag, the Appalachian Trail, and other mountainous destinations for a scenic day of exercise and camaraderie. These weekly hikes feature both rigorous and less strenuous trails, and include hikers ranging in age from seven-year-old strollers to senior trekkers. While the club welcomes newcomers on its frequent expeditions, for a $5 membership fee you'll receive the hiking and potluck-dinner schedule in the quarterly bulletin, which may tempt you to begin a regular Sunday hiking habit. Trips are $10 to $15.

Center Hiking Club
5367 Holmes Run Parkway
Alexandria, VA 22304
Ms. Marion Knight
703/751-3971

Established in 1939, this sociable group of long standing, sponsors everything from leisurely walks to rigorous treks. You may choose from local, weekday evening hikes, Saturday and Sunday hikes at the mountains and seashore, or week-long Adirondack excursions. Hikes often include picnics or post-hike dinners. The club also sponsors bicycling, cross-country skiing, horseback riding, members-only camping trips, and other outdoor adventures. Occasional historical hikes have included excursions through Arlington and Rockville, and hikes along old trolley and rail lines. Other special events are announced in the members' quarterly bulletin. With the diversity that over 800 members bring to a club, there is plenty of room to initiate and organize other group activities.

Mountain Club of Maryland
8442 Each Leaf Court
Columbia, MD 21045
Mr. Steve Williams
410/377-6266

Realizing that weekdays aren't workdays for everybody, the Mountain Club of Maryland has scheduled a variety of weekday hikes. The group also maintains trails, occasionally paddles canoes, roams through mountainous terrain, and treks across cityscapes. A large number of retired adults meet for the popular "Midweek Leisure Hikes." Out-of-the-Ordinary midweek hikes have included the "City Cultural Hike" and the "Baltimore: Market to Market" hike. Trips vary in length and difficulty, and include backpacking and overnight hikes. Attendance ranges from four to 30 people, and advanced registration is usually required. Hikes are often announced in local newspapers, although membership provides trip schedules and advanced registration.

Northern Virginia Hiking Club, Inc.
7640 Bland Drive
Manassas, VA 22110
Ms. Stephanie Williams
703/369-0888

If you take to the trail with this 170-member club, you will receive a quarterly schedule of Saturday and Sunday hikes held year round. Hikers meet in the Northern Virginia area and carpool to the George Washington National Forest, the Shenandoahs, and other nearby trails for 4- to 16-mile day hikes. The club sponsors some overnight camping and backpacking, too. Membership is $5 per year for individuals and $8 per year for families. Non-members are welcome on hikes, but must pay $1 per hike.

Wanderbirds Hiking Club
6806 Delaware Street
Chevy Chase, MD 20815
301/654-3749

Travel at your own pace on a long or short hike with the Wanderbirds, who depart by bus every Sunday morning at 8:00 a.m. and usually return by 6:00 p.m. All hikers are issued maps and are accompanied by one member acting as a "start," and another as a "sweep," to bring up the rear and keep track of independent wanderers. Hikes sometimes fill up and reservations are suggested. Although membership is not required, members receive the hiking schedule for advanced registration, and enjoy meetings and special events.

Horseback Riding

Washingtonians will discover riding classes, organized trail rides, and other equestrian activities everywhere from the Rock Creek Park Horse Center (202/362-0117) in the Capitol's own back yard, to stables in the Blue Ridge Mountains and Shenandoah Valley. In addition to the equestrian clubs profiled below, you may want to try Brundage Stables (703/759-2474) and Elk Mountain Trails (301/834-8882) for more information. See the *Volunteer* chapter for opportunities to work with horses and riding programs. Polo enthusiasts will want to explore the Potomac and Middleburg Polo Clubs profiled on page 71.

Capitol Hill Equestrian Society (CHES)
1199 Longworth House Office Building
Washington, DC 20515
202/225-3261 Ms. Debbie McBride
703/751-9375 Ms. Mary Flowers

Join this organization and you may be saddling-up for a trail ride next weekend. CHES members of all riding levels enjoy events and excursions which include moonlight, overnight, and all-day picnic rides, as well as trips to horse farms and horse shows, a fall steeplechase party, and lectures on polo, jousting, evening, and training. CHES also schedules monthly meetings, and publishes a monthly newsletter featuring a lengthy list of area horse activities and information on lessons, and leasing, boarding, buying, or selling horses. Members often receive discounts at area supply shops and on lessons at participating stables. CHES's 300 members pay annual dues starting at $20.

Trail Riders of Today (TROT)
12937 Kentbury Drive
Clarksville, MD 21029
301/588-TROT

TROT is a civic association which works to expand, preserve, and improve equestrian trails. Members gather at meetings, receive a newsletter and trail maps, and meet regularly with public officials, developers, and citizens' groups. "Fun-raising activities" include spring competitive trail rides, pleasure rides, and trail clearing outings. Membership is $8 per family.

Motorcycling

Motorcycling may elicit yesteryear's images of Jack Nicholson in *Easy Rider*. Today, however, motorcycling is gaining a broad spectrum of enthusiastic riders through club meetings, classes, rides, races, and other special events. You're bound to find fellow motorcycling companions and day trip riding partners by exploring the offerings sponsored the organizations below.

American Motorcyclist Association (AMA)
P.O. Box 6114
Westerville, OH 43081
800/AMA-JOIN

The AMA publishes *American Motorcyclist*, which includes information on motorcycling events across the country.

The Motorcycle Safety Foundation (MSF)
2 Jennifer Street, Suite 150
Irvine, CA 92718
800/447-4700

Call this number for information on MSF-sponsored courses offered throughout the metropolitan area.

Motorcycle Times
Winding Road Enterprises
2550 Albert Rill Road
Westminster, MD 21157-3453
410/374-6282

The once difficult task of finding motorcycle clubs has been simplified by Winding Road's publication, *Motorcycle Times*. Published and distributed free from motorcycle dealerships, this magazine features an annual directory issue with complete listings of the hundreds of Mid-Atlantic clubs. The publication also features an Events Calendar that announces club meetings, rides, races, and other special events.

LadyRider
1015 Madison Lane
Falls Church 22046
Ms. Wills Shores
703/237-2824

Monthly rides to the shore, the mountains, and other scenic destinations are in the path of the Lady Riders, a club for women of all ages with all sizes of motorcycles. The club also sponsors overnight rides and occasional trips to rallies and shows, as well as weekend rides for groups of up to 20 members. Current members encourage interested women to attend the monthly meetings in Falls Church. Men are admitted as associates of the club and may accompany LadyRider rides. Dues are $12 per year and include a monthly newsletter.

Potomac Area Road Riders (PARR)
P.O. Box 9006
Alexandria, VA 22304
301/248-6710

One of the most active motorcycling clubs in the area, PARR includes women and men motorcyclists of all ages. Touring and sport bikers, Harley riders, and cafe racers are welcome to attend PARR-organized events which have included Poker Runs along popular motorcycling routes, and annual January 1st Polar Bear Runs that draw up to 200 people for a winter ride starting at the Dixie Pig on Richmond Highway in Alexandria. PARR also schedules members-only activities such as summer overnight rides, a July 4th picnic, and an annual banquet during the first weekend in December.

Prospective members are welcome to attend PARR's business meetings every second Tuesday of the month and/or social get-togethers every fourth Thursday of the month. Annual dues of $12 include subscription to the newsletter, the *Spoke 'n Word*.

Rock Climbing

Mount Everest soars high above distant horizons, but Washington mountaineers have discovered challenging opportunities to learn and enjoy rock climbing in the capital city's own back yard. Clubs and classes profiled below offer adventures for rockclimbers and adventurers throughout the area.

Mountaineering Section of the Potomac Appalachian Trail Club
118 Park Street SE
Vienna, VA 22180
703/242-3501

This group scales the rocks each weekend at Great Falls, Carderock, Sugarloaf, and occasionally in the Shenandoahs, West Virginia, and New York State. In the heart of the winter, ice climbers may journey to the frigid peaks of Shenandoah National Park and the White Mountains of New Hampshire. This group also sponsors monthly meetings, slide shows, training clinics, potluck dinners, and an Annual Mountain Film Festival. Call the number above for a recorded schedule of events and further information. Membership is $15 per year and includes a monthly newsletter.

Outdoor School
P.O. Box 815
Great Falls, VA 22066
703/759-7413

If you've ever visited Carderock or Great Falls on a weekend afternoon, you're likely to find climbers and rapellers crawling along the sheer, rock walls which tower above the Potomac River. Many of these climbers may be students of the Outdoor School, which operates recreational rock climbing classes on weekends from April through November. The day-long classes are generally taught in groups of four, and often a number of groups will climb together.

Classes are $80 and include all equipment. Frigid temperatures and winter snow won't deter the most avid rock climbers, who practice throughout the year at the School's indoor climbing facility on 850 Avery Road, in Rockville, Maryland. Inside this "warehouse," you'll find simulated rock cliffs nearly 20 feet high, complete with cracks, pockets, and holes. Call ahead for information on lessons and practice time.

For more information on rock climbing trips and lessons, also contact:

Inner Quest, Inc.
Route 1, Box 271 C
Purcellville, VA 22132
703/478-1078
703/668-6699

Washington Women Outdoors, Inc.
P.O. Box 345
Riverdale, MD 20738
301/864-3070

Outdoor Excursions
P.O. Box 24
Boonsboro, MD 21713
703/821-5220

Skiing

Washington skiers don't let the perennial dearth of snow spoil their fun: they hit the slopes with local ski clubs that sponsor day trips to local slopes, weekend jaunts on cross country trails, and an array of social activities with friendly groups of fellow skiers. As club representatives may change annually, the best way to find a ski club to suit your style is to contact the Blue Ridge Ski Council of Clubs (301/587-2073), an association of ski clubs which has compiled a comprehensive list of clubs sponsoring trips, meetings, and other events that will lift any skier's spirits. The Ski Chalet's main store at 2704 Columbia Pike, Arlington, Virginia, 22204, (703/521-1700) also offers information on local ski clubs. These clubs are located throughout the metropolitan area and usually welcome new members. To find the right fit, you may want to test-run the circuit and attend a club meeting.

The Ski Club of Washington, D.C., the largest, year-round ski club in the nation, offers ski trips and more, and is profiled at the on page 92. Other ski clubs affiliated with Blue Ridge Ski Council of Clubs include:

* Arlington Hall Ski Club
* Baltimore Ski Club
* Columbia Ski Club
* Crabtowne Skiers, Inc. (Annapolis)
* Frederick Ski Club
* Fredericksburg Ski Club
* Little Heiskel Ski Club (Hagerstown)
* NASA/Goddard Ski Club
* National Capital Handicapped Sports
* Pentagon Ski Club
* Southern Maryland Ski Club

Cross-Country Ski Touring Section
Potomac Appalachian Trail Club
118 Park Street, SE
Vienna, VA
Mr. Dave Holton
703/242-1334 (Ski Info Line)

Cross-country skiers will discover new ski trails and friendly companions at this local club. During the season, members carpool every weekend to overnight destinations and trails in Maryland, Pennsylvania, Virginia, West Virginia, and New York. The club's pre-season "Learn to Ski Weekend" prepares beginning skiers to enjoy the sport on their own or to join the club's regularly scheduled events. The club publishes a frequent newsletter, and occasionally sponsors summer and fall activities which have included biking and hiking events. The club's 150 members range in age range from 20's to 70's. Annual membership dues start at $9. Trip costs vary.

Fitness & Health

Get in shape and stay in shape without the expense of private health clubs. Local park and recreation departments, YMCAs, YWCAs, and JCCs offer a wide range of inexpensive fitness and health programs, which often include aerobics, water aerobics, and weight training (see resources in *Parks, Recreation and Community Centers*). Local hospitals offer comprehensive and affordable community health education programs; call the hospital nearest you for details on individual programs. If you prefer the private fitness center route, run your fingers through the lengthy "Health Club" section in the Yellow Pages for a thorough listing of private clubs, where you're bound to find aerobics classes, racquetball leagues, and other fitness programs.

Life Dynamics
Washington Adventist Hospital
7600 Carroll Avenue
Takoma Park, MD 20912
Ms. Judy Lichty
301/445-0755

The Life Dynamics program offers a well-rounded selection of aerobics, aqua-dynamics, and other exercise classes. These classes meet once or twice a week and cost between $40 and $60 for approximately 10-week sessions. Life Dynamics also offers educational programs which have included "Weight Adjustment for a Healthy Lifestyle" and other health-related classes.

AND A FINAL NOTE: School I.D.s are not always prerequisites to joining local university sports and health clubs. You can take advantage of a long roster of athletic and fitness programs at locations such as Georgetown University's Yates Field House and American University's Sports Center, and through George Washington University's President's Club Membership. Fair weather players may enjoy the outdoor pools, golf courts, and tennis courts at other institutions such as Mount Vernon

College and the University of Maryland, and residents 60 and older will appreciate the University of the District of Columbia's Bodywise program. Call the numbers below for further information:

American University
Sports Center
2400 Massachusetts Avenue, NW
Washington, DC 20016
202/885-3000

George Washington University
President's Club Membership
600 22nd Street NW
Washington 20520
202/994-6650

Georgetown University
Yates Field House
Washington, DC 20057
202/687-2400

Mount Vernon College
2100 Foxhall Road, NW
Washington, DC 20007
202/625-4642

University of the District of Columbia
Bodywise
1100 Harvard Street, NW Room 114
Washington, DC 20009
202/727-2778

University of Maryland
College Park, MD 20742
301/403-4299 (Golf/Tennis)

⚜

Culinary Washington
Cooking up a Storm

Regardless of whether you live to eat, or eat to live — Washingtonians will discover the joy of cooking in a vast array of cooking classes and culinary societies which reflect the diverse international community around us. Both special evening cooking courses offered for singles, and wine appreciation classes present the perfect opportunity to socialize with others who share your tastes. Food cooperatives dot the metropolitan area and are another way to meet like-minded people. If you have always wanted to prepare a Chinese banquet, or learn more about French wine, read on.

Media Alert! The *Washington Post* publishes a listing of area cooking classes every fall.

Continuing Education Cooking Classes

Local continuing education programs offer a diverse selection of cooking and wine appreciation classes, often at some of the most reasonable rates in town. These programs are taught at local public schools, community colleges, and recreation and community centers. They provide an extensive curriculum for everyone from the beginning baker to the expert chef, and include menus from appetizers to desserts to the "ABC's of Wine." In addition to the examples profiled below, consult the resources in *Education* and *Parks, Recreation, and Community Centers* for culinary programs offered in your area.

Montgomery County Public Schools (MCPS)
Division of Adult Education
12518 Greenly Street
Silver Spring, MD 20906
301/929-2025

Feast your eyes on MCPS' Adult Education course catalogue, which features a range of culinary classes including International Cuisine, Vegetarian Cooking, Soups, Stews, and Breads, and Entertaining and Holiday Fare. After taking Basic French Cooking, seven two-hour sessions, you'll be able to create (and pronounce) everything from quiche lorraine to porfiteroles au chocolat. Other palate-pleasers include Tasty Quick Breads, Festive Brunches, Chinese Cooking, and Vegetarian Natural Foods. Courses are generally offered on weekends and weekday evenings. Fees range from $20 to $60.

Fairfax County
Public Schools Adult Education
Department of Adult and Community Education
7510 Lisle Avenue
Falls Church, VA 22043
703/506-2231

This extensive menu of courses features cooking and healthy gourmet, baking, entertaining, international cooking, restaurants and tours, and holiday foods. Most classes feature demonstrations, student participation, meals and/or tastings. Courses have included Pizza and Breads, Mediterranean Light, Thai Treasures, and a Chocolate Workshop. Students interested in assisting instructors may receive limited "scholarships." Fees range from $15 to $63.

Cooking Schools and Classes

Private cooking schools and classes throughout the metropolitan area offer weekday evening and weekend classes for chefs of all levels. Most courses are held in the fall and spring at culinary institutions, catering companies, bakeries, and private homes. Individual and series classes include varying degrees of demonstration and hands-on participation. Some courses offer tastings and recipes, while others include dinners complete with wine and dessert. The profiles below are divided into Comprehensive Classes; American, International, Healthy, and Vegetarian Cuisine; and, Cakes & Confections. Bon appétit!

Comprehensive Classes

California Cooking
1710 37th Street, NW
Washington, DC 20007
Ms. Carol Mason
202/333-2448

Weekly classes on foods of the Mediterranean, France, the American Southwest, and Asian countries of the Pacific Rim include mostly lectures and demonstrations. Fees are $35 per class.

Fête Accomplie
3714 Macomb Street, NW
Washington, DC 20016
202/363-9511

This elegant French catering establishment offers periodic evening classes on everything from pizza to chocolate truffles. Classes include demonstration, participation, and tastings. Fees start at $35 per class.

Judy Harris Cooking School
2402 Nordok Place
Alexandria, VA 22306
703/768-3767

Calling New Cooks, Fast & Fresh Fish Cookery, Garlic Lovers Dream, All About Herb dinners, French country cooking, new wave pizzas, and hearty winter pastas are among the popular fare at the Judy Harris Cooking School. Students also enjoy the school's extensive herb garden and vegetable plot, as well as a Virginia Country Restaurant Tour and Chinatown Trip. Ms. Harris, who has taught these classes for 15 years, offers three-hour evening and day classes from September through June. Her classes of 12 to 18 students feature both participation and demonstration and emphasize technique and creativity. Fees range from $32 to $55 per class and include a complete dinner with wine or traditional drink.

Kitchen Coach
1541 North Longfellow Street, Suite 24
Arlington, VA 22205
Sheila Kische
703/534-9464

The Kitchen Coach offers one night classes including an introductory class called The World of Beans and Grains, Quick and Easy Gourmet Soups in about 20 Minutes, Versatile Pasta Entrees in about 20 Minutes, Cajun and Creole cooking, Easy Holiday Hors D'oeuvres, and Sin Free Desserts. While the "Coach" has instructed fall and spring evening classes for 20 years, she claims the same dish is rarely presented twice. In addition to demonstrations, an emphasis on techniques, and class participation, students learn the nutritional and historical background of the foods. Class size averages 8 to 12 people, and fees of $30 per class include generous food tasting and recipes. You might even catch "The Coach" juggling some ingredients!

L'Académie de Cuisine
5021 Wilson Lane
Bethesda, MD 20814
301/986-9490
301/652-7970 (Fax)

Imagine learning to simmer, stir, and saute under the watchful eyes of some of Washington's most celebrated chefs. L'Académie de Cuisine, one of the most prestigious cooking schools in the area, offers these intriguing possibilities in its ongoing series of classes. Held in well-equipped kitchens in downtown Bethesda, L'Académie sponsors special one-time events and workshops such as a Pasta Workshop. L'Académie also offers four to six-week courses, such as Basic Techniques of Cooking and Basic Pastry, as well as full and part-time professional courses such as the Culinary Career

Training Program. The curricula includes French, Italian, Asian, American Indian, vegetarian, and low-fat cuisine, as well as wine tasting, baking, and food science. The L'Académie's training is rigorous, and its rewards, scrumptious! Class fees range from $18 to $60, and up to $12,000 for the professional course.

Specialty Courses

America's Healthy Table

2800 Wisconsin Avenue, NW Suite 403
Washington, DC 20007
Ms. Joyce Winslow
202/686-1747

America's Healthy Table features low fat, low cholesterol American regional cuisine taught by a Cordon-bleu trained chef and food writer for *Bon Appétit* magazine. In hands-on classes, students cook and enjoy four course dinners, learn principles of  creating ethnic, regional favorites in a new healthy way. The series of four classes meet Wednesday evenings from 7:30 until 9:30, and the class fee includes food, instruction, and recipes. Series themes have included Santa Fe Cuisine, French and Cajun Cuisine, Superb Rice, Peas, Beans, and Fish Dishes; Wonderful, Guiltless Holiday Fare. The series of four classes costs $140.

The Chinese Cookery, Inc.

Ms. Joan Shih
301/236-5311

Eight levels of Chinese cuisine include Szechuan, Hunan, Basic, Advanced, and Gourmet I, II, and III. The Chinese Cookery also offers classes in Japanese Sushi and Mongolian Firepot cooking. Each level of five weekly classes is held weekday evenings and Saturday afternoons. Fees are $125.

Cooking with Class

2940 North Westmoreland Street
Arlington, VA 22213
703/534-3365

Elegant appetizers await the arrival of les etudiants de cuisine at this small, intimate French cooking class. After preparing an entire meal, the student chefs enjoy the fruits of their labor: an exquisite French feast. Fees are $40 per class.

Dining With Heart

2800 Wisconsin Avenue, NW, Suite 403
Washington, D.C. 20007
202/686-1747

This national program sponsors a course taught by a Cordon-bleu trained chef and former food writer from *McCall's* Magazine for those individuals ages 35 to 65 who have suffered heart attacks or are concerned about high cholesterol. Students are taught to make "easy but delicious" low-cholesterol, low-calorie meals through lectures, demonstrations, tastings, and cardiologist-approved recipes to take home. Fees are $100 for a series of five classes.

Greek Cooking Class
11215 Gainsborough Road
Potomac, MD 20854
301/299-6467

During a series of classes from October through May, a dozen would-be chefs gather in this Greek home for classes in the art of Grecian cuisine. While some enroll in all seven classes, other participants choose only three or four. Classes include student participation, full meals, wine, desserts, and recipes. Fees are $20 per class.

Introduction to Indian Cooking
1600 Huntcliff Way
Gambrills, MD 21054
410/721-7060

For the past 20 years, this series of six demonstration and participatory evening classes has introduced Washingtonians to the art of Indian cuisine. The class series is $125.

Mimmetta
1919 Eye Street, NW
Washington, DC 20006
202/659-4447

Student chefs can gather at the Sicilian restaurant owned by author-chef Mimmetta LoMonte to study the fine art of Italian and Sicilian cooking. Classes are held on weekends, and prices vary depending on the particular class.

Paris Cooks
1619 34th Street, NW
Washington, DC 20007
Ms. Elizabeth Esterling
202/333-4451

This caterer and dessert chef is in her 17th year of teaching demonstration classes on easy, elegant French cuisine. Class is limited to five students, and includes complete meals to savor after the diligent preparation. Fees of $175 include five sessions held in both the fall and spring.

Gail's Vegetarian Meals
11 Devon Road
Silver Spring, MD 20910
301/565-0674

Teacher Gail Naftalin, nutritionist and caterer, specializes in delicious healthful cuisine. Expand your repertoire and taste fabulous vegetarian food. Strictly vegetarian classes are offered in four and eight-part evening series beginning monthly. Four session courses are $80. The Vegetarian Sushi Workshop (taught weekends) is $22.

Robyn Webb's A Pinch of Thyme Cooking School
Robyn Webb Associates
325 North West Street
Alexandria, VA 22314-2120
703/683-5034

This expert in the field of nutrition and cooking will "give you the recipe for a whole new world of delicious and nutritious cooking possibilities." A Pinch of Thyme classes are designed to teach low fat and healthy cooking that also saves time. Course fees range from $80 to $199, and include such offerings such as Cooking for Singles: Timesaving Meals for One or Two, Cooking With Five Ingredients or Less, and Where's the Beef?: Vegetarian Cooking 1990s Style.

Cakes & Confections

The baking classes listed below should tempt both beginning bakers and candy connoisseurs:

Baked by Beryl
Beryl Loveland
P.O. Box 1584
North Springfield, VA 22151
703/256-6951
703/750-3779 (Fax)

Connie's Confectionary
8931 Woodyard Road
Clinton, MD
301/868-9444

Designer Cakes
4001 North 9th Street
Arlington, VA 22203
703/525-0358

Obbie's Dessert School
716 Lowander Lane
Silver Spring, MD 20901
301/434-3131

The Pastry Institute of Washington, D.C.
6925 Willow Street, NW
Washington, DC 20012
202/726-0790

Some of the world's greatest pastry chefs are in the metropolitan area, and this school offers demonstrations and classes to everyone who would like to learn from them. Regardless of experience, classes are offered as demonstrations, 3-day special sessions, and the full six-month pastry course in their Takoma Park location. Classes range from $40–$4,000.

Culinary Clubs
American Institute of Wine and Food (AIWF)
P.O. Box 7664
Arlington, VA 22207
703/276-7786

A consummate menu of tempting events is offered throughout the metropolitan area by this local chapter of AIWF, comprised of approximately 50% professional members in the wine and food industry, and 50% "dedicated consumers" with an "active interest in

fine food, wine, and related fields." The local chapter organizes
monthly wine tastings, receptions, workshops, and other social and
educational activities. Local excursions have included trips to choco-
late factories, apple orchards, smokehouses, and Virginia wineries.
AIWF has also sponsored "Marketplace Tasting," a public extrava-
ganza of exhibits, demonstrations, and tastings with a guest appearance by the renowned Julia Child. AIWF events range from small,
intimate dinners to large culinary celebrations. Dues begin at $35, and members re-
ceive invitations to all events, which run from $10 for a wine tasting to $100 for an
elegant dinner.

Vegetarian Society of the District of Columbia
P.O. Box 4921
Washington, DC 20008
301/589-0722

Potluck dinners, picnics, lectures, restaurant evenings, and other activities are sponsored by the Vegetarian Society, the oldest vegetarian organization in the country.
The society's newsletter includes a calendar of events, a survey of vegetarians' favorite restaurants, book reviews, news articles, roommate services, cooking classes, and
recipes. Members also receive discounts on vegetarian meals at participating restaurants. Membership starts at $12 and programs vary in cost.

Food Cooperatives

According to *Bethesda Coop News*, food cooperatives enhance our sense of "community and involvement" and attest to the "feasibility of applying democratic con-
trols to economic affairs." Modern cooperatives emerged during Europe's Industrial Revolution as Europeans sought to operate the stores and factories where they
worked. American food cooperatives, run by the people and for the people with
substantial savings for all, appeared in the 1930's and grew in popularity during
the late 1960's. Today, area food co-ops are managed by members and an elected a
board of directors. Co-ops offer the chance to save money, buy high quality gro-
ceries and produce, meet your neighbors, take a cooking class, and participate in
community enterprise.

Bethesda Co-op
6500 Seven Locks Road
Cabin John, MD 20818
301/320-2530

"Food for people, not for profit," is this food co-op's maxim. This co-op's fall and
spring evening cooking classes have included Mexican Cuisine, International Vegetarian Cooking, and Creative Vegetarian Dishes ($20 per class or $100 for six classes).
Free monthly newsletters and meetings provide the Co-op community with ample
food for thought. The Bethesda Co-op is open to the public, but members who
volunteer three hours a week receive 15% discounts on all purchases.

Other area co-ops include:

Glut Food Co-op
4005 34th Street
Mt. Ranier, MD 20712
301/770-1978

The Uncommon Market
1041 South Edgewood Street
Arlington, VA 2220
703/920-6855

Senbeb Natural Food Co-op
5924 Georgia Avenue, NW
Washington, DC -20011
202/726-5566

Women's Community Bakery
737 7th Street, SE
Washington, DC 20003
202/546-7944

Takoma Park-Silver Spring Food Coop
623 Sligo Avenue
Silver Spring, MD 20910
301/588-6093

Washington Wine Connoisseurs: Classes and Organizations

Les Amis du Vin
2302 Perkins Avenue
Silver Spring, MD - 20910
301/588-0980

Les Amis du Vin (the Friends of Wine) invites its 2500 local members to monthly wine tastings and special events, which range from an annual "Octoberfest" celebration featuring German beers to an exquisitely prepared French dinner. Costs for these events range from $10 to $100. This organization offers its worldwide membership of wine lovers a bi-monthly magazine, travel opportunities, and discounts at local wine shops on selected "wines of the month."

Introduction to Wine Appreciation
First Class
1726 20th Street, NW
Washington, DC 20009
202/797-5102

Beginners sample 40 different wines and learn how to taste and appraise wine. Three evening sessions are offered once every two months. Classes include 35 to 40 people and cost approximately $80 per person.

Wine Tasting Association
1225 Eye Street, NW
Washington, DC 20005
Mr. Mark Phillips
202/682-4733

Established in September 1990, this local non-profit association hosts both formal and informal weekly events at embassies, art galleries, and other elegant locales throughout the metropolitan area. The 700-member association, generally consisting of people in their 30s and 40s, sponsors tastings, classes, dinners, and parties. "Feature Events" have included everything from horseback riding and winery tours to holiday champagne tastings. In addition, volunteers are welcome to "pour, mingle, set up, and clean up." Annual dues start at $50, and events range from $10 to $50. Although all events are open to the public and anyone can receive a free monthly calendar of events, members receive substantial discounts at restaurants, wine stores, and at Association events. ⚜

Dance
Stepping Out

If you love to dance but don't have a partner, there are hundreds of opportunities to kick up your feet in the metropolitan area. For those who are concerned about kicking up two left feet - have no fear. Many groups offer an introductory hour to assist beginners or provide special sessions for the less experienced. In most folk, ethnic and country western dancing, each person dances with a number of partners in a friendly, unpretentious atmosphere. For other groups, especially square and Scandinavian dances, prior instruction ensures a smoother start for the participants. All of the organizations in this chapter offer lessons or referrals,  and they are glad to provide more information for prospective dancers. Another excellent source of instruction is your local recreation center (see *Parks, Recreation, and Community Centers*).

Those who prize the classic discipline of ballet or the freedom of modern dance will find many private studios in the area, as well as classes at most area recreation departments, community centers, and colleges. These organizations offer instruction and studio space. Their bulletin boards are among the best sources of information for auditions, ensembles, and solo appearances.

The chapter is divided into the following sections:
* Diverse Dances
* International, Ethnic, & Folk Dancing
* Square and Contra Dancing
* Country Western Dancing
* Renaissance Dancing
* Big Band, Swing, and Jazz Dancing

Media Alert!

Dancing: A Guide to the Capital Area, by Pat McNees, is available from the author at 10643 Weymouth Street, #204, Bethesda, MD 20814. This guide is as entertaining as it is informative, with descriptions, histories, and social commentary on more than a dozen kinds of folk and social dancing to be found in the metropolitan area. Listed are more than 200 area dance groups, halls, and classes, most with information on times, programs, and places. The guide costs $8, and is also available from the Bethesda Travel and Language Center.

Diverse Dances

Dance Place
3225 8th Street, NE
Washington, DC 20017
202/269-1600

This non-profit center for contemporary and ethnic dance is literally in constant motion in its efforts to expand the dance experiences of all Washingtonians. The area's foremost presenter of contemporary dance concerts, Dance Place hosts works by local, national, and international dancers and choreographers. Classes in modern dance are offered for adults and children at all levels of experience. Outreach programs take dance into the community, and "Inreach" events draw special groups to Dance Place for free matinee programs. Dance Place is also active in international exchange, presenting dance and music from around the world and enabling Washington artists to perform abroad. Membership at Dance Place is $30, and includes reduced rates for performances, two complimentary tickets, invitations to special receptions, and a periodic newsletter.

The Folklore Society of Greater Washington (FSGW)
P.O. Box 5693 Friendship Heights Station
Washington, DC 20016
703/281-2228

Dance is only one aspect of the program at FSGW, which sponsors weekly square and contra dances at Glen Echo Park (Sunday evenings, March through November), English Country dance at Church of the Ascension in Silver Spring (Wednesdays) and international dance in Foggy Bottom (Thursday evenings). The FSGW has also offered instruction in vintage dances including waltz, polka, tango, foxtrot. The FSGW's monthly newsletter includes information on all of its own dance events, as well as notices of other dance events around town. Also see *Arts*, "Multidisciplinary Organizations".

Glen Echo Park
National Park Service
7300 MacArthur Boulevard
Glen Echo, MD 20812
301/492-6282 (Events line)
301/492-6229 (Park Offices)

The Spanish Ballroom at Glen Echo Park may be the site of more swirling and spinning than any other room in Washington. Dances are held three times a week from mid-March through November in the spacious but unheated and unairconditioned ballroom. Temperatures aside, the Ballroom is a favorite spot for area dance enthusiasts.

Friday Night Dances feature squares, contras, and country dances which start at 8:30 pm and cost $5. Lessons in contra dancing are offered from 7:30 to 8:30, and while all are invited to observe, to participate you must register for month-long series ($32). For information on classes, call 301/492-6229.

Saturday Night Dances feature swing, big band, rhythm and blues, and Cajun dancing. Lessons take place between 8:00 and 9:00 p.m., and the dancing begins at 9:00. Admission is $7 to $10 and the lessons are free. For big band information call 301/492-6229; for swing dance information, call 301/340-9732.

Sunday Night Dances are generally geared toward intermediate and advanced square and contra dancing. Dances run from 7:30 to 10:30. Admission is $7. For information, contact the Folklore Society of Greater Washington, 703/281-2228.

In addition to the instruction preceding dance events, Glen Echo offers weekend, weekday, and evening classes in a variety of dance styles. Classes include ballet, modern dance, jazz, dancercise, creative movement for older adults, music and movement improvisation workshop, improvisation, equal movement (an integration of dance movements, fitness strengthening, and yoga relaxation), and body awareness/stretch/relaxation. Classes in traditional dances include Morris Dancing, rock, swing, jitterbug, waltz, and the 8-count Lindy, a dance form of the 1920's. Fees for traditional dance classes range from $26 to $69. Classical and modern classes range from $80 to $296, depending upon the number of classes per week.

Golden Rays
Ms. Raedina Winters
703/370-1466

The Golden Rays are a group of Senior women who still enjoy tap dancing in their retirement years. Classes are sponsored by Fairfax County at the Lincolnia Senior Center and the Little River Glen Senior Center, and participants must be at least 55 years old. The dance group appears at retirement homes, clubs, organizations, and even special festivals such as the Elderfest in Washington, D.C., and the National Cherry Blossom Parade. The beautifully costumed group presents a rockette style tap dance revue to such tunes as "Chorus Line," "Tea for Two," and "When I'm Sixty Four." There is no class fee or cost of membership.

Joy of Motion (JOM)
Dance Center, Inc.
5207 Wisconsin Avenue, NW
Washington, DC 20015
202/362-3042

Joy of Motion offers classes for everyone, "whether you're dancing for your health or career." A non-profit organization created in 1976, JOM offers technique classes such as jazz, tap, modern dance, and ballet. Fitness classes such as Aerobics and Body Sculpture and high energy classes like Street Jam and Jazz Funk are also available. JOM also sponsors workshops, performances, community programs, and performance opportunities. Prices vary, and it is possible to pay by the class, the semester, or with a class card valid for 10 to 30 classes.

Herb Fredricksen
12-B Linda Court
Gaithersburg, MD 20877
301/840-2056

Bavarian and Austrian, as well as cowboy and swing dancing and tango and the waltz, are all among the steps taught by Herb Fredricksen through the Montgomery County Recreation Department, City of Gaithersburg Department of Parks and Recreation, the Smithsonian associate program, and a number of independent programs.

International, Ethnic and Folk Dance
African Dance

African Heritage Center
4018 Minnesota Avenue, NE
Washington, DC 20019
202/399-5252

The motto of this organization, "A people without a culture are a people without a future," is born out by activities that celebrate African American heritage. The Center offers classes in African, modern, jazz, and creative dance for all ages, and sponsors a Big Ladies Elder Company that welcomes mature members of the community to train and perform. The African Heritage Dancers and Drummers are the Center's most visible representatives, and their colorful programs reach over 50,000 children and young people each year.

Ceili

The Blackthorn Stick
P.O. Box 222
Riverdale, MD 20737
301/474-4641

A ceili, literally "a friendly gathering," comprises more than just an Irish social dance: it is a festive celebration that traditionally involves dancers of all ages. The Blackthorn Stick's celebrations feature live music, soda bread, libations, and dance. This is group dancing, so partners are not a requirement, and goodwill and high spirits prevail. The door prize at the club's monthly dance is a blackthorn walking stick fashioned in Ireland. The fee is $7.50 in advance or $10 at the door. Classes are offered on a weekly basis, but not at the ceili itself.

Greater Washington Ceili Club
P.O. Box 23363
Alexandria, VA 22304

This club sponsors monthly dances at Cherry Hill Park, at 9800 Cherry Hill Road in College Park. Instruction is available. Membership dues are $12 per year, and dance fees are $7 for members, $10 for non-members.

Northern Virginia Ceili Club
10114 Glenmere Road
Fairfax, VA 22032
703/978-8265

Monthly dances are held (September through June) in Fairfax City, Virginia. Free instruction. Fees are $7 for adults, $3 for children under 16, children under 6 are free.

Clogging

Media Alert!

The Daily Clog
95 East Wayne Avenue, #312
Silver Spring, MD 20901
Ms. Julie Mangin
301/495-0082

The *Daily Clog* is the area's best source of information on clogging, a distinctive form of American folk dancing that combines African and Indian influences with folk dances from the British Isles. Free-style clogging can be found on the second and fourth Thursday evenings at The Chicken Place, 11201 Grandview Avenue in Wheaton, where for $5 cloggers converge to dance to live music from 8:30 p.m. to 11:30 p.m. Several clogging clubs and classes are listed below.

Cranberry Cloggers
Ms. Diane Rowe, Director
703/534-1279

The director of this club also teaches clogging through the Fairfax County Department of Recreation.

English Country Dance

Metropolitan Washington Country Dance Society
7613 Fountaine Bleau Drive
Apartment 2112
New Carrollton, MD 20784
301/577-5018

One English country dance enthusiast, asked to describe this form of folk dance, said there is simply "no more fun in the world — it's magic." The magic in this case may be in the live music that accompanies the dancing. A relative of American square and contra dances, English country dancing is more stately and sedate, and has been compared to a choreographed walk. Performed primarily in lines but also in circles and sets, this dancing is an ideal introduction to folk dance in general, and beginners are easily absorbed into the group. At the Society's bi-monthly dances, beginners are urged to join in at the start of the evening, since the dances are progressively more complicated. It is much better to move early and watch later! Dances are taught and then danced without callers, though prompting is provided as necessary. The dances are held on the second and fourth Saturdays of the month at the Sligo Middle School on Dennis Avenue in Silver Spring, and the fee is generally $4 per evening. Singles are welcome.

Morris Dance

Foggy Bottom Morris Men
6704 Westmoreland Ave.
Takoma Park, MD 20912
301/270-2014

This ancient men's ritual dance from the Cotswold region of England has traditionally used the sounds of bells on shin pads, clashing sticks and snapping of handkerchiefs in an exuberant dance to awaken the earth in Spring and bring forth good harvests in the Autumn. The Foggy Bottom Morris Men meet on Thursday evenings from 8-10 p.m. in Takoma Park. They find Morris dancing historic, fun, and an aerobic workout. No prior experience is necessary; an interest in traditional music and customs are required and a sense of rhythm and some lightness of feet is helpful ! During the year they perform at gatherings of Morris groups from this area and beyond.

Indian Dance

Nritya Rangam Cultural Association, Inc.
4216 Underwood Street
University Park, MD 20782
301/864-6976

The sinuous movements of Indian dance and the haunting music of the sitar, tabla, and harmonium are taught, performed, and presented by this association. The aim is to reach all persons interested in the music and dance of India. Classes are held for various skill levels at the Prince George's Plaza Community Center (6600 Aldelphia Road, Hyattsville, 301/864-1611) on Sunday afternoons. An ensemble of the Association has performed a program entitled "Glimpses of India" at many universities and other sites throughout the area. Class tuition is $38 per month. Private instruction is also available.

Israeli Dance

Israeli Folk Dance
Jewish Community Center of Greater Washington (JCCGW)
6125 Montrose Road
Rockville, MD 20852
301/881-0100

There are more than 1000 dances in the Israeli folk repertoire that reveal the influences of cultures from Spain to India. Dancers of all ages and all levels of experience are welcome at the Wednesday evening classes at the JCCGW. Beginners are taught at 7:00 p.m., intermediate dancers at 8:00 p.m., and requests are accepted from 9:00 to 11:00. The fee is $3 for JCC members, $3.50 for students, and $4 for all others. Folk dance is but a part of the JCCGW's active dance department, which involves over 400 students in ballet, modern, jazz, tap, and American folk dancing.

The Jewish Community Center of Northern Virginia at 8900 Little River Turnpike in Fairfax, Virginia (703/323-0880) also offers Israel folk dance programs. You may also contact Ms. Dorothy Solomon (301/656-3391) for information on intermediate and advanced dancers who meet on Mondays at Temple Israel in Silver Spring.

Scottish Dance

St. Columba's Scottish Country Dance Group
4354 Warren Street, NW
Washington, DC 20016
202/363-0976

A descendant of French court dances and antecedent of square and contra dancing, Scottish Country Dance places great emphasis on both steps and music. Lines of couples progress through set steps without the aid of a caller, though beginners who are "tolerably mobile" will find they can do the simpler steps right away. Not technically a form of folk dancing, Scottish country dancing has always belonged to all classes of society, from Mary Queen of Scots to the present Queen of England, hence the "Royal" in the Royal Scottish Dance Society (RSDS) with which this club is affiliated. The activity is still quite democratic, with more experienced dancers willing to help newcomers through the paces. It is not necessary to arrive with a partner. Though one is encouraged to follow the classes through the semester ($30), it is possible to drop in on the Tuesday evening sessions ($2).

Scottish Country Dance Society of Washington (SCDS)
5034 Eskridge Terrace, NW
Washington, DC 20016
202/966-3595

Washington Branch
3320 Kaywood Drive
Falls Church, VA 22041
703/820-7060

Northern Virginia Branch
P.O. Box 20313
Alexandria, VA 22320
703/379-5779

The Northern Virginia Branch of the SCDS meets on Wednesdays at Durant Recreation Center, Alexandria, Virginia. The Washington Branch meets Mondays at the National Institutes of Health, in Bethesda, Maryland, and Tuesdays at the Washington Episcopal School in Bethesda, and also publishes a quarterly newsletter. Both branches are affiliated with the Royal Scottish Country Dance society, headquartered in Edinburgh.

Spanish Dance

Spanish Dance Society (SDS)
4201 Cathedral Avenue, NW, Suite 1023
Washington, DC 20016
(703) 527-8326

The discipline in Spanish dance is as strict as that in ballet, but the click of heels, the swirl of skirts, and the clack of castanets are part of a distinctly different dance form. Flamenco, regional, and Spanish classical dance are all taught by this chapter of the Spanish Dance Society in conjunction with the dance department of the George Washington University. Classes are offered at all levels, and follow the international SDS syllabus. The Society's performing ensemble often appears at the Smithsonian, the Kennedy Center, and numerous folk festivals. Students must register for classes on a semester basis, but need not be enrolled at GWU to participate. The fee schedule varies.

Sam and Sarah Stulberg
2001 Merrimac Drive
Stafford, VA 22554
703/527-8998

Dancers who appreciate variety should visit the Key Elementary School in Arlington, Virginia, on Tuesday evenings. For more than 25 years, the Stulbergs have offered instruction in dances from around the world under the auspices of the Arlington County Department of Recreation and Parks. There is an emphasis on Balkan dances, but you may also encounter Russian, Japanese, English, or a dozen other forms of dance. The dances chosen each week depend partly on the group that assembles (usually about 30 people), and may be done in circles, lines, squares, or couples. Experience and partners are not necessary, and instruction is offered throughout the evening. The cost is $3 per session. The Stulbergs can also steer you to groups that meet in other areas on different nights.

Mel and Phyllis Diamond
301/871-8788

This couple schedules international dances on Mondays at Leland Community Recreation Center (4301 Willow Lane, Chevy Chase). They also teach classes of all levels at the Center.

Charles and Ruth Toxey
301/229-0455

These enthusiasts of international dance offer instruction in Washington, D.C. on Wednesdays from 8:15 p.m. until 10:00 p.m. at the Guy Mason Recreation Center on Wisconsin Avenue, and on Fridays from 7:30 p.m. until 9:30 p.m. at the Chevy Chase Community Center.

Foggy Bottom Folkdancers
202/547-6419

Eastern European dance is the fare at St. Mary's Episcopal Church located on 23rd Street between G and H streets, one block from the Foggy Bottom Metro station. Instruction is offered from 7:30 to 9:00 p.m., and requests are from 9:00 to 10:45 on Thursday nights.

Mt. Vernon International Folk Dancers
Ken or Pat Krogh
703/780-2393

These dancers meet Wednesdays at Mt. Vernon Unitarian Church, in Alexandria, Virginia.

Square and Contra Dancing
Washington Area Square Dancers Cooperative Association (WASCA)
5004 Colonial Drive
Camp Springs, MD 20748
301/899-6657

Western-style square dancing is a wonderful diversion from everyday cares, but you still need to mind the music and the steps. There are over 3000 calls to contend with, and once you have mastered about 70 of them, you may join over 5000 Washingtonians in one of the 150 square dance clubs in the metropolitan area. WASCA can guide you to lessons, classes, dances, and to Babe Mitchell, the WASCA newsletter editor, who will happy to route you to dances at your skill level in your area. For $10 a year you may subscribe to the newsletter, *Calls n' Cues*, which lists all of the participating clubs, when and where they meet, and who calls. The newsletter also includes a list of beginners' classes and a variety of articles, poetry, and club news. In addition to western-style square dancing, WASCA keeps tabs on a number of contra, round, and clogging clubs.

Country Western Dancing
Northern Virginia Country Western Dancing Association
P.O. Box 384
Merrifield, VA 22116-0384
703/860-4941

Pat McNees, author of *Dancing: A Guide to the Capital Area*, describes country western dancing as "a cowboy version of ballroom dancing. . .it makes you feel like you are in the nonsmoking section of Marlboro Country." This form of couples dancing includes the two step, waltz, shuffle, and western swing. The NVCWDA sponsors two dances each month, and publishes a newsletter full of local country western dance events. The NVCWDA can also direct you to nearly a dozen night spots in the area that cater to country western dancers.

Renaissance Dancing

Thrir Venstri Foetr
15900 Pinecroft Lane
Bowie, MD 20716-1739
301/390-4089

Though the name is Old Norse for "three left feet," the skillful execution of medieval, renaissance, and old English country dances proves the dancers have no such thing. Beginners are welcome at Tuesday evening rehearsals at the University of Maryland, College Park. The group performs annually at the Maryland Renaissance Festival, where dancers emphasize audience participation.

Big Band, Swing and Jazz Dancing

Big Band Society (BBS)
Ed Walker Chapter
P.O. Box 6103
Silver Spring, MD 20916
202/BIG BAND (244-2263)

There are usually more than 200 people at the BBS monthly dances in Wheaton, where the music is provided by regional bands of up to 18 players. The 1200 BBS members not only bring music and dance of the past into the present, but they sponsor fundraisers and scholarships to ensure the future of big band music. The annual Big Band Festival held each spring at Chantilly High School draws student musicians from around the area, who compete for trophies and three $1000 scholarships. A monthly newsletter includes information on upcoming BBS events, news of the BBS family, and a "Datebook" of events around town. Annual dues are $20, and each dance costs about $13.

Capital Vintage Dance Society
403 G Street, NE
Washington, DC 20002
202/543-7178

"Vintage" dances — those popular between 1840 and 1930 — are celebrated by this society at special events that feature live music, dance cards, and refreshments. Workshops offer a chance to brush up on dances from the waltz and polka to ragtime and foxtrot. Special events have included a tango workshop followed by a "Tango Tea," and a 19th-century ball at which period costume is encouraged. The Society is affiliated with the Folklore Society of Greater Washington, whose members receive a reduced rate for events. The cost for dances is $12 to $15, and weekend workshops average $50.

Potomac River Jazz Club
3608 35th Street, NW
Washington, DC 20016
703/698-7752

Though this group concentrates on the music, there is a dance floor at each of its monthly events. (See *Arts*, "Music Societies and Organizations".)

Washington Swing Dance Committee
3601 Upshur Street
Brentwood, MD 20772
301/340-WSDC (9732)

These folks have the reputation of sponsoring the best swing dances in the area. Their highly energized affairs roll back the decades with live bands that provide the music for swing, jitterbug, boogie-woogie, and rock n' roll. Workshops scheduled one hour before the dance begins allow everyone to brush up their steps. The $7 fee is refunded if you volunteer to help for an hour during the dance. ⚜

Education
Mind Over Matter

According to *The 1993 Places Rated Almanac*, the metropolitan Washington area is ranked sixth in the country for the number of educational options available here. Evening and weekend courses cater to those of us who don't have the luxury of becoming full-time students. Being an international center, Washingtonians have access to lectures by the brightest scientists, political leaders, and artists in the world. Along with degree programs offered at the renowned universities in the area, community colleges, local public schools, and community centers have impressive course catalogues and are often conveniently located in your own neighborhood. The local library is also a valuable source of information on nearby classes, seminars, workshops, and special programs. Open universities offer one night courses, and several innovative programs have been designed specifically with singles or senior citizens in mind. As  classes and fees are subject to change, contact the school or program of your choice for a current course catalogue. In most cases, local residents often receive discounts, and seniors, retirees, and the unemployed may be eligible for tuition waivers and/or substantial discounts.

Uniquely Washington

Many of the nation's leading educational and cultural institutions are located here in the nation's capital, allowing metropolitan residents to take advantage of an exceptional selection of courses and other special programs. The Smithsonian Institution's Associate Program is in a class by itself, but other organizations offer equally stimulating, if less numerous, programs. Depending on your interests and talents, be sure to consult our other chapters. For instance, a host of courses in the humanities, the fine arts, and the studio arts is previewed in *Arts*. The Writer's Center's literature classes, L'Academie de Cuisine's culinary seminars, Alliance Français' French instruction, and the Montgomery County Historical Society's genealogical classes are but a small sampling of the additional educational opportunities to be explored.

Smithsonian Institution Associate TSA (Resident Program)
1100 Jefferson Drive, SW
Washington, DC 20560
202/357-3030

Antarctic Adventure. Murder They Wrote. Why the Mona Lisa Smiles. Nuts and Bolts of Robotics. The Okra Dance Company. Only in Washington and only through TSA can you choose from more than 2000 such programs a year. Virtually every day, TSA offers a wide selection of courses, film series and premieres, lectures, seminars, tours, studio arts classes, and performing arts programs. All of TSA's current programming is listed in the monthly Associate available at the TSA office or by calling the number listed above.

The Smithsonian's Campus on the Mall is TSA's "non-credit university," which offers a remarkable array of courses in art and architecture, humanities, international studies, performing arts, science, and special topics taught by a prestigious "faculty" of renowned scholars and speakers. Two-year certificate programs are also available in art history, international affairs, Asian and Western civilization, and music connoisseurship. Other offerings include Weekends on the Mall and Daytime Courses. Current courses are listed in the *Campus on the Mall* quarterly brochure.

Of special interest is the year-round Smithsonian After Dark Supper Series, when TSA presents cocktails and dinner followed by lectures and discussions at the Smithsonian Castle. Special series have included Jazz Evenings at the Smithsonian for Young Professionals, and A Culinary Journey Through China featuring illustrated lectures, tastings, receptions, and a Chinese lunch. TSA also presents Superstar Seminars with outstanding academics, and Young Associates and Family Activities that include the lively Discovery Theater and the annual Kite Festival. Other offerings include Friday Evening for Singles, a series of lectures, concerts, demonstrations, and informal receptions that recently featured The Sophisticated Traveler in the '90's: Unique Places in America. Singles Evenings: Conversation and Canapes, is a quarterly series of four lectures, each followed by champagne and hors d'oeuvres and attended by some 250 people. A breakfast lecture series, Tuesday Mornings at the Smithsonian, is especially popular with Washington seniors. TSA also offers a wide range of special tours to historic sites, private art exhibits, Broadway musicals, museums, vineyards, and natural sites such as wild West Virginia's Cliffs and Caverns.

TSA programs are generally held in Smithsonian museums, and range from evening lectures and weekend seminars to six to eight-week courses. While TSA membership is not required for registration, members receive at least a 25% discount on class fees (which may range from $8 to over $200), the *Associate* and *Smithsonian* magazines, and free invitations to special events. Membership starts at $45 and is one of the best entertainment bargains in the Washington area.

The Washington Adventurer...

The Smithsonian National Associate Program also arranges worldwide study tours and seminars, research expeditions, and learning adventures. Especially popular are the Smithsonian Countryside Study Programs, tours and seminars held in villages and small towns all over the globe. In 1992, over 14 tours included 10 to 14-day excursions to France, England, Mexico, Greece, and the Czech Republic.

Other cultural classes and educational programs include:

American Youth Hostels (AYH)
Potomac Area Council
P.O. Box 28607 Central Station
Washington, DC 20038
202/783-0717

AYH members have enjoyed educational programs such as a Discover America lecture series on topics including Oregon, Mississippi, and Transcontinental Train Adventures. Slide shows, a Whole World Adventure series, theater outings, and other special programs complete AYH's educational and cultural activities. Events with hostelers from around the world have included language roundtables, film nights, a Bastille Day Celebration, and a tour and dinner in Washington's Chinatown. Members receive a Calendar of Events and other publications listing local AYH activities and services. Membership starts at $25, is open to all ages, and includes discounts on most AYH programs. While some AYH programs are free, others vary considerably in cost (also see *Athletics and Outdoor Adventures,* and *Volunteer*).

Friends of the National Zoo (FONZ)
Office of Volunteer and Educational Services
The National Zoological Park
Washington, DC 20008
202/673-4955

FONZ hosts an Audubon Lecture Series and classes and workshops on everything from beginning nature photography to veterinary studies. Less traditional classrooms include field trips to local sites such as the Chincoteague National Wildlife Refuge and more exotic locales such as the Galapagos Island. FONZ social calendars feature champagne breakfasts with the zookeepers, the summer concert series, and special events and festivals. Membership starts at $24 and includes members-only tours and events, exhibit previews, discounts on classes, and FONZ publications. Several FONZ programs are open to the public and fees start at $7. Some programs, such as the popular summer concerts, are free.

Jewish Study Center (JSC)
1747 Connecticut Avenue, NW
Washington, DC 20009
202/265-1312

The JSC offers courses on Jewish texts, prayer, language, philosophy, and social issues. Frequent activities include wine and cheese receptions, Shabbat dinners, tours, and other special events. The JSC also sponsors a work-exchange program, in which students donate time to pay for class tuition. While some classes are free, others range from $15 to $185 for a 12-session series. JSC members, Jewish Community Center members (see *Parks, Recreation, and Community Centers*), and certain area congregations receive substantial discounts on most classes. JSC membership starts at $36.

Kennedy Center Performance Plus
The Kennedy Center for the Performing Arts
Washington, DC 20566-0001
202/467-4600

Behind the Kennedy Center's stage curtains and bright lights, Washingtonians can meet famous performers, directors, and producers during discussions, lectures, demonstrations, symposia, backstage tours, and receptions. These events are listed in Kennedy Center News, available at the Kennedy Center and mailed to members of the Friends of the Kennedy Center (see *Arts, Volunteer*). Events range from $6 for single classes, to $150 for a luncheon/ dinner lecture series preceding NSO concerts.

Library of Congress
First Street and Independence Avenue, SE
Washington, DC 20540
202/707-6400

Though known to many as the city's most elegant place to pore through a card catalogue, the Library of Congress is much more than the nation's book repository. It is the largest and most accessible collection of human intellectual achievement in the world. Anyone over high school age may use the Library. The Library's monthly *Calendar of Events* — free upon request at the information counter or by calling 202/707-2905 — lists lectures, exhibitions, film screenings, poetry readings, and dramatic performances. Recent exhibitions have included "Rome Reborn: The Vatican Library and Renaissance Culture," priceless books and manuscripts never allowed outside the Vatican Library before, and "Scrolls from the Dead Sea," featuring twelve fragments of the oldest known copies of the Old Testament. The Library's impressive Chamber Music Series is now held at the National Academy of Sciences Auditorium during the renovation of the Coolidge Auditorium (call 707-5502 for details). Some of these free public events are followed by wine and cheese receptions where the audience is invited to meet the speakers and mingle informally.

National Geographic Society
1600 M Street, NW
Washington, DC 20036
202/857-7700

Travel to the Brazilian rainforests or the Antarctic tundra with the National Geographic's Society's Tuesdays at Noon, a lecture and film series for lunch-hour adventure. Other events held at the Society's Gilbert H. Grosvenor Auditorium include illustrated lectures, musical and dance performances, storytelling, and a series of travel film/lectures. Special events scheduled frequently throughout the year include lectures with biologists, anthropologists, historians, and other experts. Washingtonians may journey to virtually every corner of the globe during these programs, which range in price from the free Tuesdays at Noon to class series starting at $15. Free parking is available at some events.

Washington National Cathedral
Massachusetts and Wisconsin Avenue, NW
Washington, DC 20016-6098
202/537-8990

The Washington National Cathedral sponsors a wealth of educational opportunities in religious history, architecture, and the fine arts. Tours, concerts, films, demonstrations, readings, lectures, conferences, open houses, retreats, and other events are listed in the Cathedral's *Calendar*. Special opportunities include gardening workshops with the Cathedral's All Hallows Guild and a Medieval Workshop where you may create stained-glass windows or clay model gargoyles. The Tour and Tea program on Tuesday and Wednesday afternoons, which includes an hour-long tour given by a Senior docent followed by an authentic British tea in the tower, overlooking the entire city, is an educational event not to be missed. An especially active volunteer program offers further opportunities for involvement with this historic Washington institution. Also see *Volunteer*.

Continuing Education Classes

Continuing education programs are more popular than ever, and include classes and workshops offered at area universities, community colleges, public schools, and community education centers (profiled below according to location). Generally scheduled throughout the year on weekday evenings and weekends, and with fees a fraction of the cost of regular tuition, these non-credit, non-degree programs offer accessible, affordable opportunities for all. Innovative classes feature everything from Chinese Detective Fiction to Astronomy Overnight, in departments which include anthropology, art history, studio arts, economics, education, government, history, international affairs, languages, literature, music, psychology, philosophy, public policy, religion, science, sociology, theater and performing arts, women's studies, and writing.

Local Universities: The Consortium of Universities of the Washington Metropolitan Area includes American, Catholic, Gallaudet, George Mason, George Washington, Georgetown, Howard, and Marymount Universities, Mount Vernon and Trinity Colleges, the University of the District of Columbia, and the University of Maryland-College Park. College graduates and/or upper-level undergraduates interested in degree programs may enroll in courses at these universities on a space-available basis. Prerequisite, admission policies, and costs vary considerably. Virtually every university also offers an ambitious menu of lecture series, readings, films, concerts, and performances — often for free. Choose a campus and call the general number for further information.

DISTRICT OF COLUMBIA

Georgetown University
School for Summer and Continuing Education
Washington, DC 20057-1038
202/687-5942

If you always wished you had taken art appreciation or Western civilization, now is your chance: Georgetown University offers one of Washington's most diverse and extensive curricula of non-credit courses in the arts and sciences. With everything from Writing Mysteries to Islamic Fundamentalism, this university offers courses in art history and appreciation, literature, writing, communication, classics, religion, psychology, philosophy, history, international affairs, economics, and public policy. Courses on issues of local interest have included Politics, Scandal and People: Political History of the District of Columbia, and A Potomac River Overview: Its Geography and Natural and Human History. Georgetown also offers classes in foreign languages, the studio arts, and theater and music appreciation classes, as well as innovative music theater workshops (see *Arts*). Tuition ranges from $50 to $200.

Mount Vernon College
Division of Continuing Studies
2100 Foxhall Road, NW
Washington, DC 20007
202/625-4501

Situated in the tranquil neighborhood along Foxhall Road, Mount Vernon College offers courses in a wide range of subjects including the fine arts, photography, and personal development. The classes are primarily geared towards working adults, and small class size offers more personal service for the students. The cost is $300 per credit hour.

U.S. Department of Agriculture (USDA) Graduate School
South Agriculture Building, Room 1033
14th Street and Independence Avenue, SW
Washington, DC
202/720-5885

The USDA Graduate School offers evening and weekend courses in more than 50 areas which include professional and personal enrichment. The foreign language courses are especially popular, ranging from introductory Spanish to conversational Lithuanian. Other courses in environmental studies, horticulture, and natural history have included

Landscape Plants of Fall, Bird Life, and Geology, featuring field trips throughout the Central Atlantic. Those with a creative bent should consider courses such as Creative Photography and Introduction to Cartooning. Fees generally start at $100 per course.

MARYLAND
Johns Hopkins University School of Continuing Studies
Odyssey Program
34th and Charles Streets
Baltimore, MD 21218
410/516-7428

The Odyssey Program is a comprehensive, non-credit liberal arts certificate program offered at Johns Hopkins' Baltimore campus. Odyssey courses in the humanities include ancient civilizations and anthropology, foreign languages, national and world affairs, performing arts, art and architecture, film, literature, and creative writing. Some of the unusual offerings in Odyssey's science curriculum have included Ecology and the Environment, which featured lectures and field trips around the Chesapeake Bay, and a social sciences course on implications of the aging U.S. society. Two to ten-session courses range from $45 to $260.

Montgomery College
Continuing Education
Mannakee Street
Rockville, MD 20850
301/279-5188

Montgomery College offers "life enrichment" courses in art, literature, writing, graphic arts, music, languages, and photography at campuses throughout the county. These courses are often designed with beginners in mind and include offerings such as Know-nothing Photography. If you can find middle C you may consider taking How to Play the Piano Despite Years of Lessons. Courses of local interest have included The C&O Canal: A Living History, and Gardening Basics for the Metropolitan Area. Most non-professional courses are $30 to $150.

Montgomery County Public Schools (MCPS)
Division of Adult Education
12518 Greenly Street
Silver Spring, MD 20906
301/929-2025

MCPS' Adult Education course catalogue is nothing short of an extra-curricular extravaganza: you'll find classes in the studio arts, photography, music, cooking, writing, languages, and personal growth. MCPS Adult Education has offered everything from Luscious Linguini and Chinese Watercolor to group piano and home carpentry. A miscellaneous selection of courses has featured Irish Genealogy, Ancient Rome and Greece, U.S. Foreign Policy, and Sailing and Seamanship. Classes are held at public schools in the county throughout the year. Fees vary considerably from $20 to $200.

National Institutes of Health

Foundation for Advanced Education in the Sciences (FAES)
One Cloister Court, #230
Bethesda, MD 20814-1460
301/496-7976

FAES is in its 34th year of educating Washington residents, especially those considering a new career in the sciences. In addition to a host of professional programs and AMA-approved medical courses, you'll find several offerings in the liberal arts which have included Introduction to the History of Medicine as well as courses in art history, studio arts, and photography. A diverse selection of language courses includes Introduction to Chinese Literature, Spoken Russian, and Italian for Beginners. Evening courses at the college and graduate level may require prerequisites. Fees are $60 per credit hour.

Prince George's Community College

Continuing Education and Evening Programs
301 Largo Road
Largo, MD 20772-2199
301/322-0875

PGCC offers classes in fitness, floriculture/horticulture, music, photography and video production, and personal growth. Highlights have included Motorcycle Rider Safety, Discover Scubadiving, and Astrology in Action. Travel study courses include out-of-town trips to Frank Lloyd Wright's Fallingwater in Pennsylvania, hikes to Calvert Cliffs, and international excursions to England, France, and Germany. Classes are held at the college on weekday evenings and weekends. While tuition varies considerably, most courses range from $25 to $250.

Prince George's County Public Schools Adult Education

William Paca Instructional Services Center
7801 Sheriff Road
Landover, MD 20785
301/386-1512

A small selection of courses in history, art, cooking, personal growth, and parenting are featured at this continuing education program. Most courses are one to four sessions and have included The Arts of Early China and Gourmet Cooking. Fees range from $8 to $35.

VIRGINIA

Northern Virginia Community College (NOVA)

Community Education
8333 Little River Turnpike
Annandale, VA
703/323-3168

NOVA's Community Education Program offers evening and weekend noncredit courses at its Annandale, Alexandria, Loudoun, Manassas, and Woodbridge campuses. Courses have included:

❈ Inventor's Workshop
❈ Assertiveness
❈ Stress Management
❈ Conversational Spanish
❈ Chinese I - Mandarin
❈ Coping with Difficult People
❈ Creative Writing
❈ Photography
❈ Speedreading
❈ Sign Language
❈ Fundamentals of Interior Design

Class fees begin at $25.

University of Virginia

Division of Continuing Education
Northern Virginia Center
2990 Telestar Court
Falls Church, VA 22042-1279
703/876-6900

Since its founding in 1819 by native son Thomas Jefferson, the University of Virginia has offered innovative programs in higher education. The tradition endures at today's Division of Continuing Education, which offers a variety of credit and non-credit courses, seminars, and special programs in art history, history, literature, music, political and cultural studies, science, social studies, and writing. Courses have included an American studies series on 20th-century musical traditions, and the culture and history of the Soviet Union. Fees may range up to $173 per credit hour, depending on subject and number of sessions.

Virginia Public School Adult Education

Virginia public schools offer a range of opportunities for bona fide "fun" classes. In addition to liberal arts and science courses in music history, international studies, literature, travel French, and the studio arts, you'll find other unusual classes such as bike tune-up, attracting and identifying backyard birds, camera workshops, beginning genealogy, and the "ABC's of Wine Selection." Truly, there's everything from calligraphy to pilot training. Fees start at $30, with substantial discounts for Virginia residents.

Alexandria City Public Schools
Community Education
3330 King Street
Alexandria, VA 22302
703/824-6845

Fairfax County Public School Adult Education& the Fairfax County Department of Recreation
7510 Lisle Avenue
Falls Church, VA 22043
703/506-2200 or 703/506-2340

ArlingtonCounty Public Schools Adult Education Department & the Department of Parks, Recreation and Community Resources
855 North Edison Street
Arlington, VA 22205
703/358-7200

Open Universities

First Class
1726 20th Street, NW
Washington, DC 20009
202/797-5102

Courses taught by local instructors and experienced practitioners in the field include offerings in Looking Good, Career Options, New Discoveries, Creative Arts, Meeting People, Feeling Good, Writers' Workshops, Washingtonia, Business Scene, Sporting Life, Tours, First Class Fun, and Home Work (home improvement). Fees start at $20.

The School of Artsights and Insights
11226 South Shore Road
Reston, VA 22090
703/471-6327 Ms. Nannette Hoffman
703/620-4616 Mr. and Mrs. John Fleet

The School of Artsights and Insights offers short term courses in private homes, using the open university model. Classes last from one to four evenings, and are an "alternative to movies or television." Course offerings, which are listed in the school's bi-monthly catalogue, will feature, for example, evening discussions on various issues, a four session course called Slimmer You, and a poetry writing workshop.

Strictly Seniors

American University's Institute for Learning in Retirement (ILR)
4400 Massachusetts Avenue, NW
Washington, DC 20016
202/885-3920

ILR offers an affordable, enriching educational experience for Washingtonians over 50 years of age. As a membership organization, ILR participants design their own curricula of noncredit courses, lectures, and tours. Seniors may choose from over 100 study groups, which meet for two hours once a week in two, ten-week terms to explore subjects including foreign languages, history, literature, the arts, and the social sciences. Fees are $155 per semester or $250 fall through spring.

Elderhostel
75 Federal Street
Boston, MA 02110
617/426-7788

"Studying there is half the fun," proclaims Elderhostel, a progressive education program which offers week-long classes in the liberal arts and sciences for adults ages 60 and over. Inspired by the youth hostels and folk schools of Europe, Elderhostel was founded in 1975 and today includes over 1700 educational and cultural institutions in all 50 states and 10 Canadian provinces. In 1990, a record 250,000 hostelers enrolled in specialized programs ranging from "Cicero to computers... politics to poetry... from Maine to Manitoba.... Wollongong to Wales." 'Hostelers' live in dormitories and may enroll in up to three non-credit classes taught by college professors and other renowned instructors. Course size varies from 20 to 50 students. There are no exams, grades, or homework. Most courses, profiled in the course catalogue, presuppose only a "lifetime of experience and an inquiring mind."

More than a third of Elderhostel participants are single, and many others travel with a spouse or traveling companion. Most choose a destination of interest and enroll in a course there. Some 'Elderhoppers' make their way across the country, or take a course or two on their annual winter pilgrimage south to Florida. Others really take to the spirit of hosteling, and embark on raft trips down the Colorado River with Elderhostel's Outdoor Adventure. The programs in Maryland and Virginia feature courses in Chesapeake Bay ecology, colonial Williamsburg, and the Civil War (only 5% of the hostelers enrolled in these programs, however, are actually from the area). For the surprisingly-low cost of $300, hostelers enjoy classes, meals, accommodation, extracurricular activities, fieldtrips, and cultural events for the entire week. Elderhostel also sponsors programs in over 47 countries overseas which cost up to $4000. Full and partial 'hostelships' are available. Obtain the catalogue by calling the number listed above or by forwarding a postcard with your name and address.

Evergreen Society

Johns Hopkins University School of Continuing Studies
203 Shaffer Hall
Baltimore, MD 21218-2691
410/516-6055

These seniors enjoy seminars, workshops, and study discussion groups on a wide range of subjects such as art, history, literature, politics, world affairs, science, and the environment. The faculty is comprised of the University's professors and experts in the Washington community. Social outings include lunchtime activities and field trips to cultural events. Classes are held in Columbia, Maryland, at the Columbia Center of the School of Continuing Studies (on Wednesdays), and in Baltimore at the Grace United Methodist Church (on Tuesdays, Thursdays, and Friday mornings). Past courses have included: Great Books, State of the World 1991, The Jewish Roots of Christianity, The Age of Light Opera and Operetta, and Writing Your Personal Experiences and Memoirs. Special activities include performances and lectures during lunch, and field trips to cultural events. Membership is required. The annual dues of $340 include admission to all Evergreen programs. ⚜

Gardening
Earthly Delights

For centuries gardens have been a source of tranquility and beauty. One way to enjoy Mother Nature and put down roots in the community is to join other green thumbs in the peaceful pursuit of gardening. Gardening clubs, horticultural organizations, and plant societies offer classes and workshops, garden tours, volunteer opportunities, and other special programs. Community garden plots organized by non-profit organizations, park and recreation departments, community centers, and gardening extension services offer residents access to small sections of land for personal use. The resources in this chapter can be considered small seeds; joining one of the groups will most likely reap new friendships and the sense of accomplishment that beautifying our surroundings can bring.

Media Alert!

Beauty and Bounty: One-Day Nature Trips In and Around Washington, D.C., by Jane Ockershausen Smith (Mclean: EPM Publications, 1983) introduces you to "more than 150 of nature's refreshments within a day's drive of Washington, D.C."

The *Washington Post's* Thursday *Washington Home* Section devotes several pages to gardening information and events. You may also want to listen to the gardening radio shows produced by WGTS, 91.9 FM, on Tuesdays from noon until 1:00 p.m., and WRC, 980 AM, on Saturdays from 7 a.m. until 10 a.m.

Horticultural Programs

Gardens, conservatories, and wild flora are abundant in this area, where each season brings a new flowering of color, scent, and growth.

The organizations profiled below not only provide the enjoyment of their own facilities, but make their resources available to the home gardener.

American Horticultural Society (AHS)
7931 East Boulevard Drive
Alexandria, VA 22308
Ms. Stephanie McLellan
703/768-5700

The AHS offers comprehensive horticultural programs which serve gardeners nationwide. Events include a National Youth Gardening symposia, which is geared towards educators but is open to the public, special plant celebration days, and an annual plant show. The AHS also sponsors a Gardeners' Information Service, a data-base of horticultural organizations and programs which is available to members (800/777-7931). There is also an active docent program. In addition, the AHS organizes educational travel/tour programs to garden sites around the world, and publishes the *American Horticulturist.* Membership starts at $35.

Brookside Gardens
The Maryland-National Capital Park and Planning Commission
1500 Glenallan Avenue
Wheaton, MD 20902
301/949-8230

The magnificent 50-acre Brookside Gardens, run by the Maryland-National Capital Park and Planning Commission, offers a wide variety of educational programs, guided tours, and horticultural information services. Program activities have included lectures on Italian gardens, Brookside azalea walks, workshops on composting, and tours of other area gardens such as Hillwood and Longwood. Volunteers at Brookside meet other garden enthusiasts by leading tours, answering gardening questions, and assist-ing in the library. To cultivate and share your gardening/landscaping know-how, call to request an educational programs schedule and information on volunteer activities.

Horticulture Program of Friends of the National Zoo (FONZ)
Office of Volunteer and Educational Services
National Zoological Park
Washington, DC 20008
202/673-4955

FONZ volunteers enjoy the flora and fauna while assisting National Zoo gardeners on the Zoo grounds and in the greenhouse. The Zoo asks volunteers for two to three hours a month and attendance at a monthly meeting. See *Volunteering.*

National Arboretum
3501 New York Avenue, NE
Washington, DC 20002
202/475-4858

This well-kept Washington secret extends over 444 acres of woods and gardens in the city's northeastern corner. It boasts the most extensive collection of azaleas in the country (more than 70,000), as well as rhododendrons, hollies, boxwoods, maples, cherry trees, dogwoods, and other flora. You'll also find 53 miniature trees, some of which are over 350 years old. The Arboretum often needs volunteer gardeners to work in its truly glorious gardens; call for current opportunities.

U.S. Botanic Garden
Maryland Avenue and First Street, SW
Washington, DC 20024
202/226-4082

The U.S. Botanic Garden, the "Capitol Hill Conservatory," is a series of intercon-nected glass and stone buildings and greenhouses containing orchids, cacti, and a wide variety of rare and unusual plants. The Botanic Garden displays plants from around the world and features four annual plant and flower exhibits. Gardeners can volunteer their services—call the public programs office for more information.

THE SPRING EVENT:

The Behnke Nurseries Company
11300 Baltimore Avenue (U.S.1)
Beltsville, MD 20705
301/937-1100

This company celebrates the onset of spring with a free series of gardening seminars, generally scheduled from February through April. Past classes have included Gardens in Jeopardy, Back to the Basics, Spring Planting Inspirations, Aquatic Gardening, and specialty seminars in mums, azaleas, and rhododendrons. Other nurseries in the area offer similar programs. Wolf Trap Nursery, for instance, offers free bonsai classes throughout the year as well as two annual workshops to help you build your own bonsai (9439 Leesburg Pike, Vienna, Virginia, 22180, 703/759-4244).

Gardening Clubs and Plant Societies

Whether you have an extensive plot in the backyard or simply a pot on the windowsill, you can find advice, competition, and camaraderie in many places. The organizations profiled below cater to both general and specialized interests, and include plant enthusiasts of all ages.

Gardening Clubs

Over 100 garden clubs in the metropolitan area allow those with green thumbs to share their talents and display their horticultural triumphs. Social events can be as important as soil culture, and each club has its own calendar of meetings, shows, fund raisers, and excursions. Meeting times vary, and many clubs have evening or weekend meetings that enable members to accommodate their busy schedules. Because many clubs have limited membership, and openings often do not occur frequently, it is best to consult the National Capital Area Federation of Garden Clubs, profiled below to locate the clubs that are currently accepting new members.

National Capital Area Federation of Garden Clubs
5831 Fitzhugh Street
Burke, VA - 22015
Ms. Jo Sellers, Membership Chair
703/451-7037

You don't have to actually dig in the dirt to join the National Capital Area Federation of Garden Clubs, Inc., but you must have a love of the land and a healthy respect for the environment. This 40-year old Federation, a local offspring of the parent National Council of State Garden Clubs, includes 133 neighborhood clubs with a total of 4200 members. In addition to monthly club meetings, you'll find opportunities to meet other gardeners beyond your neighborhood at District club meetings and state conventions. The Federation strongly encourages recent retirees to join to make up for lost time out-of-doors. Annual dues entitle members to a number of benefits, including the quarterly "Capital Gardener," regular gatherings of day, evening, and Saturday clubs, lunchbreak "Brown Baggers," and occasional fashion shows, fundraisers, teas, and international events. Volunteer activities include decorating at the Botanical Gardens' "Christmas Green Show," as well as staffing the gift shop and leading tours at the National Arboretum. Federation president Mrs. William Butcher can suggest local garden clubs to prospective members based on the interests and schedule of the gardener and the openings available in the individual clubs.

Plant Societies

Washington area residents with a predilection for a particular plant may find other aficionados at area plant societies, which include: African violet, azalea, bonsai, bromelial, cactus and succulent, camellia, chrysanthemum, daffodil, dahlia, daylily, gloxinia, herb, ikebana, iris, lily, orchid, rhododendron, rock garden, and rose societies. These groups vary in size from 20 to 700 members (there appears to be a special fondness for roses). Activities may include speakers, slides, lectures, plant sales, cutting exchanges, shows, garden visits, newsletters, auctions, and picnics. For more information about plant societies, contact Brookside Gardens (301/949-8227), the National Arboretum (202/475-4815), the National Capital Area Federation of Garden Clubs (301/924-4718), or the U.S. Botanic Gardens (202/225-8333). Dues typically range from $5 to $20.

The Herb Society of America, Potomac Unit
P.O. Box 1055
Springfield, VA 22151
703/451-7037

Parsley, sage, rosemary, and thyme are just the beginning for the 85 members of this society, whose aim is to promote the "use and delight" of herbs. The group holds four meetings a year that are open to members and non-members alike, and participates in a number of local horticultural activities that include the maintenance of several local herb gardens, an annual herb plant sale at the National Arboretum, and a number of culinary and craft workshops, symposia, and study groups. A newsletter, The Potomac Potpourri, features information regarding meetings and activities.

National Capital Orchid Society
8905 Linton Lane
Alexandria, VA 22308-2731
Richard Grundy
703/360-6920

This gathering of orchid growers owes its existence to a U.S. Navy lieutenant who was so overwhelmed by the orchids he saw in the jungles of New Guinea during

World War II that he sought out other enthusiasts in the Washington area. The group has been affiliated with the American Orchid Society since 1947, and now has several hundred members in and around Washington. Meetings are held at the National Arboretum on the third Monday of each month. Almost weekly activities are held for all interested in this exotic plant to meet and mingle. Auctions and an October orchid show are among the annual highlights, and a monthly newsletter features growing tips, dispels myths, and tells of upcoming events.

Potomac Rose Society
831 Azalea Drive
Rockville, MD 20850
301/279-0028

If your rose garden has been a source of more frustration than pleasure, the Potomac Rose Society can help you to produce more blooms than bugs. A major priority of the society is to "assist and encourage the beginning rose grower," and monthly meetings, workshops, and two dozen experts offering free advice make it possible. The society's award-winning, monthly newsletter is read by rose growers nationwide and is full of practical advice. The frequent meetings held in McLean, Virginia are free and open to the public. The society is affiliated with the American Rose Society, and all members receive the national organization's quarterly digest. Basic membership is $17.50.

Community Garden Plots

Community garden plots are a valuable resource for apartment dwellers and other metropolitan residents who love to garden but who find themselves without ground to till. To find your own garden plot, you may contact one of the sources profiled below: (1) Garden Resources of Washington (2) Parks, Recreation and Community Centers, and (3) Gardening Education Resources: Extension Services. Patience is a prerequisite, as you'll encounter more landless gardeners than organized gardens and long waiting lists for the area's limited number of public garden plots.

Garden Resources of Washington (GROW)
1419 V Street, NW
Washington, DC 20009
Ms. Judy Tiger
202\234-0591

GROW offers a cornucopia of gardening opportunities by helping individuals and groups of all income levels and all ages to start self-sufficient community garden plots in and around public housing, church grounds, senior citizens' centers, homeless shelters, park lands, and private lots. Volunteers are encouraged to coordinate special events and to teach informal workshops on organic gardening and food preservation. If you're not up to organizing a new gardening

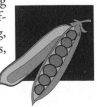

effort, GROW welcomes volunteer "Gardening Angels" to install, design, clean up gardens, and work regularly in established gardens with children and seniors (see *Volunteering*).

Parks, Recreation, and Community Centers

E a c h metropolitan jurisdiction has its own system of community gardening: plot sizes vary; some sites have water and some do not; some are restricted to organic gardening methods; some sites are plowed, and some have activities organized by volunteer gardeners. Registration dates and procedures also vary, although most systems run on a first-come-first-serve basis, with priority given to returning gardeners. The one constant is the nominal charge. Application and/or registration dates usually fall between January and March. Contact one of following administrative offices (before January) for information and application procedures in your area.

DISTRICT OF COLUMBIA

D.C. Department of Recreation and Parks
Youth and Urban Gardens Program
3149 16th Street, NW
Washington, DC 20010
Mr. William C. Hash
202/576-6257

National Park Service, National Capital Region
Rock Creek Park Superintendent
3545 Williamsburg Lane
Washington, DC 20008-1207
202/282-1063

Fort Dupont Park
National Capital Parks-East
c/o Fort Dupont Activities Center
1900 Anacostia Drive, SE
Washington, DC 20020
202/426-7723

Oxon Hill Farm
1900 Anacostia Drive, SE
Washington, DC 20020
301/839-1176

MARYLAND

Prince George's County
Department of Parks and Recreation: Park Permits
6600 Kennilworth Avenue
Riverdale, MD 20737
301/699-2415

City of Gaithersburg
Department of Parks and Recreation
Garden Plot Program
502 South Frederick Avenue
Gaithersburg, MD 20877
301/258-6350

City of Rockville Civic Center
603 Edmunston Drive
Rockville, MD 20851
301/309-3001

Mr. Raymond Heinen
2306 Hildarose Drive
Silver Spring, MD 20902
301/681-7898
(Mr. Heinen manages the plots on Briggs Cheney Road between Rt. 29 and Cloverly in Montgomery County, which no longer administers a garden plot program).

VIRGINIA

Arlington County Extension Service
3308 South Stafford Street
Arlington, VA 22206
Ms. Charlotte Hudson
703/358-6400

**Alexandria Chinquapin Recreation Center
Department of Recreation, Parks, and Cultural Activities**
3210 King Street
Alexandria, VA 22302
Ms. Margaret Orlando
Garden Park Manager
703/931-1127

**Green Springs Gardens Park
Fairfax County Park Authority**
4603 Green Spring Road
Alexandria, VA 22312
Ms. Faye Ghuneim/Mr. Jim Dewing
703/642-5173

Gardening Education Resources: Community Extensions Services

Local Extension Services offer a variety of gardening activities, including community garden programs, horticultural and environmental workshops and lectures, master gardening training courses (50 hours of training for 50 hours of volunteer work), and information hotlines.

DISTRICT OF COLUMBIA

**Cooperative Extension Service,
University of the District of Columbia
Attn: Horticulture or Gardening**
CESUDC 901 Newton Street, NE
Washington, DC 20017
202/576-6993

MARYLAND

**Prince George's County
Cooperative Extension Horticulture Office**
6707 Groveton Drive
Clinton, MD 20735
800/342-2507 (Maryland callers only, Monday through Friday 8:00 a.m. to 1:00 p.m.)
301/868-8780

Montgomery County Cooperative Extension Services
301/590-9650 (Monday through Wednesday 10:00 to 12:00 a.m.)
800/342-2507 (Monday through Friday 8:00 a.m. to 1:00 p.m.)

VIRGINIA:

**Arlington County Extension Services
Fairlington Center**
3308 South Stafford Street
Arlington, VA 22206
703/358-6400

**Fairfax County, Agriculture and Information Center
Agricultural/Horticultural Division**
12011 Government Center Parkway, 9th Floor
Fairfax, VA 22035-1109
703/222-9760
703/324-5326

Sowing Seeds of Peace and Understanding
International Peace Garden Foundation
1700 K Street, NW Suite 902
Washington, DC 20006
202/296-5331

If digging in the garden is not your cup of tea, but the idea of promoting the peaceful surroundings a garden provides is appealing, the International Peace Garden Foundation can use your help. The Foundation was created with the vision of sponsoring a chain of tulip gardens around the world. The gardens are planted in international capital cities near historic landmarks to promote peace and friendship. Each spring tulips bloom in Ottawa, Warsaw, Berlin, Budapest, and here in Washington. The Foundation hosts international events year-round, sponsoring scholarships, artist exchanges, and tours of the gardens. Volunteers are needed in every aspect of the Foundation: to help coordinate events, liaison with garden and artist associations, plan tours overseas, sell crafts for fundraising. ⚜

Historical Washington
Preserving the Legacy

The nation's capital is filled with famous sites and monuments that stand as milestones in our country's dramatic development. For those interested in knowing more than the standard facts and figures, a historical society can provide detailed pictures of days gone by. Local historical societies sponsor activities celebrating our rich heritage and preserving the past for future generations. Living history and re-enactment clubs bring various eras to life by focusing on specific periods in world history using costumes, language, and lifestyles dating from medieval times to the Civil War. Antiquarians hold classes and demonstrations of antique tools and crafts, sharing their knowledge of the lifestyles of our ancestors.

Historical Societies

From the National Trust for Historic Preservation to the Friends of Fairfax Station, historical societies throughout the metropolitan area offer classes, tours, monthly meetings, and other special programs. These societies also organize annual town festivals, preserve local historic landmarks, maintain historic sites, and sponsor community events. Volunteers who share a love of history often operate these societies by staffing museums and working farms, leading tours, teaching workshops, and coordinating events. Volunteer docents often dress in authentic costume and demonstrate period crafts and trades. Most societies require minimal dues and publish newsletters announcing upcoming events. Below you will find descriptions of national historical societies followed by profiles of local societies in Washington, D.C., Maryland, and Virginia.

National Societies

National Trust for Historic Preservation
1785 Massachusetts Avenue, NW
Washington, DC 20036-6412
202/673-4000 Main Office
202/673-4141 Public Information

This organization, chartered by Congress in 1949, includes over 250,000 national members who contribute to the preservation of this country's historic and architectural heritage. The local chapter sponsors unique activities every month at historic properties throughout the area, which have included a James Madison Birthday Celebration at Montpelier in Orange County, Virginia, a Kalorama House Tour in Washington, D.C., and a Woodlawn Christmas at Mount Vernon. Garden parties, dog shows, craft workshops, and special exhibitions are also featured on the local chapter's agenda. Membership starts at $15 and includes free admission to historic properties nationwide, exclusive invitations to National Trust seminars and domestic and international study tours, and several National Trust publications.

Washington, D.C. Historical Societies

The local historical societies profiled below celebrate the city's historical and architectural legacy bequeathed by outstanding architects such as the great French visionary Pierre L'Enfant.

The D.C. Preservation League (DCPL)
1511 K Street, NW, Suite 739
Washington, DC 20005
202/737-1519

"Don't Tear It Down" was the former name of this preservation society, which once stormed the barricades surrounding the Old Post Office in a victorious effort to save the building from destruction. Today, the DCPL's continued successes have earned the organization a reputation for excellence. In addition to preserving the city's "eclectic architectural splendor," the DCPL sponsors several public education programs. Each spring, an education series explores a different aspect of local architectural history, preservation, and development. Other events have included award galas, bicycle tours of historic neighborhoods, preservation auctions, architects' office tours, and special exhibits. A quarterly newsletter provides comprehensive coverage of local preservation and development issues, and includes a "Preservation Calendar" of upcoming events. Membership dues start at $25 ($15 for students and senior citizens).

Historical Society of Washington, D.C.
1307 New Hampshire Avenue, NW
Washington, DC 20036-1507
202/785-2068

In this transient city where change accompanies each new administration, it's comforting to know that someone is keeping track of things. Thus, with a declared mission to "preserve, collect and teach" the history of the city, the Historical Society of Washington, D.C. sponsors tours, lectures, workshops, exhibits, book signings, luncheons, and receptions. Especially popular walking tours have included "Communities and Museums: The Anacostia Story" and "Tour of Civil War Monuments and Memorials." The Society offers varying levels of membership, which afford such benefits as invitations to the annual Garden Party and free workshop passes. Founded in 1894, the Society is housed in one of Washington's best-preserved Washington mansions, a spired and turreted relic from the Gilded Age. This turn-of-the-century palace was built by local brewer Christian Heurich, whose brewery once operated on the site of the Kennedy Center. Membership dues begin at $35, and program fees range from $3 to $10.

Maryland Historical Societies

Granted by charter to Lord Baltimore in 1632, Maryland originally included land that is now part of the Federal City of Washington, D.C. Today, residents of Maryland's Prince George's and Montgomery Counties celebrate and preserve their local heritage through the following historical societies.

Historic Medley District, Inc. (HMD)
P.O. Box 232
Poolesville, MD 20837
301/972-8588

Montgomery County originally included five election districts. The former northwestern Medley District was named for John Baptist Medley's Tavern, a popular watering hole that doubled as a voting center and civil court. Since 1974, the HMD and its 100 members have been devoted to the restoration, preservation, maintenance, and appreciation of historic buildings in the former Medley District. HMD sponsors programs on current issues of historic preservation, local history, architecture, and genealogy. This organization also conducts tours to unusual historic sites, and invites the public to attend many of its lectures, barn dances, and guided tours.

Historic Takoma, Inc.
P.O. Box 5781
Takoma Park, MD 20912

Developed as a small railroad suburb in 1883, Takoma Park today extends through parts of the District and Montgomery and Prince George's County. Historic Takoma, Inc. dedicates itself to the preservation of the area's architecture and history by sponsoring periodic walking tours with local historians, by erecting markers at historically significant sites, and by acquiring an extensive collection of historical photographs and artifacts. The group also sponsors ongoing educational activities such as lectures and workshops. At monthly Board meetings, members plan the holiday open house, historic preservation projects, and other special events. The more than 150 members receive a quarterly newsletter with updates on member activities and neighborhood events.

Montgomery County Historical Society
111 West Montgomery Avenue
Rockville, MD 20850
301/762-1492

Montgomery County, chartered in 1776, was named for American Revolutionary War hero Richard Montgomery. The society, devoted to collecting, preserving, and interpreting Montgomery County history was formed in 1944, and today offers lecture series, walking tours, workshops, classes, and volunteer programs. Especially popular are the fall and spring genealogy classes. Other favorite events include the Holiday Open House, a spring wine tasting, and a Halloween evening where story-tellers recount the tales of infamous Montgomery County ghosts. The Society's 850 members receive a monthly newsletter and invitations to special events.

Peerless Rockville Historic Preservation, Ltd.
P.O. Box 4262
Rockville, MD 20850
301/762-0096

This 800-member society focuses on the preservation of Rockville's historic struc-tures and sites by sponsoring house tours, program talks, workshops, slide shows, receptions, and special events including a Victorian Ball and a New Year's Day Brunch. Members research Rockville history, plan house tours and "progressive dinners," paint fences, do yardwork, prepare food, write newsletters, serve on committees, or contribute legal or financial expertise. The society owns several historic properties, including a schoolhouse and a cemetery, and has adopted projects such as restoring Montgomery County's Red Brick Courthouse.

Prince George's County Historical Society
P.O. Box 14
Riverdale, MD 20738
301/464-0590

This county, named for Prince George of Denmark, was first visited by Captain John Smith and his crew in 1608. Over three hundred years later, the Prince George's County Historical Society began to chronicle the county's history through exhibits, events, and monthly meetings on subjects ranging from architectural trends to the Civil War. The Society's bi-monthly meetings are held at the Marietta site, 5626 Bell Station, Glenn Dale, Maryland, 20769.

Surratt Society
The Historic Mary E. Surratt House and Tavern
P.O. Box 427
9110 Brandywine Road
Clinton, MD 20735
301/868-1121

The Historic Surratt House and Tavern was once the home of Mary Surratt, the first woman executed by the U.S. government for her alleged complicity in Presi-dent Lincoln's assassination. Over 1000 members belong to the Surrat Society, which maintains the unique House and Tavern and encourages ongoing research into the Lincoln tragedy. The Society sponsors monthly meetings, exhibits on the site's history and 19th-century Southern Maryland lifestyles, and special events such as a bi-annual John Wilkes Booth Escape Route Tour, Civil War reenact-ments, and a Victorian Christmas by Candlelight. Surrat Society members may serve as docent guides, and all receive a monthly newsletter announcing upcoming events and pertinent historical information. Membership begins at $5.

Other Maryland historic societies include:

Chevy Chase Historical Society
P.O. Box 15145
Chevy Chase, MD 20825

Darnestown Historic Society
13700 Darnestown Road
Darnestown, MD 20878
301/926-4723

Gaithersburg Heritage Alliance
5 South Summit
Gaithersburg, MD 20877
301/869-1063

Historic Society of Germantown
P.O. Box 475
Germantown, MD 20875
301/972-0795

Hyattsville Preservation Association
P.O. Box 375
Hyattsville, MD 20781

Kensington Historic Society
P.O. Box 425
Kensington, MD 20895

Woodside Civic Association
8816 First Avenue
Silver Spring, MD 20910
301/589-7345

Virginia Historical Societies

In Virginia, whose native sons include George Washington, Thomas Jefferson, and Robert E. Lee, you'll find a historical society in virtually every town. In addition to the following profiles, other historical societies flourish in Burke, Falls Church, Lorton, Fairfax City, and other locales throughout Virginia.

Media Alert! **Northern Virginia Association of Historians (NVAH)**
c/o Ross Netherton
306 North Virginia Avenue
Falls Church, VA 22042

Northern Virginians interested in local history may write to the NVAH for *The NVAH Directory of Northern Virginia History Organizations* ($5). This directory profiles Northern Virginia historical societies, genealogical societies, and historic preservation groups. It includes valuable information concerning meeting times, dates, and places, names of contacts, membership, activities, and publications. The directory also features local historical libraries and special collections, and local government historical preservation agencies.

Alexandria Society for the Preservation of Black Heritage, Inc.
P.O. Box 3527
Alexandria, VA 22302
703/931-5330

Founded in 1980 to preserve the oldest African American Baptist church in the metropolitan area, this small historical society collects, preserves, and promotes the early history and impressive contributions of the African American community of Alexandria, Virginia. The Society's primary goal is to support the Alexandria Black

History Resource Center by providing volunteer manpower and matching grants for exhibits and receptions at the Black History Museum. The Center's varied activities include walking tours of the community and cultural and historical presentations on the lifestyles of Alexandria's African American community. Special tributes and youth programs have included a city-wide Martin Luther King Poster Contest and storytelling sessions for young children. Future events include a lecture series, memorial dinners, and the African-American Ethnic Fair. The Society welcomes interested residents to attend meetings scheduled at 7:30 p.m. on the second Monday of each month at the Resource Center, 638 North Alfred Street, Alexandria, VA, 22314, (703/838-4356). Annual dues start at $10 for individuals and $25 for organizations.

Arlington Historical Society and Museum
P.O. Box 402
Arlington, VA 22210
703/892-4204 (Museum)

Arlingtonians interested in the county's history, antiquities, art, and literature should explore this society, whose 350 members organize annual meetings, promote Historic Arlington Day, and coordinate tours and receptions that have included a holiday house tour by candlelight, and a George Mason Bus Tour to honor the nation's "Father of the American Bill of Rights." The Arlington Society also publishes a monthly newsletter and operates a historical museum at 1805 South Arlington Ridge Road, Arlington, Virginia, 22202.

Friends of Fairfax Station, Inc.
P.O. Box 7
Fairfax Station, VA
703/631-5100

The Friends of the Fairfax Station have meticulously recreated the 1850's railroad depot known as Fairfax Station. It is operated as a museum, gift shop, and community meeting room used by many local clubs, associations, and private groups. The museum is open to the public the first and third Sundays of the month from 1:00 until 4:00 p.m. The annual calendar includes craft shows, Civil War events, a December model train display, and semi-annual meetings featuring local authors and experts speaking on topics of historic interest.

Great Falls Historical Society
P.O. Box 56
Great Falls, VA 22066
703/759-2206

Founded in 1977, this society sponsors monthly meetings which usually feature guest speakers and slide presentations. In addition to preservation, education, and genealogical programs, this society also sponsors special celebrations and banquets, tours and dinners at historic sites, and an Annual Virginia Ham and Harvest Dinner. Events are generally open to the public. Meetings are held on the second Wednesday of the month, September through May, at the Grange Hall in Great Falls.

Historic Vienna, Inc.
P.O. Box 53
Vienna, VA 22183
703/830-2852

Since 1976, the 100 members of Historic Vienna, Inc. have operated the Freeman Store and Museum in a general store built before the Civil War. Volunteer members also sponsor an annual Antique and Crafts Fair, Heritage Awards, walking tours, programs to restore historical landmarks, and author luncheons where authors and members discuss recent publications of historical interest. Most events are open to the public.

Other historical societies in Virginia include:

The Alexandria Historical Society
301 Saint Asaph Street
Alexandria, VA 22314

Burke Historical Society
9330 Burke Lake Road
Burke, VA 22015

Falls Church Village Preservation and Improvement Society
P.O. Box 6824
Falls Church, VA 22040
703/532-0884

Historic Centreville Society
P.O. Box 1512
Centreville, VA 22020
703/830-1882

Historic Fairfax City, Inc.
10209 Main Street
Fairfax, VA 22030

Herndon Historical Society, Inc.
P.O. Box 234
Herndon, VA 22070

Kenmore
1201 Washington Avenue
Fredericksburg, VA 22401
703/373-3381

Lorton Heritage Society
c/o A.P. Sullivan
7605 Devries Drive
Lorton, VA 22079
703/550-9389

History at Home

These organizations are for anyone interested in surrounding themselves with historic artifacts on a daily basis. Weekend collectors of antiques as well as those curious about old-fashioned ways of life will discover others of the same ilk during activities and field trips with these groups.

American Antique Arts Association (AAAA)
P.O. Box 426
Temple Hills, MD 20757-0426
301/449-5372

For more than a decade, antiquarian Orva Heissenbuttel would find herself at the close of her classes surrounded by a host of antique enthusiasts, all of whom wanted to know where they could continue to learn about antiques, art, crafts, architecture, and local history. The interest was so great that twenty years ago she organized the AAAA to promote the appreciation, study, and preservation of these arts. There are now 1000 members in 15 chapters throughout the metropolitan area. The AAAA's monthly meetings feature speakers and discussions, and special events that include tours, daytrips, study groups, and annual fund raisers that benefit a number of local museums and historic sites. A bi-monthly journal has program information for all chapters. Membership is open to all interested persons. Dues are determined by each chapter, and range from $7.50 to $15 per year.

Potomac Antique Tools and Industries Association, Inc.(PATINA)
6802 Nesbitt Place
McLean, VA 22101
703/821-2931

PATINA is an educational organization of antique tool collectors, tool users, and tool historians. More than 2000 area tool enthusiasts come together for the March Antique Tool Show and Auction, and some proceeds from this event are donated to other tool-related organizations and museums. The group meets bi-monthly and the September meeting is usually an overnight trip to a historical site of interest. Past locations have included Colonial Williamsburg in Virginia and the Gruber Wagon Works in Pennsylvania. Membership is on a family basis; the $12 dues for the primary member entitles their spouse and the rest of their family to participate in events.

Historical Reenactment and Living History Programs

Do you often feel as though you were born into the wrong century? Would you feel more at home in a Civil War parade or crossing swords at midnight? If you want to escape to the long-gone days of the American Revolutionary War, the English Civil War, or the medieval era, join one of the several reenactment clubs or living history programs in the metropolitan area.

Historical reenactment clubs focus on the wars which have changed the course of history. They portray military units of virtually every war, including the Roman, Napoleonic, and medieval wars, the War of 1812, and the Crusades. American Revolutionary and Civil War units are particularly popular in the Washington metropolitan area. Through extensive research of military units and their history, uniforms, accoutrements, and weaponry, these clubs simulate battle reenactments and organize encampments, parades, demonstrations, and other special events. Reenactment clubs are generally restricted to men, although occasionally women portray nurses, laundresses, cooks, and others who shouldered the duties which historically fell to the distaff. Bear in mind that these clubs involve considerable costs, as the necessary uniform and equipment generally amount to more than $600.

Living history programs, on the other hand, emphasize the lifestyles of a particular period. In these programs, men, women, and children demonstrate the clothing, crafts, food, and etiquette of a particular era. Many historical societies profiled earlier incorporate extensive living history programs in their calendar of events, as do several reenactment clubs in their demonstrations of camp life.

Historical Reenactment Clubs

Below you'll find profiles of American Civil and Revolutionary War clubs, medieval clubs, and a miscellaneous assortment of historical reenactment clubs. The best way to discover additional clubs is to consult with the following organizations, ask your local historical society, or attend a small, local reenactment event in the Washington area and speak with the reenactors. These events are generally published in the *Washington Post* Weekend.

AMERICAN CIVIL WAR CLUBS

Media Alert!

Finding Fun & Friends in Washington is a book that is useful in helping all Washingtonians — new or old-timers — get to know their home city. The book has something to offer just about everyone: sports enthusiasts, aspiring actors and singers, hikers, bikers, tropical fish fans, dog lovers, political junkies. If you're looking to get involved in any number of ways, then Finding Fun and Friends is the book for you. Whether you're a recent college graduate, or a retiree looking for more productive ways to spend your time, we have the book for you.

The Washington area, steeped in the momentous history of the American Civil War and dotted with over 100 Civil War sites, is home to hundreds of recreated Civil War regiments. The following monthly publication features schedules of Civil War reenactment events and occasionally profiles Federal and Confederate units. Write to the address below for further information.

Camp Chase Gazette
P.O. Box 707 B
Marietta, OH 45750

Fifth New York Volunteer Infantry
Civil War Federal Unit
c/o Mr. Brian Pohanka
P.O. Box 1601
Alexandria, VA 22313

Founded in 1971, the Fifth New York Volunteer Infantry is one of the oldest Civil War reenactment clubs and living history organizations in the Washington area. It is also one of the most colorful, as members sport the braided jacket, baggy red trousers, and tasseled fez of the Zouave uniform that made their forbearers so conspicuous on the battlefields of Virginia. Presently numbering approximately 70 members who range in age from 12 to 50, plus a ladies auxiliary, the Fifth New York seeks to honor and perpetuate the memory of the original regiment by authentically recreating the drill, camp life, and battle tactics of a Civil War era infantry company. Yearly events include battle reenactments in Virginia, Maryland, and Pennsylvania, as well as living history demonstrations at National Parks such as Manassas, Antietam, and Gettysburg. The Fifth New York welcomes new "recruits" who share an interest in researching and recreating that stirring era of American history.

Fifty-Fourth Massachusetts Volunteer Infantry, Company B
c/o Captain Jack Thompson
807 Duke Street
Alexandria, VA 22314
703/836-5272

Despite the fact that 187,000 Black Americans served in the Union Army during the Civil War, their bravery and sacrifice in the cause of freedom was largely ignored until the filming of the motion picture *Glory*. The 54th Massachusetts Volunteer Infantry regiment was recreated in October of 1988 to support the filming of the feature movie, in which Company B's portrayal helped to raise awareness of Black contributions to the preservation of the Union and abolition of slavery. Since 1988, the regiment has "enlisted" over 100 men in the Washington area to serve in the ranks of the 54th Massachusetts Infantry. The group serves as a living monument to commemorate and honor the men who sacrificed their lives in the American Civil War. In order to achieve an accurate portrayal of African Americans in the Civil War, the unit welcomes physically fit men with a strong interest in historical interpretation. The unit meets approximately once a month during the summer for various battle reenactments, living history encampments, interpretive work for the National Park Service, parades, school presentations, and training sessions and drills. Annual dues are $30.

Forty-Ninth Virginia Infantry
Civil War Confederate Unit
c/o Mr. Tony Meadows
3006 Albany Court
Dale City, VA 22193
703/690-0245

The 49th Virginia Infantry regiment wears the grey uniform of the Confederate Army of the American Civil War. The original regiment was led by Governor William Smith, commander of the regiment that fought from 1861 through the end of the War. Today's reenactors honor the Confederate regiment through battle reenactments and camp life at Civil War sites, living history demonstrations at local schools, and special events such as the Confederate Army's Memorial Day march through Richmond, Virginia to Hollywood Cemetery, the burial ground of Smith and other Confederate heroes. Like other reenactment groups, "soldiers" reenact battle scenarios while men, women, and children portray camp life authentically recreated down to the period tools, mourning clothes, and 19th-century etiquette. Members of the unit also take care of local graves of the original soldiers from the 49th Infantry. This group of fifty or so "19th-century people and 20th-century friends" started in 1985. Although its close-knit members are drawn from the Mid-Atlantic region, most are from Northern Virginia. Membership dues are $15 and include a quarterly newsletter and invitations to a summer picnic, Christmas party, and other special events.

AMERICAN REVOLUTIONARY WAR CLUBS
First Maryland Regiment
2531 Ennalls Avenue
Wheaton, MD 20902
Mr. Bill Deuterman
301/946-5397

The First Maryland Regiment celebrates the American Revolutionary War and other 18th-century battles through reenactments, encampments, military demonstrations, and parades. This club performs as the honorary guard at Mount Vernon and the official reenactment group at National Colonial Farm in Accokeek. It is also a frequent participant in events at Williamsburg, Fort Frederick, and other historic locales. The club sponsors several events per month during the summer and the holiday season, and at least one event a month during the rest of the year.

First Virginia Regiment of the Continental Line
9124 Rockefeller Lane
Springfield, VA 22153
Mr. Jim Garner
703/644-1066

In 1975, the First Virginia Regiment was recreated by a group of more than 50 men and women who portray Revolutionary War soldiers and camp life. Today, "historians, business executives, government employees, students, teachers, and artisans" continue to double as 18th-century citizen/soldiers and their families. The regiment performs tactical and camp demonstrations, participates in parades and battle reenactments.

MEDIEVAL CLUBS
Markland Medieval Mercenary Militia
P.O. Box 715
Greenbelt, MD 20768-0715

The medieval traditions and arts are brought to life every Tuesday evening at the University of Maryland Armory, where up to 60 enthusiasts arrive for dance, music, swordfights, and other activities popular in the Middle Ages. At these weekly events, members also plan special activities such as jousting events, medieval feasts, and nearby sailing expeditions on the club's Viking ship. A popular Markland celebration is the December 21 festival "to banish strife and war and bring back the sun." This event includes feasting, drinking, and general merry-making. Special oaths, candle-lighting ceremonies, and the "Maltese" ring dance also commemorate the occasion. Markland members are encouraged to adopt Viking names and wear authentic attire. The Black Knight and other medieval characters from Markland often appear at the annual Maryland Renaissance Festival. Markland, incidentally, is the name which Viking explorers chose for the southern part of the New World. Markland members receive *The Plague* (the club newsletter, not the epidemic), which features articles on medieval history and upcoming events.

Society for Creative Anachronism
9704 Beechwood Avenue
Lanham, MD 20706
Mr. Steve Kiefert, Seneschal
301/731-0673

This is the local branch of the nationwide organization which was founded over a quarter of a century ago to celebrate the history and culture of the medieval and renaissance eras. Members organize recreational events almost every weekend at various locations throughout the Mid-Atlantic region, otherwise known as "Barony Storvik," or Old Norse for the Great Bay. Activities have included seminars, an English Tavern feast, a Christmas Ball, and authentic recreations of medieval combat including archery and swordfighting tournaments. Members adopt medieval names, dress in authentic attire (loaner garbs are available for first-time Society goers), and develop specialties in different aspects of medieval and renaissance life that include crafts, heraldry, costuming, armor, music, dancing, cuisine, and brewery. A monthly newsletter, *Drekkar*, updates the several hundred local members on upcoming events.

OTHER REENACTMENT CLUBS:

English Civil War Society of America
Mr. Bob Giglio
2016 Amherst Road
Hyattsville, MD 20783-2806
301/422-9015

The English Civil War Society consists of two armies which are based on the actual two sides that fought in the conflict. Interested people of all ages and walks of life are invited to become members of the Society, which makes "every effort to achieve authenticity of drill, dress, equipment and a seventeenth century atmosphere while being run in a military manner." Events involving the Society have been presented at Fort Mifflin in Philadelphia, Jamestown, and well over a dozen other sites throughout the eastern United States. For more information, send a self-addressed, stamped envelope to the address above.

Hampden's Regiment
English Civil War Parliamentarians
9512 Dubarry Avenue
Seabrook, MD 20706-4025
301/577-3457

Legio XX (20th Roman Legion, Mid-First Century A.D.)
9416 Rhode Island Avenue
College Park, MD 20740
Mr. Matthew Amt
301/345-0582

Light Infantry Company of the 46th Regiment
American Revolutionary War British Regiment
1006 Laredo Road
Silver Spring, MD 20901
Mr. Ed Safford
301/681-2624

Milipes Normanorum
Norman Knights
Mr. Tom Ball
209 South Main Street
Northeast, MD 21901
410/287-9318

St. Mary's City Militia
P.O. Box 1311
Front Royal, VA 22630
Mr. Tom Calloway
703/635-8710

Westphalian Association
German Mercenaries of Thirty Year's War
11947 Andrews Street
Wheaton, MD 20902
Ms. Veronica M. Stanley
301/946-6665

Wolfes' Company
Hundred Year War
3727 Monmouth Place
Burtonsville, MD 20866
301/890-7594

Living History Programs

For a different perspective on historic Washington, consider the events and volunteer activities of the living history programs detailed below that offer especially enriching opportunities to share in the capital city's past.

Fairfax County Park Authority
Division of Historic Preservation (DHP)
3701 Pender Drive
Fairfax, VA 22030-6067
703/759-5241 Calendar of Events
703/759-4360 Volunteer Coordinator

The DHP sponsors a wealth of historical programs such as Music of the Federal Period, Civil War Encampments, Sully by Candlelight and Evening at the Tavern. Other programs feature festivals, open houses, art shows, banquets, blacksmithing and woodcarving demonstrations, and more. One of the best ways to immerse yourself in Fairfax County history is to join the friendly staff of over 150 volunteers who interpret and preserve the county's historical traditions and cultural heritage. This volunteer staff acts as touring and teaching docents, special program aides, and assistant curators. Volunteers also press cider, bake biscuits, stir apple butter, and reenact Civil War battles. Other activities include open hearth cooking, story-telling, and 19th-century gardening. Volunteers receive frequent newsletters, celebrate at an annual "Soiree" and a cocktail party at Sully Historic Site, and enjoy champagne brunches, frequent meetings and training programs, and field trips to local museums and historic houses. An application, interview, and training program is required of each volunteer, and a "job bank" matches volunteer interests, activities, and skills.

Historic Alexandria Docents (HAD)
Founded in 1749 by Scottish merchants, Alexandria was originally a prosperous seaport town of cobbled streets, row houses, and a picturesque waterfront. Today, members of HAD celebrate this city's maritime heritage and colonial charm as regular volunteers at five local historic properties. Each property features a different period of Alexandria's heritage. "Light Horse Harry" Lee once lived in the gracious early-19th-century Boyhood Home of Robert E. Lee. Other prominent Alexandrians made the Carlyle House Historic Park and the Lee-Fendall House their elegant homes. Gadsby's Tavern Museum was once a favorite haunt of General Washington. The Lyceum, Historic Site and Museum celebrates the town's yesteryears through exhibitions and public programs. Through activities that include training sessions, meetings, lectures, demonstrations, and tours, these volunteers broaden our knowledge and appreciation of Alexandria's history, traditions, customs, architecture, and decorative arts.

Listed below are the historic properties and programs in Alexandria:

The Boyhood Home of Robert E. Lee
607 Oronoco Street
Alexandria, VA 22314
703/548-8454

Carlyle House Historic Park
121 North Fairfax Street
Alexandria, VA 22314
703/549-2997

Gadsby's Tavern Museum
134 North Royal Street
Alexandria, VA 22314
703/838-4242

Lee-Fendall House
614 Oronoco Street
Alexandria, VA 22314
703/548-1789

The Lyceum, Alexandria's History Museum
201 South Washington Street
Alexandria, VA 22314
703/838-4994

National Park Service (NPS)

Volunteer-in-Parks
1100 Ohio Drive, SW
Washington, DC 20242
David Larsen, Volunteer Coordinator and Curatorial Services
202/619-7077

NPS volunteers participate in a variety of diverse programs which include serving as guides at popular attractions such as the Vietnam Veterans Memorial and the White House. At the Antietam National Battlefield, volunteers dress in period costume and demonstrate the latest in cannon-firing techniques. Contact the number above for information about these and other opportunities with the national parks in the capital area (also see *Volunteer*). ⚜

International
Foreign Affairs

While exploring the streets of the capital one's ears pick up snatches of many different languages spoken by those who have come from foreign lands to make their home here. The diverse community is reflected in the array of international organizations and activities to be found in and around the metropolitan area. Cultures from every continent are represented by embassies and ethnic organizations sponsoring special functions and exotic festivals, many of which are open to the public. A myriad of language classes are also available, as well as activities to help international newcomers feel welcome. The following organizations all contribute to the city's vibrant international atmosphere. Participating in their activities can open up new doors for those of us who have grown up stateside.

International and Ethnic Organizations
Alliance Française
2142 Wyoming Avenue, NW
Washington, DC 20008
202/234-7114

Dedicated "to promoting an appreciation of French language and culture and fostering friendly relations" between the French and American people, the Alliance Française is the largest network of French language and cultural centers in the world. The Washington chapter is one of 1300 around the globe and one of 175 in the U.S. Language courses, lectures, concerts, films, exhibitions, museum tours, and receptions offer members ample opportunity to enhance language skills and meet fellow francophiles. A modest membership fee entitles members to a newsletter, use of an extensive library and video-cassette collection, and invitations to special events.

American Czech and Slovak Association (ACSA)
1511 K Street, NW, Suite 1030
Washington, DC 20005
202/638-5505; 202/638-5308 (Fax)

The common denominator among members of ACSA is not ethnicity but a shared interest in Czech and Slovak culture, business, and academia. The Association's 2000 members are Americans with or without Czech or Slovak backgrounds who enjoy weekly events that have featured embassy functions, concerts, lectures, and conferences. Language classes and nine ACSA committees, including Business Roundtable, Legal Affairs, and Government Relations, offer enriching opportunities for further involvement. An important conduit for cultural exchange, ACSA arranges for Americans to teach English in Czech and Slovak Republics. A social highlight is the annual ACSA Merit Awards, organized in cooperation with both embassies, to recognize individuals and organizations making significant contributions to bilateral cooperation. Membership starts at $35 for individuals ($15 for students) and includes a subscription to the monthly *ACSA newsletter*.

American Turkish Association of Washington, D.C.
P.O. Box 57073
Washington, DC 20037
202/363-2136

Founded in 1965 to foster mutual understanding between the American and Turkish peoples, this Association of several hundred members sponsors more than 30 social, educational, cultural, and charitable activities each year, including a colorful Turkish bazaar. The Turkish Ambassador has been one of the distinguished speakers of the Association's lecture series. Other events have included concerts, theater performances, exhibitions, the annual Republic Day Ball, and a three-day "Istanbul on the Potomac" festival. Language classes, teacher workshops, and programs with local Turkish students further strengthen cultural ties between the two nations. A monthly newsletter features articles on the politics, economics, and culture of Turkey and the United States. There are modest annual dues.

The Arab-American Cultural Foundation
1204 31st Street, NW
Washington, DC 20007
202/337-9670

A Lebanese flutist at Georgetown University's Gaston Hall, Egyptian jewelry and Algerian films at the Alif Gallery, and Palestinian dramatic productions at the Kennedy Center are just some of the events sponsored by this organization. Fostering understanding of and appreciation for Arab culture has been the Foundation's mission since it was founded in 1978. The Alif Gallery in Georgetown has served as both an exhibition center and as Foundation headquarters since 1983, and its outstanding exhibits are complemented by a series of lectures and poetry readings. Donations are invited.

The Asia Society
Washington Center
1785 Massachusetts Avenue, NW
Washington, DC 20036
202/387-6500

Celebrate the cultures of Asia and the Pacific with the local Asia Society, which offers an intriguing array of cultural, historical, and educational programs. There are over

1200 members in the Washington chapter of this national organization, which was founded in 1956 by John D. Rockefeller, III. Specialists and non-experts alike are encouraged to participate in the Society's activities. More than 50 programs each year include lectures, seminars, performances, films, and classes, as well as special events. An "Arts in the Embassies" series presents the visual and performing arts of Asia, and a series of "Ambassadors' Briefings" features addresses by distinguished members of the diplomatic corps. Members receive a newsletter listing all Asia-related events in the Washington area, including those not sponsored by the Society. Many events are held at the Society's Dupont Circle facility. Membership begins at $35.

Brazilian-American Cultural Institute, Inc.
4103 Connecticut Avenue, NW
Washington, DC 20008
202/362-8334

Anyone interested in the culture and people of our largest southern neighbor will find plentiful opportunities for fellowship and exchange at the Brazilian-American Cultural Institute. Art exhibits, recitals, Brazilian films, and lectures are only a part of the offerings enjoyed by the Institute's nearly 900 members. From four to five events are scheduled monthly, from September through June, and attendance at individual events may range from 5 to over 100 participants. An active language program offers instruction at all levels, from beginning to advanced. Membership in the Institute begins at $20; fees for language classes vary.

Global Nomads International
P.O. Box 9584
Washington, DC 20016-9584
703/993-2975

Did you spend your salad days as a diplomat's son in India? Or as a missionary's daughter in Brazil? Or at a Peace Corps worksite in Africa? You will find many such common experiences among the members of Global Nomads International, an association for people who have lived abroad before adulthood, due to a parent's occupation. GNI's local chapter, Global Nomads Washington Area (GNWA) sponsors potluck suppers, discussions, and occasional retreats to bring together the club's 80-plus members. As might be expected, the level of global awareness is high in this club, where members share common aspects of their unusual childhood and the way it has shaped their unique vision of the world.

The Goethe Institute
1607 New Hampshire Avenue, NW
Washington, DC 20009
202/319-0702

The Goethe Institute of Washington is one of 150 centers in 69 countries devoted to promoting German language and culture. Newly relocated in a magnificent turn-of-the-century mansion (formerly a Presidential guest house) near Dupont Circle, the Institute currently hosts a series of free, weekly German-language films. Unlike most

Goethe Institutes worldwide, the Washington center does not offer language instruction, though it does plan to augment its offering of cultural programs in the future.

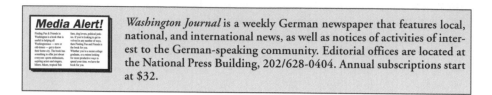

Media Alert! *Washington Journal* is a weekly German newspaper that features local, national, and international news, as well as notices of activities of interest to the German-speaking community. Editorial offices are located at the National Press Building, 202/628-0404. Annual subscriptions start at $32.

The International Club of Washington
1800 K Street, NW
Washington, DC 20006
202/862-1400

The International Club, founded as a meeting place for Washington's diplomatic and international community, is located on a site containing soil from virtually every country in the world. Among its 1200 members are most of the world's ambassadors to the United States. The Club's chef is renowned, as are special "Country Nights" that feature international cuisine, receptions, and entertainment provided by the hosting embassy. Ambassadorial luncheons, theatre nights, monthly mixers, wine and food tastings, and art exhibitions are among the Club's special events. Reciprocal agreements offer members privileges in clubs across the country and abroad. Initiation and monthly fees are applicable.

Irish American Club of Washington, DC
P.O. Box 11094
Washington, DC 20008
301/567-9332

If your heritage entitles you to the wearin' o' the green, the Irish American Club welcomes you to join its convivial crew. Monthly meetings at various Knights of Columbus Halls are followed by refreshments and social hours. The recent addition of an Irish football team has boosted the average attendance, especially among the younger crowd. Annual parades in Alexandria and Washington are a special part of the club's activities, with fundraisers and work parties taking place weeks before St. Patrick's Day. Members are kept informed of the area's activities through the club's newsletter, which lists concerts, folk festivals, and pub events. Membership fees are nominal.

The Italian Cultural Society of Washington, DC (ICS)
2010 Linden Lane
Silver Spring, MD 20910
301/585-9730

Though Roma, Firenza, and Venezia may be distant destinations on the Mediterranean horizon, you can savor the Italian flavor here at home by joining the local ICS. Since 1953, this organization has celebrated all aspects of Italian culture, history, and language. A number of special interest groups explore Italian music, arts, folklore, current events, and, not surprisingly, Italian cooking. A monthly cena amichevole, an Italian potluck supper, features a sumptuous feast of regional specialties as well as an informal opportunity to make friends and practice conversational Italian. The Society's language program offers classes at all levels in more than 20 locations throughout the metropolitan area. Monthly meetings also feature "planned programs and impromptu fellowship" for the society's 375 members. The membership fee is $25, and there is a separate fee for language classes.

Other Italian organizations in Washington include:

National Italian American Foundation (NIAF)
666 11th Street, NW Suite 800
Washington, DC 20001-4596
202/638-0220

This organization serves as an important political voice for Italian Americans nationwide. The NIAF also sponsors tours to Italy and publishes a newsletter and a quarterly cultural magazine with information on events and programs and issues across the U.S. of interest to Italian Americans. In October, the NIAF sponsors its Gala Award Weekend, which is the largest meeting of Italian-Americans in the country. The two day conference, which focuses on Italian-American issues and which is attended by many celebrities, culminates in the presentation of an award to a prominent Italian-American. In recent years the award has gone to Danny DeVito and Sophia Loren.

The Order Sons of Italy in America
219 E Street, NE
Washington, DC 20002
202/547-2900

The 11 local lodges of the Sons of Italy sponsor social and cultural activities such as community service projects, art exhibits, dances, guest speakers, and monthly meetings. Men and women of all ages share equal status in this organization, which promotes Italian cultural heritage, fosters business and educational exchange between the U.S. and Italy, represents the interests of Italian Americans on Capitol Hill, and contributes to the professional development of members and their families. The organization donates millions of dollars each year to educational and charitable causes around the world and sponsors an extensive National Mentor Program that pairs young adults and professionals in 20 fields. Dues vary from lodge to lodge.

The Japan-America Society of Washington, DC, Inc.
606 18th Street, NW
Washington, DC 20006
202/289-8290
Founded in 1957 to "promote friendship and understanding between the people of the United States and Japan," this society now has 3000 members in the metropolitan area. Lectures, films, and symposia concentrate on all aspects of Japanese society, culture, politics, and economics, while exhibits, performances, and workshops feature

Japanese arts, crafts, and skills. Language classes are offered for beginning to advanced students, and a library provides access to a host of Japanese literature. The Society's largest annual event is the "Matsuri," featuring handicrafts, food, dance, music, Bonsai, origami, and other Japanese arts and crafts. Special events include a traditional Japanese Moonviewing Party, with stories, food, and special moonviewing poems. Events are held at many locations, including the Duke Ellington School for the Arts, the Kennedy Center, the Brookings Institution, and the Walters Art Gallery inBaltimore. Membership fees begin at $40.

Japan Information and Culture Center
Embassy of Japan
Lafayette Centre III
1155 21st Street, NW
Washington, DC 20036
202/939-6900

Japanese history, literature, music, art, education, politics, economy, and Japan/U.S. relations are among the topics explored in programs offered by this branch of the Japanese Embassy. Seminars and lectures, films, demonstrations, exhibitions, performances, and other cultural activities are scheduled about once a month at the Center's auditorium and exhibition hall. The Center's library, inquiry center, and education programs are open and free to all those who wish to know more about Japan.

Meridian House International
1630 Crescent Place, NW
Washington, DC 20009
202/667-6800

Founded in 1960 to promote international understanding "through the exchange of people, ideas, and the arts," Meridian House International administers a number of programs that serve foreign diplomats, scholars, and visitors, as well as Americans preparing to live abroad. For local residents, the Meridian House programs offer an international perspective through art exhibitions, concerts, conferences, lectures, performing arts programs, and workshops. Addresses by ambassadors and cabinet members, events such as Flamenco dance programs and chamber music recitals, and exhibitions featuring the graphic arts of Yugoslavia or African ceremonial arts provide glimpses of life on other continents. Most activities are held in either the Meridian House or the neighboring White-Meyer House, both of which were built for retiring diplomats at the turn of the century. Volunteers are welcome in a number of capacities, and notice of Meridian House activities are sent to all Meridian House International supporters (see *Volunteer*).

Metro Area Russian Services (MARS)
1000 Connecticut Avenue, NW Suite 9LL
Washington, DC 20036
301/961-4652

MARS publishes an entertaining, monthly newsletter featuring "all things Russian" from local events to international issues and Moscow lore. This organization has also sponsored several "Russian Nights" at local restaurants for newsletter subscribers and others. MARS offers Russian language instruction and tutoring utilizing three Muscovite teachers. In addition, there is an intermediate-level Russian language conversation group. MARS also has a movie club, so newsletter subscribers can watch a large variety of Russian language movies. The number listed above will provide general information on the organization. There are also three "MARSLines" that provide recorded information concerning the group's activities: 202/828-3060, 202/828-3057, and 202/828-3053. Annual subscription to The *MARS Newsletter* is $20.

Mexican Cultural Center
2829 16th Street, NW
Washington, DC 20009
202/728-1628

Monthly events at the Mexican Cultural Center include art exhibitions, seminars, films, and receptions. Call for information on current course and seminar offerings. Tours are also given on request. Most events are open to the public and are usually free. The Center's galleries are open Tuesday through Saturday from 11 a.m. to 6 p.m. The Center maintains a mailing list and sends announcements of upcoming events.

Order of American Hellenic Educational Progressive Association (Ahepa)
1909 Q Street, NW
Washington, DC 20009
202/232-6300

Ahepa is a charitable and educational organization with several thousand members in the Washington area and over 60,000 members nationwide. Men belong to the Order itself, women join the Daughters of Penelope, and younger generations belong to either the Sons of Pericles or the Maids of Athena. Monthly meetings of the local chapters support Ahepa's philanthropic mission, which includes medical research, disaster relief, academic scholarships, and homes for the elderly. Local activities may range from athletic and social events to discussions of global politics. Annual dues to the national organization are $20, while fees for local chapters vary.

Society for the Preservation of the Greek Heritage
5125 MacArthur Boulevard, NW
Washington, DC 20016
202/363-4337

Preserving the treasures of the past and promoting the cultural heritage of Greece are the twin missions of this national organization, which has over 800 members in the Washington area. The six to eight annual events include lectures, benefits, and concerts, and are held at locations which include the Greek Embassy, Meridian House International, and the Cosmos Club. The events of a recent year featured several lectures on Greek history and heritage. Membership fees start at $15 and include increasing benefits at each level of giving.

The Washington Group
P.O. Box 11248
Washington, DC 20008
Mr. Nick Babiak, President

TWG is an association of Ukrainian-American professionals who welcome non-Ukrainians with an interest in their homeland. The group features a regular schedule of speaker forums (1-2 times per month) and receptions for guests, who are often cultural and political figures from Ukraine. TWG also sponsors an annual leadership conference in October, which consists of three days of receptions, dinners, speakers, and panels. The social highlight of the year falls on August 24, when TWG celebrates Ukrainian Independence Day. All events highlight Ukrainian culture and history. Full membership, $50 per year, entitles members to voting privileges. There are also associate, student, and overseas memberships, and all members receive the monthly *TWG News*.

Embassy Events

Garden parties and sparkling receptions are for the most part "invitation only" affairs, but many of Washington's diplomatic missions welcome more casual visitors to a range of cultural activities which include films, lectures, theater, concerts, and exhibitions. Events co-sponsored with museums, universities, and societies such as the Organization of American States greatly increase the range of possible programs, as does the active interest and participation of many embassies in the Smithsonian's "Campus on the Mall" program (see *Education*). Programs generally feature the work of artists, musicians, and experts from the country represented and often include an informal reception. Many of the programs, scheduled at museums, arts centers, and elegant embassies, are free of charge. The following are among the embassies that sponsor cultural programs open to the public, and several maintain a mailing list. Once on the list, you will discover a host of fascinating and often unpublicized events.

The Embassy of Austria
3524 International Court, NW
Washington, DC 20008
202/895-6700

The Embassy of Belgium
3330 Garfield Street, NW
Washington, DC 20008
202/333-6900

The Embassy of Bolivia
3014 Massachusetts Avenue, NW
Washington, DC 20008
202/483-4410

The Embassy of Canada
501 Pennsylvania Avenue, NW
Washington, DC 20001
202/682-1740

The Embassy of Chile
Cultural Department
1732 Massachusetts Avenue, NW
Washington, DC 20036
202/785-1746

The Embassy of China
2300 Connecticut Avenue, NW
Washington, DC 20008
202/328-2500

The Embassy of Colombia
2118 Leroy Place, NW
Washington, DC 20008
202/387-8338

The Embassy of Egypt
2310 Decatur Place, NW
Washington, DC 20008
202/232-5400

The Embassy of the Federal Republic of Germany
4645 Reservoir Road, NW
Washington, DC 20007
202/298-4000

The Embassy of Finland
3216 New Mexico Avenue, NW
Washington, DC 20016
202/363-2430

The Embassy of Guatemala
2220 R Street, NW
Washington, DC 20008
202/745-4952

The Embassy of Hungary
3910 Shoemaker Street, NW
Washington, DC 20008
202/362-6730

The Embassy of Indonesia
2020 Massachusetts Avenue, NW
Washington, DC 20036
202/775-5200

La Maison Française
The Embassy of France
4101 Reservoir Road, NW
Washington, DC 20007
202/944-6090

⚜

The Royal Netherlands Embassy
4200 Linnean Avenue, NW
Washington, DC 20008
202/244-5300

The Royal Norwegian Embassy
2720 34th Street, NW
Washington, DC 20008
202/333-6000

The Embassy of Spain
2700 15th Street, NW
Washington, DC 20009
202/337-7172

The Embassy of Switzerland
2900 Cathedral Avenue, NW
Washington, DC 20008
202/745-7928

The Embassy of Ukraine
3350 M Street, NW
Washington, DC 20007
202/333-0606

The Embassy of Venezuela
1099 30th Street, NW
Washington, DC 20007
202/342-6846

Washington's Literary Life
By the Book

After being bombarded by technological advances at work, many people are returning to the simple joy of reading books for pure pleasure. Bookstores have emerged as a place for Washingtonians to mix and meet. Along with the blossoming of bookstore/cafes that serve cappucinos and cranberry tarts to accompany discussions and booksignings, area literati may select from such diverse venues as the Elizabethan Folger Library or a rustic log cabin in Rock Creek Park to enjoy the written word. Seminars, readings, and workshops are also offered in community art centers. The National Press Club is a haven for professional writers and journalists; local literary organizations and continuing education programs sponsor events for bibliophiles and budding authors. Opportunities for sharing a love of literature through tutoring and literacy programs are in the *Volunteer* chapter under Mentoring and Tutoring.

Media Alert! On the first weekend of every month, the "Literary Calendar" of The *Washington Post Book World* announces upcoming literary events throughout the city.

Readings, Discussions, and Other Literary Events

Share your latest literary masterpiece at a local arts center, or meet the new Poet Laureate at the Library of Congress; attend a lunch hour poetry reading at the Martin Luther King library, or enjoy the more esoteric programs of the Jane Austen Society. Explore the organizations profiled below and you're likely to find a program to suit your literary leanings.

Rock Creek Gallery, formerly The Art Barn
2401 Tilden Street, NW
Rock Creek Park
Washington, DC 20008
202/244-2482

Monthly poetry readings have featured international poets such as Alicia dejoux and Fouzi El-Asmar. Still other readings are open to anyone wishing to share his or her latest literary creation. These events are held at the Rock Creek Gallery on the third Thursday of the month at 8:00 p.m., and are free and open to the public (donations requested). Membership in the Rock Creek Gallery Association starts at $25, and includes a newsletter that features announcements of invitations to gallery openings and wine and cheese receptions, craft demonstrations, slide shows, dances, children's festivals, and other special events (see "Visual Art Centers," in *Arts*).

Folger Shakespeare Library
Folger Poetry Series
201 East Capitol Street, SE
Washington, DC 20003
202/544-7077

The silence of scholars prevails in the Folger's Reading Room, but the Great Hall and Elizabethan Theater reverberate with the voices of writers, musicians, actors, and visitors from around the world. The Folger Poetry Series "expresses the library's commitment to the literary arts and to the continuing legacy of Renaissance humanism." Both emerging and established writers read from their poetry, conduct seminars, and participate in literary salons, conferences, and symposia. Of particular interest is the PEN/Faulkner Series, a series of author readings held on Friday evenings from October through May. Each reading is often followed by question and answer sessions, book signings, and receptions or dinners. PEN poets have included William Styron, E.L. Doctorow, and John Updike. Some events are free and open to the public, while others range from $5 to $25 and require advance reservations. Call the number above for a calendar of events.

The Folger produces more than 60 events each year that include not only poetry readings, but concerts of early music performed by the Folger Consort, exhibits and gallery talks, garden tours, Shakespearean festivals for children in grades 4 through 12, and the annual Shakespeare's Birthday Open House. Making all this possible is a devoted corps of volunteers and an especially active docent program; call for further information on scheduled events and volunteer opportunities.

Gaithersburg Lyric Society
Gaithersburg Public Library
18330 Montgomery Village Avenue
Gaithersburg, MD 20879
301/840-2515 Library

Since 1979, this society has sponsored free monthly meetings for those wishing to stop by and read their poetry or prose. Participants are limited to five minutes, and informal discussions follow. Occasionally, guitar players and singers contribute their musical talent to this small group, whose members gather at the Gaithersburg Public Library on the first Tuesday of every month.

Jane Austen Society of North America (JASNA)
7204 Brookstone Court
Potomac, MD 20854
Ms. Betty Woods
301/365-7858

December 16 is a momentous date for JASNA, when Janeites celebrate the author's birthday and delight in the elegant, 19th-century social satire created by Jane Austen. The 225 members of the local chapter find unending inspiration in the author and her works, and meet for events that include tea-and-cucumber-sandwich receptions, concerts featuring the music of the 18th-century, lessons in 18th and 19th-century card games and dancing, local tours, and small discussion groups. The local chapter also publishes The Austen Scribbler, highlighting news of Austen-related events and activities in the area. Many of the Society's 3000-nationwide members converge at the annual fall conference for lectures, workshops, musical and dramatic presentations, special tours, and a banquet featuring menus drawn in part from Austen's novels. During this three-day tribute to the writer and her works, enthusiastic members often dress in period costume and engage in "fanciful debates over favorite characters" of a particular novel. JASNA members are "scholars and enthusiasts, amateurs and professionals," whose $15 annual dues include several publications including the literary journal *Persuasions* and the semiannual newsletter, *JASNA News*. For further information, contact Vicki Barie, 2650D Matheson Way, Sacramento, CA, 95864.

Joaquin Miller Cabin Poetry Series
Beach and Military Drives
Rock Creek Park, Picnic Area #6
Washington, DC 20015
202/726-0971

Mailing address:
1411 Kennedy Street, NW
Washington, DC 20011

Aspiring Thoreaus and admirers of poetry may indulge in the Joaquin Miller Cabin Poetry Series held every summer in Rock Creek Park under a shower of stars. These romantic summer soirees include eight programs every Tuesday night at 7:30 in June and July, in which poets read to an audience of 40 to over 100 listeners. The audience includes a faithful corps of 20 who return year after year, as well as curious bikers, joggers, and other passersby. Following the informal reading, the poets and listeners are invited to a wine and cheese reception at the nearby home of program director Jacklyn Potter. A selected committee chooses 17 poets in an open competition (poets may submit their work in January and February). The unusual locale merits a historical note: Joaquin Miller, a late 19th-century poet who shocked the conservative capital by sporting a huge sombrero, flashy bandanna, and bushy mustache, built this cabin in the woods to "retreat from the perils of civilization." Later, an informal group of 20 poets read by kerosene lantern inside the cabin, a tradition which eventually evolved into the current series which has been sponsored for nearly 20 years by Word Works Press. The Park Service is in the process of installing an interpretive wayside near the cabin to tell about both Miller and the poetry series.

Library of Congress
Poetry and Literature Program
First & Capitol Streets, SW
Washington, DC 20540
202/707-5394

The oldest continuing literary series in the metropolitan area, the poetry readings at the Library of Congress have been a capital attraction since the 1930's. National Poet Laureates, who have included such literary giants as Joseph Brodsky, Mark Strand, and Robert Penn Warren, open the October to May season and serve as the master of ceremonies. Poets and other writers invited to read from their works have included Tom Stoppard and Garrison Keillor. Special events have featured the readings of T.S. Eliot in celebration of the late poet's birthday. This free series is attended by 50 to 200 people and includes a post-reading reception providing a chance to meet and mingle. Call the number above for a calendar of events.

Martin Luther King Memorial Library Lunchtime Author Series
901 G Street, NW
Washington, DC 20001
202/727-1186 Library Services staff
301/654-9191 Lunchtime Authors Talks Coordinator

Every Tuesday at noon, the Literary Friends of the D.C. Public Library sponsor author talks in the main lobby of the Martin Luther King Library. Bring a brown bag lunch. Listen and ask questions as writers of both local and national renown discuss their work. The series is free, and runs from just after Labor Day through the end of June. All readers and writers are also invited, for free, to the Literary Friends' annual evening gala every autumn, honoring all Washington area writers who have published a book in the past year. Membership in the Literary Friends costs $10, less for seniors and students.

National Archives Author Lecture Series
NXI, National Archives
Pennsylvania Avenue between 7th and 9th Streets
Washington, DC 20408
202/501-5000 Recorded program update
202/501-5525 Public Affairs office

What better place to attend an author lecture and book signing than the National Archives, the home of historical documents ranging from the Declaration of Independence to the Nixon/Watergate tapes. The Archives' free, noontime author lecture series and related question-and-answer sessions draw from 10 to 300 professionals, retirees, and university students. Authors speak on issues from civil rights and foreign policy to political cartoons. The Archives' arts and culture program also sponsors playwright competitions, lectures, live performances, workshops, films, and other special events. Call for a recorded schedule of activities and monthly calendar of events.

The Red Circle of Washington
3900 Tunlaw Road, NW, #119
Washington, DC 20007-4830
202/338-1808

The Red Circle of Washington is the local branch of the Baker Street Irregulars. The group meets four times a year for dinner and discussion of the Sherlock Holmes stories. Other special events sponsored by these detectophiles include a running of The Silver Blaze at Pimlico Race Track each spring, and an occasional theatre party or film evening. Events are generally held in downtown Washington, and members are asked to pay $2.20 per year to cover the costs of a year's mailings. Each event also carries its own fees.

Sisters in Crime, Chesapeake Chapter
P.O. Box 2843
Kensington, MD 20891
301/231-9237

Mystery readers and writers, take note: the Chesapeake Chapter of Sisters in Crime holds monthly meetings for fans and friends. Featured speakers have included authors, police detectives, a Secret Service officer, forensic psychologists, and even a psychic. From 60 to 80 people usually attend. They ask probing questions, talk about mysteries, and meet others who share their interests. Meetings are held at 12:30 p.m., the first Saturday of most months at Bish Thompson's Restaurant in Bethesda, Maryland ($12-15 fee includes lunch). Annual dues are $15 (chapter), and $25 (national), and membership is open to both men and women.

Smithsonian Institution TSA (Resident Program)
1100 Jefferson Drive, SW
Washington, DC 20560
202/357-3030

The veritable literary mecca offered at TSA includes a full schedule of poetry readings, author lectures, writing seminars, and courses in the arts and humanities. See *Arts* for further information.

Washington Rare Book Group
National Capitol Station
P.O. Box 2908
Washington, DC 20013
202/994-6848

Formed in the 1970's by a group of collectors, book dealers, and librarians, the ranks of these rare book lovers have grown to more than 200 members who share an interest in collecting first editions and other unusual works, as well as socializing. Monthly gatherings are held from September to May over catered lunches, cocktails and dinners. The group also makes excursions to museums and libraries. Private tours and lectures by experts in various aspects of rare books have been offered to members, as well as field trips to special collections outside the Washington area. Annual dues are $10.

Writers' Organizations

Both amateur and accomplished writers belong to the following organizations, which feature a host of literary activities and other cerebral pleasures from writers' clubs to classes and special events.

Washington Independent Writers (WIW)

220 Woodward Building
733 15th Street, NW
Washington, DC 20005
202/347-4973

WIW was established in 1975 "to promote the mutual interest of freelance writers," and provides workshops, seminars, conferences, and a job bank for all writers from aspiring journalists to masters of fiction. Within the organization are several "Small Groups" that range from neighborhood groups to those focusing on business, the environment, fiction, nonfiction, and children's literature. These groups hold local meetings throughout the metropolitan area. Frequently-scheduled workshops and conferences have featured a popular freelance career course and an annual spring conference. Social activities include "Pubspeaks" at local restaurants, wine and cheese socials, theater outings, and holiday parties. All WIW news and events are published in *The Independent Writer*, WIW's monthly newsletter. WIW members may also purchase health insurance and legal services. Membership ranges from $45 to $120, and program fees vary considerably. Some events are open to non-members.

The Writer's Center

4508 Walsh Street
Bethesda, MD 20815
301/654-8664

Whether you have recently been compelled to compose or have a well-developed penchant for prose, you should explore the Writer's Center's workshops, readings, and writers' groups. Supported by 2000 writers, editors, small press publishers, and graphic artists, the Writer's Center is a non-profit membership organization that offers classes and workshops on the novel, fiction, stage and screen, poetry, non-fiction, mixed genre, writing and editing on the job, graphic arts, and publishing. The faculty includes a colorful assortment of accomplished writers, poets, artists, and academics. The fall and spring reading series at the Writer's Center features several monthly events, including coffeehouse-style open readings and a poetry and prose series. Most events are followed by receptions and open to the public. Not to be missed are the Center's prolific bulletin boards, filled with notices of writers' group meetings and other news of interest to aspiring authors. Membership starts at $30, and fees range from $1 to $133.

Writer's Center members receive a range of benefits which include:
❋ A bi-monthly publication, *Carousel*, featuring an extensive calendar of local literary events, writing contests, artists' retreats and conferences, writers' market listings, and feature articles

❧ *Poet Lore*, a quarterly journal of poetry and review and the oldest continuously published literary magazine in the country

❧ Discounts on workshops, readings, special events, and publications at the Center's Book Gallery, where members may also display and sell their works

❧ Access to the Center's word processing, typesetting, design facilities, and research library

Bookstores

Your local bookstore is often an ideal locale to discover unusual literary activity, from neighborhood book clubs and special readings, to celebrations commemorating authors such as Marcel Proust.

Borders Books & Music (Formerly Borders Book Shop/Rockville)

White Flint
11301 Rockville Pike
North Bethesda, MD 20895-1021
301/816-1067
301/816-2071 (Children's Books)
301/816-0259 (Music)

This spacious, comfortable bookstore recently moved to larger premises in White Flint Mall and added a Music Store, video section with screening area, and Espresso Bar. The store sponsors an extensive calendar of monthly events with lectures, readings, and book signings by local authors and well-known writers and illustrators such as Isabel Allende, Oscar Hijuelos, Mary Engelbreit, and Graeme Base. Events for kids have included live music and theater, special holiday events and book signings. There is a Storytime for Under 5's on Tuesdays at 10:00 a.m. Local musicians give an informal concert at Borders every Friday from 7:30 to 10:00 p.m. All programs are free and open to the public. Copies of the monthly calendar of events are available at the store. For further information contact Pam Kempf, Community Relations, 301/816-1040. Other Borders Book Shop locations are as follows:

Borders Book Shop
Baileys Crossroads
3532 South Jefferson Street
Baileys Crossroads, VA 22041
703/998-0404

Borders Books & Music
1801 K Street
Washington, DC 20006
202/466-4999

Borders Book Shop
Tyson's Square
8311 Leesburg Pike
Vienna, VA 22182
703/556-7766

Chapters Bookstore

1512 K Street, NW
Washington, DC
202/347-5495

Started by two defectors from some of D.C.'s larger chains, Chapters is not only one of the city's best independent bookstores but is also an exciting hub of literary activity. Readings, lectures, and poetry recitations abound here, and acclaimed guests have included Amy Tan and Martin Amis. Chapters sometimes sponsors eccentric activities, such as a recent pajama party in celebration of Marcel Proust's birthday. These events are generally free and open to the public.

Lambda Rising

1625 Connecticut Avenue, NW
Washington, DC 20009
202/462-6969

This gay and lesbian bookstore has been in Washington since 1974. A quarterly published catalogue, *Lambda Rising News*, has a circulation of 430,000. The store sponsors author readings and booksignings, and offers community bulletin boards in their DC, Baltimore, and Rehoboth Beach locations. Rita Mae Brown, David Leavitt, and Alan Ginsberg are among the authors who have read at Lambda Rising. The stores also sell tickets for plays and events of interest to the gay community.

Lammas Books & More Reading Series

1427 21st Street, NW (At P Street)
Washington, DC 20036
202/775-8218

Readings, book-signings, and workshops are the fare at Lammas Books' frequent, informal events, which are usually followed by a reception or discussion session. Alice Walker, Adrienne Rich, and several local authors have appeared at this feminist bookstore, which also sponsors special events on subjects that have included lesbian issues and rape prevention. These events are mostly attended by women, and they are free to the public.

Mystery Bookshop

7700 Old Georgetown Road
Bethesda, MD 20814
301/657-2665

Devoted followers of suspense and detective fiction will enjoy the weekly author readings at the Mystery Bookshop. A quarterly newsletter and periodic flyers announce upcoming events. All are encouraged to call or stop by the shop to be placed on the mailing list. Mystery Bookshop also sponsors the Chesapeake-Potomac Chapter of Mystery Readers International, with monthly readings, discussions, and field trips.

Politics and Prose (P&P)

5015 Connecticut Avenue, NW
Washington, DC 20008
202/364-1919
800/722-0790

This cozy, local bookstore hosts a remarkable array of programs, which include several monthly author lectures and readings that are often followed by informal discussions, receptions, and publication parties. Courses taught at P&P have included a Yeats class and a course on Spanish Literature. The P&P Book Club meets monthly at 7:30 on the second Tuesday of the month, and has discussed books such as *At Play in the Fields of the Lord* and *Palace Walk.* The bookstore stays open until midnight on Friday and Saturday nights and hosts a coffeehouse on those evenings. All events are open to the public; fees vary (many events are free, the class cost varies). A quarterly newsletter announces upcoming events. Call the number above to be placed on P&P's mailing list.

Favorite literary haunts in the city also feature author readings and events with play-wrights, actors, painters, musicians, artists, and performance artists. At Food for Thought, writers and poets gather to the tune of local musicians. At Kramerbooks & afterwords, a cafe/bookstore, literary enthusiasts may peruse the bookshelves and discuss their purchases over a delicious repast or frothy cappucino.

Food for Thought
1738 Connecticut Avenue, NW
Washington, DC
202/797-1095

Kramerbooks & afterwords
1517 Connecticut Avenue, NW
Washington, DC
202/387-1462 (Cafe)
202/387-1400 (Bookstore)
The bookstore and cafe are open all night
on the weekends.

Kramerbooks & afterwords
4201 Wilson Boulevard
Arlington, VA 22203
703/524-3200 (Books)
703/524-3900 (Cafe)

Educational Programs

Whether you want to produce a press release, publish a newsletter, or write a travel-ogue, there is a course for you at cultural institutions, recreation and community centers, and university and college campuses throughout the metropolitan area. From the Alexandria public school adult education classes to the Smithsonian Resident Associate Program, you'll find workshops and classes in (1) creative writing for aspir-ing poets, novelists, playwrights, screen writers, travel writers, and others (2) courses in literature and the humanities (3) journalism and job-related writing, and (4) desktop publishing. See *Education* for resources to classes in your area. Also consult *Literary Washington,* by David Cutler (Lanham, MD: Madison Books, 1989).

Footnotes

✻ Don't neglect to contact your neighborhood library for a schedule of author read-ings and other literary events.
✻ Choose almost any local campus and you'll discover an impressive menu of spe-cial readings and author lectures.
✻ The arts centers listed below also offer a host of literary programs (for further information on local arts centers, consult the arts councils listed at the end of *Arts*).

DISTRICT OF COLUMBIA

Market 5 Gallery
7th and North Carolina Avenue, SE
Washington, DC 20003
202/543-7293

MARYLAND

Harmony Hall Regional Center
10701 Livingston Road
Fort Washington, MD 20744
301/292-8331

Montpelier Cultural Arts Center
12826 Laurel-Bowie Road
Laurel, MD 20708
301/953-1993

Rockville Arts Place
100 East Middle Lane
Rockville, MD 20850
301/309-6900

Strathmore Hall
10701 Rockville Pike
North Bethesda, MD 20852
301/530-0540

VIRGINIA

Athenaeum (Northern Virginia Fine Arts Association—NVFAA)
201 Prince Street
Alexandria, VA 22314
703/548-0035

Arlington Arts Center
3550 Wilson Boulevard
Arlington, VA 22201
703/524-1494

Great Falls Arts Center
P.O. Box 712
Great Falls, VA 22066
703/759-7469

Greater Reston Arts Center (GRACE)
11911 Freedom Drive
Reston, VA 22090
703/471-9242

Herndon Gallery
7 Lynn Street
Herndon, VA 22070
703/476-0881

McLean Project for the Arts
McLean Community Center
1234 Ingleside Avenue
McLean, VA 22101
703/790-0123

Media Alert!

The Washington Review, the award-winning journal on arts and literature in Washington, includes reviews of recent literature by both new and established talent. Poetry, fiction, and feature articles are also included in this bimonthly publication. Subscribers receive invitations to special events. Contact the *Review* offices at P.O. Box 50132, Washington, D.C. 20091-0132, or call 202/638-0515. Annual subscriptions start at $12. ❖

Parks, Recreation and Community Centers
All in the Neighborhood

Since so many Washingtonians spend hours each week commuting to work, it is fortunate that a source of affordable fun and fitness for most area residents is within their own neighborhood. Across the metropolitan area, several hundred parks and recreation centers sponsored by local and county governments as well as other organizations like the YMCAs, YWCAs, and JCCs offer team and individual sports, aquatic programs, and activities for every interest from the arts to outdoor excursions. Programs specifically tailored for children, families, young adults, and seniors are also offered. In addition to the sports programs, seasonal events — such as Easter egg hunts, Shabbat dinners, and summer camps — help to weave together the fabric of the community.

Local Departments of Parks and Recreation

City and county jurisdictions operate differently in terms of program agenda and coordination: the information below is provided to show you what may be available in your area. Be sure to call the center nearest you (listings below) and ask for a current catalogue.

Arts

Discover your creative talents by exploring the studio classes, performance opportunities, and dance programs offered by your local community center. Drawing, painting, pottery, cartooning, stained-glass making, and a myriad of other fine arts and crafts classes will interest those with an affinity for the studio arts. Some of the area's most outstanding community theaters — such as the Alden Theatre in McLean, Dominion Stage in Arlington, and the Roundhouse Theatre in Silver Spring — are part of the local parks and recreation departments and offer wonderful opportunities for the thespian resident. These centers are also remarkable places to learn your left foot from your right, with instruction in everything from ballet and ballroom dancing to clogging, cowboy, and contra dances. Many centers also offer gallery exhibitions and performing arts programs that present local and international artists at often surprisingly-low ticket prices.

Athletics, Fitness, and Outdoor Adventures

This is the heart of many recreation departments, with courts, fields, and tracks hosting individuals, teams, and classes. For a detailed list of team sports and competitive leagues organized by local departments of parks and recreation, see *Athletics* and Outdoor Adventures. These departments may also offer a full schedule of aerobics, weight-training, yoga, and exercise classes to keep Washingtonians fit and trim. You can start by exploring below the earth (caving) and above it (rock climbing), or keep your feet well-planted on the ground with racquet sports, fencing, and martial arts. Gymnastics, equestrian events, ice skating, and sailing all offer a different perspective on gravity and the defiance thereof. The well-endowed roster of other pursuits may include gardening, fishing, motorcycling, camping, and bicycle repair.

Aquatics

Whether you're looking for swimming lessons, swim teams, scuba diving adventures, senior aerobic water exercise, or recreational swimming, try your local community pool first. The range of programs is impressive, and many facilities offer classes for the physically and mentally challenged.

Children's and Family Programs

Community centers are often ideal locales to share quality time with your children and meet other parents. McLean, for instance, offers a "You and Me Baby" exercise for new mothers and their offspring, Rockville offers a family film series, and other centers offer swim classes for fathers and their toddlers.

Education

Thousands of unusual (and affordable) continuing education classes in the arts, sciences, and other studies are offered at neighborhood public high schools and are administered by local departments of parks and recreation. See Montgomery County Public Schools, Prince George's County Public Schools and Adult Education, and Virginia Public School Adult Education under "Continuing Education Classes" in the *Education* chapter.

Nature Centers

A surprising number of ponds, parks, woods, streams, and meadows are part of the local landscape, and scores of nature centers help local residents to learn about and njoy them. Exhibits, libraries, trails, conservation areas, and archaeological sites offer opportunities to explore the out-of-doors, and programs for children, families, and indiuals range from butterfly walks to lessons in basic family ng skills.

Potpourri

Cooking classes, writing seminars, photography classes, visits to historic sites, storytelling sessions, chess tournaments, volunteer programs, bridge clubs, genealogy — trust the imagination of the program planners to find something of interest for just about everyone.

Seniors

Whatever the activity — arts, athletics, aquatics, family, nature, or potpourri — there is almost certain to be a program that is specifically designed for older adults. Senior centers operated by the parks and recreation departments are one source of programs, but other activities for the more experienced generation are integrated with those for their juniors.

REGIONAL

National Park Service, National Capital Region
1100 Ohio Drive, SW
Washington, DC 20242
202/619-7222 Office of Public Affairs
202/619-7275 Dial-a-Park Hotline

Call the numbers listed above for information on the national monuments, the White House, ice rinks, and other facilities managed by the National Park Service. The Park Service sponsors a variety of free events and activities, including Sunday morning bird walks. *Kiosk*, a monthly calendar of activities, is sent to those who request it.

DISTRICT OF COLUMBIA

District of Columbia Department of Recreation and Parks
3149 16th Street, NW
Washington, DC 20010
202/673-7671 (Recreation information)
202/673-7671 (Dial-An-Event)

The District of Columbia maintains 104 community centers and recreation facilities, each of which sponsors its own roster of programs. Program profiles are published in a bi-annual catalogue and monthly calendar distributed to local libraries.

MARYLAND

Gaithersburg Department of Parks and Recreation
502 South Frederick Avenue
Gaithersburg, MD 20877
301/258-6350

The City of Gaithersburg Recreation Guide is printed quarterly and is available at the library in Montgomery Village, all city schools, and all City of Gaithersburg facilities. There is information on courses and special events, on the activities of the Casey Community Center, the Gaithersburg Aquatic Center, and the Summit Hall Farm Park Pool.

Maryland-National Capital Park and Planning Commission & Montgomery County Parks Department (MNCPPC)
9500 Brunett Avenue
Silver Spring, MD 20901
301/495-2525

Park It! A Guide to Parks in Montgomery and Prince George's County is a colorful and easy-to-read publication, and includes maps of many of the 700 parks and facilities owned by the Commission in both Montgomery and Prince George's Counties. The publication includes information on campsites, horse stables, tennis courts, swimming pools, boating and fishing, ice skating, natural areas and historic sites, arts facilities, gardens, nature centers, and special facilities. *Park It!* is free, and *Montgomery County's Guide to Parks* is available at the regional parks for $2. For information on reserving ball fields, golf courses, picnic pavilions, etc., in Montgomery County, call 301/495-2525, and in Prince Georges County, call 301/699-2415.

Montgomery County Department of Recreation
12210 Bushey Drive
Silver Spring, MD 20902-1099
301/217-6820

The general information number listed above is a good place to begin to explore the countless programs offered by Montgomery County's 10 community centers and four senior centers. The Guide to Recreation and Leisure Services is mailed to all County residents and is available at libraries or by calling the above number. Call 301/217-6880 for information on Arts and Leisure classes.

Prince George's County Department of Parks and Recreation
6600 Kenilworth Avenue
Riverdale, MD 20737
301/699-2407

The Seasonal Guide, mailed to all Prince George's County residents, lists the classes and activities in the County's more than 35 community centers and nature centers. Although information on the County as a whole is available at the number above, more details are available at the regional offices: Northern Area: 301/445-4500; Central Area: 301/249-9220; Southern Area: 301/292-9006.

Rockville Department of Recreation and Parks
111 Maryland Avenue
Rockville, MD 20850
301/309-3340

The City of Rockville Recreation and Parks Guide, available at Rockville City Hall, the Rockville Library, and the Twinbrook Library, details several hundred offerings in aquatics, arts, sports, fitness, crafts, family events, and senior programs.

Takoma Park Recreation Department
7500 Maple Avenue
Takoma Park, MD 20912
301/270-4048

The Recreation Guide is available at the Takoma Park Recreation Department and its next door neighbor, the City Library.

VIRGINIA

Alexandria Department of Recreation, Parks, & Cultural Activities
1108 Jefferson Street
Alexandria, VA 22314
703/838-4831

In Your Neighborhood, mailed to all residents and available in libraries, recreation centers, and the Torpedo Art Factory, details the classes and programs offered at seven pools, 11 recreation centers, and numerous parks and ball fields in Alexandria.

Arlington County Department of Parks, Recreation, and Community Resources
2100 Clarendon Boulevard
Arlington, VA 22201
703/358-3313

Information on Arlington County's ten community centers and park and recreation activities is published in *Education and Recreation in Arlington,* available at all county libraries and recreation centers.

Fairfax County Department of Recreation and Community Services
12011 Government Center Parkway Suite 1050
Fairfax, VA 22035-1115
703/324-5500; 703/324-4FUN (4386)

This department of recreation and community services sponsors a wide curriculum of classes and other activities at Fairfax County's seven community centers and other locales. Profiles of these programs and more are found in *Leisure Pursuits* and *CLASSES, ETC.,* mailed to all residents and available at County libraries.

Fairfax County Park Authority
3701 Pender Drive
Fairfax, VA 22030
703/246-5574

Fairfax County Park Authority manages eight recreation centers, six nature centers, three lakefront parks and various historic sites. *PARKtakes,* the agency's quarterly listing of classes, events, services and facilities, is mailed free to subscribers. For a free subscription, call 703/246-5588.

Falls Church Department of Recreation and Parks
Falls Church Community Center
223 Little Falls Street
Falls Church, VA 22046
703/241-5077

The Schedule of Classes and Community Programs is available at the Falls Church Community Center and library.

Herndon Parks and Recreation Department
Herndon Community Center
814 Ferndale Avenue
Herndon, VA 22070
703/435-6868

A quarterly brochure with details on classes and facilities is mailed to all residents and is available at the Herndon Community Center. The more than 1000 class offerings and activities include sports, arts, festivals and fairs, theatre trips, and health and fitness. From water babies to seniors, the Herndon Community Center has something for everyone.

McLean Community Center
1234 North Ingleside Avenue
McLean, VA 22101
703/790-0123

Classes, fitness programs, a teen center, the highly acclaimed Alden Theatre, and much more are sponsored by the McLean Community Center. *The Quidnunk*, published three times a year, has all the details and is available at the Center.

Reston Community Center
Hunters Woods Center
2310 Colts Neck Road
Reston, VA 22091
703/476-4500

National touring productions join with local companies to comprise the performing arts program at this center, which also offers an aquatics program, classes to please all interests, and special events for adults and young people. The monthly newsletter, *CenterStage*, is delivered to area homes, and a complete schedule of classes and activities is published three times a year.

Vienna Parks and Recreation Department
Vienna Community Center
120 Cherry Street, SE
Vienna, VA 22180
703/255-6360

A quarterly brochure with details on all of the activities of the Vienna Parks and Recreation Department is available at the Vienna Community Center.

Public Libraries

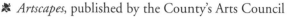

Never underestimate one of the most powerful community centers around: your local public library. Here you'll find a plethora of valuable information on community events. A recent visit to Montgomery County's Bethesda library yielded the following publications and calendars of events:

❋ *Artscapes*, published by the County's Arts Council
❋ *County Connection*, news from the County
❋ *Friends of the Library* Newsletter
❋ *Guide to Recreation and Leisure Programs*, a course catalogue for programs sponsored by the County's Recreation Department
❋ *Human Interest*, a Commission on the Humanities newsletter
❋ *In Touch*, a community activities newsletter published by the County's Office of Minority and Multicultural Affairs
❋ *Nutshell News*, a newsletter of the Maryland-National Capital Park and Planning Commission describing upcoming events at parks and nature centers

This library also featured information on the Friends of the Library's Literary Luncheon Series, a track club, a environmental volunteer group, a career changers' support group, a nearby concert performed by the Theater Chamber Players of the Kennedy Center, an upcoming theater production sponsored by the County's Recreation Department, an African American storytelling series, a nutrition group, and programs and services for women and their families.

Jewish Community Centers (JCCs)

JCCs in Washington, D.C., Rockville, and Fairfax are a rich resource for programs ranging from outdoor clubs to Judaic classes. Several of these programs are specifically designed for single/young professionals, families, and senior adults. Members receive catalogues and guides, substantial discounts on programs and activities, invitations to members-only events, and a unique opportunity to meet others in the Jewish community.

District of Columbia Jewish Community Center (DCJCC)
1836 Jefferson Place, NW
Washington, DC 20036
202/775-1765

Get your hands on the DCJCC's thick program guide, and you'll discover a world of activities of every conceivable variety. The DCJCC takes pride in being one of the most exciting institutions of its kind in Washington. Within the Cultural Arts program alone, the DCJCC sponsors the annual Washington Jewish Film Festival, as well as exhibit openings, concert series, dance performances, its own "Theater J" with three plays each year, and a number of classes. The singles-oriented adult services program includes a variety of social activities such as ski trips, after-work parties, relationship and career workshops, museum excursions and Shabbat dinners. Through its pioneering Community Services Department, volunteers reach out to the community year-round through working with at-risk children, seniors, new Americans, nursing home residents and others, and participate in building and renovation of homes and shelters, gleaning, and mentoring activities. The Youth and Family Program offers full and part-time preschools, a day camp, and a variety of special programs for kids and families. Senior Services has a kosher nutrition program and lectures, discussions and other activities. The DCJCC's Athletics Department features coed volleyball, softball, basketball, bowling, golf, soccer, cycling, hiking, and much more. To this, one can add the Judaic program's lectures, classes in Hebrew and other subjects, morning, lunch, and evening study groups and special events, and Public Affairs lectures and brunches with policy makers and journalists. The monthly newsletter, *Center in the City*, is free and available to all who ask. Membership fees range from $50 for students and senior adults to $155 for two parent families.

Jewish Community Center of Greater Washington
6125 Montrose Road
Rockville, MD 20852
301/881-0100; 301/881-0012 (TDD)

The JCC of Greater Washington has been described as a combination of the YMCA, the Kennedy Center, a day care facility, a senior center, a singles resource, and an educational institution. With the largest program of any JCC in the area and a splendid new athletics center, this description is fairly accurate. The JCC Arts Center (see *Arts*) is one of the area's most active, and other important offerings include a health club and aquatics program, a nursery and children's program, the Washington Jewish Theater, an Institute for Jewish Learning, and an extensive senior adults program. Membership fees range from about $225 for young adults to about $450 for families.

Jewish Community Center of Northern Virginia
8900 Little River Turnpike
Fairfax, VA 22031
703/323-0880

This center continues the rich tradition of JCC activities in the following areas:
* Aquatics
* Children & Teen Programs
* Cultural Arts
* Judaic Studies
* Singles/Young Professionals
* Senior Adult Clubs and Programs
* Special Events
* Sports & Fitness (includes competitive leagues & outing clubs)
* Theatre
Membership fees range from $75 for college students to $435 for families. There are also three month introductory memberships available.

Young Men's Christian Association (YMCA)

As a member of the United Way, the YMCA strives to assist all people to grow in mind, body, and spirit. There are 14 independent YMCA branches in metropolitan Washington, each of which offers programs that vary according to facilities and community needs. Programs include aquatics, community services, dance, fitness programs, gymnastics, martial arts, open and family gyms, racquet sports, recreational and competitive sports, wellness programs, and youth programs.

Sports and fitness programs may include team league opportunities in basketball, volleyball, softball, and more. You'll also find classes in strengthening and conditioning with weights, low and high-impact and bench aerobics, beginner fitness, yoga, and fencing. Martial arts possibilities include tae kwon do, judo, jujitsu, aikido kokikai, and self-defense courses. Dance courses include ballet and ballroom dancing. In the aquatics program, infants through adults may take classes varying from beginning swimming to scuba and masters swim classes. Also offered are squash, tennis, and racquetball instruction and leagues.

While health and fitness members are burning off the calories, the YMCA's Community Services at downtown Washington's YMCA runs over two dozen activities to accommodate other needs, which include tutoring sessions and English classes, basketball programs for at-risk men, children's educational programs, senior citizen fitness programs, fitness and social programs for blind and disabled adults, and other critical social services. Contact your local YMCA for specific information.

DISTRICT OF COLUMBIA

Adams Morgan YMCA Program Center
2409 18th Street, NW
Washington, DC 20009
202/332-2630

Anthony Bowen YMCA
1325 W Street, NW
Washington, DC 20009
202/462-1054

National Capital YMCA
1711 Rhode Island Avenue, NW
Washington, DC 20034
202/862-9622

YMCA Urban Program Center
3431 Benning Road, NE
Washington, DC 20019
202/398-2600

MARYLAND

Bethesda/Chevy Chase YMCA
9401 Old Georgetown Road
Bethesda/Chevy Chase, MD 20814
301/530-3725

Prince George's County YMCA
3501 Moylan Drive
Bowie, MD 20715
301/262-4342

Silver Spring YMCA
9800 Hastings Drive
Silver Spring, MD 20901
301/585-2120

Upper Montgomery County YMCA
10011 Stedwick Road
Gaithersburg, MD 20879
301/948-9622

YMCA Camp Letts
P.O. Box 208
Edgewater, MD 21037
301/261-4286

VIRGINIA

Alexandria YMCA
420 East Monroe Avenue
Alexandria, VA 22301
703/549-0850

Korean Program Center YMCA
3900 King Street
Alexandria, VA 22302
703/379-1141

Arlington County YMCA
3422 13th Street, North
Arlington, VA 22201
703/525-5420

Veterans Memorial YMCA
3440 South 22nd Street
Arlington, VA 22204
703/892-2044

Fairfax County YMCA
9124 Little River Turnpike
Fairfax, VA 22031
703/323-1222

YMCA membership fees vary according to the facilities and programs offered at each center. Fees can range up to $1,000 per year, and financial assistance may be available for youth, adult, and senior citizen memberships. Membership entitles individuals to use the YMCA facilities and often includes added benefits such as free aerobics classes.

Young Women's Christian Associations

Washington's YWCA's provide facilities for and classes in swimming, safety, fitness, and exercise. Offerings include adult and children's swimming programs, water exercise for arthritis, stroke clinics, weight training, day care and pre-school programs, and career education. Community services sponsored by area YWCAs include women's support groups. Membership is required and costs $25 per year. Program costs vary.

Washington, D.C. YWCA
624 Ninth Street, NW
Washington, DC 20001
202/626-0700

Fairfax County YWCA
Wolftrap and Gallows Road
Dunn Loring, VA 22027
703/560-1116

❖

Personal Growth
So Much in Common

Washingtonians looking for ways to add deeper meaning to their lives have many resources to choose from in the region. A host of personal growth programs throughout the metropolitan area address these needs by facilitating spiritual and emotional development. Religious organizations, continuing education courses, and a diverse range of support groups offer a haven where members and participants can openly share their feelings in the company of those who share similar concerns. In addition to the "mainstream" resources detailed below, also explore the organizations in New Age Activities and "Washington: Rest and Relaxation," profiled at the end of the chapter, to discover alternative routes to achieving spiritual development.

Well-known area social worker, Beverly H. Black, Director of the Center for Stress Management at Roundhouse Square Counseling Center in Alexandria offers the following suggestions for those who feel some discomfort when meeting new people in a group situation.

How to take that "First Step"

For some of us, joining organizations, walking up to a group of people who are already engaged in conversation, or even entering a crowded room can bring on bouts of heart palpitations and sweaty palms.

Thinking that all eyes are on us, and feeling very vulnerable, we feel we have to prove our competence, which is hard to do when we're feeling awkward. Never mind how some of us developed these painful feelings — it is possible to change our fear reactions by changing the way we approach the situations.

Try the following approaches:

1) Give yourself permission to make mistakes. Having fun socially is not about being perfect. If you goof up and say the wrong thing, it will not be a fatal blow to your social aspirations. Plan to make mistakes and keep on trying to improve.

2) Prepare to be uncomfortable for the first few months of effort. Concentrate on just attending the event. You may feel very nervous at first. Your feelings will chnge gradually after your repeated efforts.

3) Early on, you may feel that all eyes are on you, and that these eyes are critical ones. Ignore this.

4) Use visual imagery to imagine yourself successful. Instead of imagining yourself shy, awkward or tongue-tied, picture yourself as being wildly successful, saying and doing just the right thing. Your brain actually records this "success" so that when you enter the real situation, it has a memory of having been successful.

Changing ideas and behavior is hard work. Treat yourself kindly as you begin this adventure.

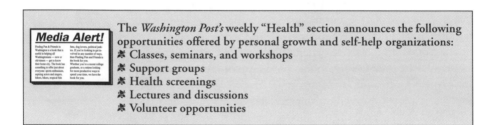

Media Alert!

The *Washington Post's* weekly "Health" section announces the following opportunities offered by personal growth and self-help organizations:
* Classes, seminars, and workshops
* Support groups
* Health screenings
* Lectures and discussions
* Volunteer opportunities

Religious Organizations

Churches, synagogues, temples, and other houses of worship foster the spiritual development of individuals and the community through weekly services, religious classes, and a diverse range of support groups. Local congregations may also sponsor community outreach projects, cultural and social events, recreational outings, sports leagues, and other activities. New members are almost always welcome to attend a religious service or function, where they may discover a study group or support group of interest, such as a bible study class or alcoholics anonymous program. Outreach committees, senior citizens' clubs, and volunteer projects at nearby soup kitchens are just of a few of the other programs offered at Washington's 2000-plus congregations of various religious faiths. For further information, consult Saturday's *Washington Post*, or *Washington '94* (Columbia Books, Inc., 1212 New York Avenue, NW, Suite 330, Washington, DC 20005). This annually-published resource (found at most public libraries) lists leading religious organizations and seminaries, and profiles several of Washington's congregations and their outreach projects, classes and support groups, and other programs.

Interfaith Conference of Metropolitan Washington
1419 V Street, NW
Washington, DC 20009
202/234-6300

This organization provides an excellent opportunity to join members of numerous faiths, races, and cultures. About 30 different religious groups and several thousand congregations participate in the Conference. Programs of interfaith dialogue, overcoming racial and ethnic polarization, and a high school youth retreat are offered annually. Each fall the Interfaith Conference sponsors the largest interfaith concert in the world. Individuals are welcome to join the Conference, as well as entire congregations.

Continuing Education Programs

Comprehensive and affordable workshops and classes help Washingtonians cope with stress, anger, divorce, parenthood, health problems, and other of life's changes and challenges in the company of those with similar concerns. These programs are offered through adult education classes at community colleges, city and county public schools, local departments of parks and recreation, and area community centers. The resources in *Education* will direct you to personal growth education programs in your area; call and request current course catalogues for further information.

Local hospitals offer a full curriculum of health education programs that provide the ideas and insights of professionally trained counselors and medical staff. For instance, Washington Adventist Hospital's "Life Dynamics" program (301/891-5716) includes a host of exercise and nutrition courses, support groups and special services, free lectures, and parent education classes. Life Dynamics also sponsors fitness programs, weight adjustment classes, diabetes and eating disorders support groups, classes in back care and CPR, and culinary classes in low-cholesterol cuisine and international vegetarian cooking. Programs generally range from $65 to $120. Other hospitals in the area offer similar programs: contact the hospital nearest you for further information.

Support Groups

Washington has an unusually diverse network of support and anonymous support groups to accommodate a wide spectrum of concerns. These groups foster and promote their members' emotional, spiritual, mental, and physical well-being in an atmosphere of acceptance and confidentiality. Some groups meet weekly to discuss and share common experiences. Other groups include a comprehensive calendar of educational and social activities. Group discussions, study groups, guest speakers, and informal activities often fill the agenda at group meetings scheduled in church halls, public buildings, hospitals, and members' homes. Through these meetings and activities, you're bound to gain the understanding and friendship of others who share similar concerns. These groups are generally free and open to the public, although they often request a small donation. If none of the organizations profiled below speak to your concerns, you may want to contact the Self-Help Clearinghouse of Greater Washington, detailed in the following Media Alert.

Media Alert!

Self-Help Clearinghouse of Greater Washington
c/o Mental Health Association of Northern Virginia
7630 Little River Turnpike, Suite 206
Annandale, VA 22203
703/941-LINK (5465)

For a comprehensive listing of the more than 600 self-help and support groups in the metro-politan area, contact the Self-Help Clearinghouse of Greater Washington. This organization — the only resource center of its kind in the area — serves individuals and groups in Northern Virginia, Montgomery and Prince George's Counties, and Washington, D.C. It not only pub-lishes a self-help group directory, but it distributes a newsletter, refers individuals to existing resources and helps to form new self-help groups, provides consultations to member groups, and conducts frequent seminars and workshops throughout the metropolitan area. Member-ship fees for the Mental Health Association of Northern Virginia (starting at $25 for individu-als and small groups) include several benefits such as a free directory and invitations to special events.

AIDS Support

Whitman Walker Clinic
1407 S Street, NW
Washington, DC 20009
202/797-3576

The Whitman Walker Clinic, now a model for similar clinics in San Francisco and New York, was founded as the Gay Men's VD Clinic in 1973 and is now D.C.'s premiere community-based provider of AIDS ser-vices to people of all orientations. The Clinic provides a variety of support services for people with AIDS and their families and friends (see *Volunteer*).

Divorce and Separation

Divorce Recovery Support Group
3901 Rugby Road
Fairfax, VA 22033
703/631-2100

This group is sponsored by the Fairfax Church of Christ and provides a safe environ-ment for accepting, healing, and growing through separation or divorce. The group schedules weekly meetings and social events and is open to anyone.

New Beginnings, Inc.
13129 Clifton Road
Silver Spring, MD 20904
301/384-0111

This support group, for recently separated and divorced men and women, schedules regular discussion meetings, supplemented by expert speakers, on issues such as coping with being alone and building new relationship skills. Social activities include potluck dinners, dances, and weekend retreats. Members meet in each other's homes and are eligible to join up to two years after their divorce. Membership is $40 the first year and $30 annually thereafter.

Parenthood

Parent Education Network of Greater Washington (PEN)
2306 Henslowe Drive
Potomac, MD 20854
301/294-9604

Dedicated to supporting parents through education and providing a social network and environment, PEN has nine chapters in the District, Maryland, and Virginia. Each chapter is organized around parents with children in the same age group (beginning at the newborn stage and up to ten-year-olds) so topics and speakers are developmentall appropriate and interesting to al members. Annual dues are $20-30 per year.

Single Parenthood

Montgomery County Single Parents, Inc. (MONTCOSP)
5 Hardwick Place
Rockville, MD 20850
301/468-5735

This non-profit, volunteer organization for single parents and their children organizes an extensive calendar of activities that features adult social events and discussion groups, educational workshops, and family programs. Included in this crowded calendar are monthly brunches and new member orientations, community service projects, family boating and picnic dinners, a Speaker-of-the-Month series, and TGIF parties. Special events include a Mother's Day Dinner Dance hosted by MONTCOSP Dads. Members generally range from 30 to 60 years of age. While MONTCOSP activities are centered in Montgomery County, members live throughout the metropolitan area. Membership is $25 annually, and includes a monthly newsletter announcing scheduled activities. Special programs, which vary in price, generally cost under $5.

Parents Without Partners
c/o Smith, Buckland, & Associates
401 North Michigan Avenue
Chicago, IL 60611
312/644-6610
800/637-7974

Parents Without Partners began in 1957 as a handful of single parents gathered in the basement of a Greenwich Village Church. Today the national organization has 135,000 members. Six local chapters of 200 to 3000 metropolitan Washingtonians host weekly meetings open to all single parents. This organization offers a diverse selection of social activities to help single parents re-integrate with other single adults, and provides a comfortable setting for separated families to have fun. Family activities include picnics, hikes, camping, and bowling. Members may take advantage of the organization's substantial resources, including "The Single Parent Clearing House," a library devoted to single parenting, and *Single Parent Magazine*. Membership is required, and fees average $30 annually.

Single Parents Raising Kids (SPARK)
P.O. Box 1631
Wheaton, MD 20915
301/598-6395

Family, friendship, and information are the cornerstones of SPARK, whose activities include diverse program of family, social, and educational events. Discussion and support groups, speaker programs, day trips to Washington's parks, museums, and art and sports attractions, and wine and cheese parties are included in SPARK's calendar of events. Interested single parents may attend SPARK's orientation sessions, generally held on the first Sunday of each month. Members may live anywhere in the metropolitan area but must have children under 18 years of age. Special programs are generally under $4, while annual dues are $18.

Smoking

Freedom From Smoking
American Lung Association of Maryland
814 West Diamond Avenue, Suite 270
Gaithersburg, MD 20878
301/990-1207

"It's a matter of life and breath" is the familiar slogan of the American Lung Association, which sponsors Smoking Cessation Clinics throughout the metropolitan area. Through the Clinics' Freedom From Smoking support group programs, smokers may find the encouragement needed to quit smoking permanently. Smokers attend seven sessions over six weeks which include suggestions on relaxation techniques, how to avoid weight gain, and ways to build a healthier lifestyle. The cost of the program is $80.

Widowhood

Widowed Person's Service
American Association of Retired Persons (AARP)
601 E Street, NW
Washington, DC 20049
Ms. Marjory G. Marvel, Senior Program Specialist
202/434-2260

AARP, the leading lobbying and service organization for senior citizens, sponsors free support groups for widowed persons of all ages as part of an outreach and support program. These groups meet throughout the greater Washington area.

Women Only

Commission for Women Counseling and Career Center
(formerly A Woman's Place and New Phase Career Center)
255 North Washington Street
NationsBank Building Fourth Floor
Rockville, MD 20850
301/279-1800
301/279-1034 TTD

The Commission for Women was established by the Montgomery County government in 1972 to advocate equal rights for women. Today the Commission serves residents of Montgomery County and employees of the Montgomery County government as a women's resource, activity, and counseling and career center in Rockville, Maryland. The Center offers personal, career, and financial counseling, seminars and workshops on personal growth and career development, referrals to resources for assistance, and information on current job openings. Support groups have included a job search and networking group, a "coping with job loss" group, a displaced homemaker program, and M.A.M.S. (middle-aged moms). Single-day seminars and six-session workshops have included "Sexual Harassment in the Workplace," "Divorce Legal Seminars," and "Building Self-Esteem." Appointments and registration are required. All programs are held at the center and most sessions are $6.

Just Friends
P.O. Box 20741
Alexandria, VA 22320
703/550-6291

This new organization was started by two women who realized how difficult it can be to form friendships in Washington. Just Friends is not a same-sex dating service, but a service for women who want to find others with similar interests. Some group outings are also planned. For $30, new members describe their interests and are added to the published list of participants. The list of descriptions is then circulated bi-monthly, and like-minded members can contact each other.

The Women's Center
133 Park Street
Vienna, VA 22180
703/281-2657

Serving more than 60,000 individuals each year, the Women's Center is one of the largest and most comprehensive resources for women and their families in the Washington metropolitan area. A private, nonprofit community resource, the Center provides counseling, education, and referral services dealing with the personal, professional, legal, and financial concerns of women. A professional staff of psychologists and social workers, career counselors, attorneys, and financial planners enables the Center to assist women with these four interrelated areas of their lives. The Center's year-round support groups include those for women, men, singles, moms, single parents, and divorced individuals, as well as those for compulsive overeaters, co-dependents, victims of incest, adult children of alcoholics and dysfunctional families, and others who suffer from low self-esteem or PMS. Group membership requires an initial interview. Workshops meet every week throughout Northern Virginia for a monthly fee of $60. In addition to individual and group counseling, the Center offers more than 200 single-day seminars and six, eight, and ten-week workshops on such topics as managing motherhood, changing careers, legal aspects of separation and divorce, and personal financial planning. The Center also sponsors an annual Leadership Conference for Women, and a Summer Health Series which has included classes such as "Total Fitness through Exercise and Nutrition" and "Stress Management for Women in the '90's." Other programs have featured book signings and receptions, workshops on topics such as basic auto maintenance and repair, and "Potomac Parties," a series of special events including a relaxing spa day, a mystery dinner party, and an elegant breakfast at historic Oakwood. A newsletter includes a complete calendar of events. A modest fee is charged for all workshops and counseling services; a limited sliding fee schedule is available.

Young Women's Christian Association (YWCA)

The YWCA sponsors several women's support groups to help women through divorce, separation, widowhood, single parenting, and the single life. These groups also address anger, depression, and sexuality. Membership is required and costs $25 per year. Program costs vary.

Washington, D.C. YWCA
624 Ninth Street, NW
Washington, DC 2001
202/626-0700

Fairfax County YWCA
Wolftrap and Gallows Road
Dunn Loring, VA 22027
703/560-1116

Anonymous Support Groups

A substantial network of anonymous support groups helps Washington residents find mutual understanding and confidential support for problems such as alcohol and drug abuse, depression, and anxiety disorders. Members exchange common experiences, discuss ways to solve their problems, and often establish lasting friendships.

Alcoholics Anonymous (AA)

Washington, DC/Prince Georges and Montgomery County Intergroup
4530 Connecticut Avenue, NW Suite 111
Washington, DC 20008
202/966-9115

Northern Virginia Intergroup
380 Maple Avenue West #301
Vienna, VA 22180
703/281-7501

AA is "a voluntary, worldwide fellowship of men and women from all walks of life who meet together to attain and maintain sobriety." AA's 500 to 600 Washington metropolitan groups hold over 1900 weekly meetings free to anyone with a desire to stop drinking. Some meetings are open to family and friends, while closed meetings are strictly for alcoholics. All AA participants follow a 12-step program which outlines a practical approach to recovery. By following these guidelines and working closely with other members, addicts learn to stop drinking and face the challenges of daily living. AA also coordinates a 24-hour phone support service and publishes the *New Reporter*, a monthly newspaper featuring news of AA groups, articles on alcohol and alcoholism, and updates on social events. To find out about AA groups, Al-Anon groups for friends and family of alcoholics, and other anonymous groups in your area, call one of the numbers listed above.

Depression and Related Affective Disorders Association (DRADA)
Meyer 3-181, 600 Wolfe Street
Baltimore, MD 21205
410/955-4647

One out of every 10 persons will suffer from an affective disorder at some point in their life, according to DRADA, a local nonprofit organization. Many do not even realize the fact that depression and other affective disorders are treatable illnesses. In cooperation with the Johns Hopkins University School of Medicine, DRADA promotes education, support services, and research in the area of affective disorders. DRADA sponsors support groups throughout the Baltimore and Washington metropolitan areas whose members provide a "supportive environment for sharing experiences and solutions to problems common among those living with these illnesses." Members include patients, families, mental  health professionals, and others. Membership is $25, and includes a quarterly newsletter, announcements of DRADA meetings and programs, and other DRADA publications.

Narcotics Anonymous (NA)
P.O. Box 515
Greenbelt, MD 20770
301/731-7221 (Maryland)
202/399-5316 (Washington, D.C.)
703/281-8638 (Virginia)

NA is a nonprofit, community-based society of recovering narcotics addicts who meet regularly to help each other to "stay clean." The only requirement is the desire to stop using narcotics. Modeled after the 12-step AA approach, NA sponsors hundreds of regular weekly meetings throughout the Washington area. The basic premise of anonymity allows addicts to attend meetings without fear of legal or social repercussions. Two types of meetings include those open to the general public, and those for addicts only. Members talk about their experiences and recovery from drug addiction, and often lead group discussions. Meetings are informally structured and may also feature guest speakers and question-and-answer sessions. NA is funded entirely from donations by members and the sale of recovery literature.

Overeaters Anonymous (OA)
Central office: 703/642-3437

OA sponsors nearly 180 support groups of five to 40 people who meet weekly throughout the area. Washingtonians with anorexia, bulimia, and other eating disorders may find a supportive group of encouraging folks who try to overcome their addiction to food through the well-known 12-step process established by Alcoholics Anonymous.

New Age Activities

There are many nontraditional paths to spiritual enrichment in Washington. Those in search of metaphysical guidance may begin by exploring the vast spectrum of non-denominational ministries that offer unique philosophies, credos, and alternative approaches to spiritual and communal enrichment that are sometimes called "new age activities." These activities are fostered through support groups and weekly services, lectures and study groups, channeling meetings and crystal sales, and guided meditations and special celebrations. A valuable resource to the organizations which sponsor these activities is a local, quarterly publication, *Pathways*, profiled below.

Media Alert!

Finding Fun & Friends in Washington is a book that is useful in helping all Washingtonians — new or old-timers — get to know their home city. The book has something to offer just about everyone; sports enthusiasts, aspiring actors and singers, bikers, hikers, tropical fish fans, dog lovers, political junkies. If you're looking to get involved in any number of ways, then Finding Fun and Friends is the book for you. Whether you're a recent college graduate, or a retiree looking for more productive ways to spend your time, we have the book for you.

Pathways
6926 Willow Street, NW
Washington, DC 20012
202/829-3289

Free *Pathways: A Journal and Resource Guide to Personal and Social Wellness in the D.C. Area,* provides information to improve the quality of your life "physically, mentally, emotionally, and spiritually." *Pathways* is a hefty quarterly publication with feature articles, a directory to the area's new age organizations, and a calendar of local events. Chapters include: classes and learning centers, goods for growth, metaphysical sciences, psychology and therapy, retreats and adventures and classifieds. You'll find everything from yoga classes and Sunday services to holistic dentists in *Pathways,* which distributes throughout the Washington and Baltimore metropolitan areas and offers a two-year subscription for $10.

Washington: Rest and Relaxation

Stress reduction and relaxation are two keys to a longer life. These organizations specialize in ancient methods of working out the mental kinks and muscular tension.

Potomac Massage Training Institute (PMTI)
4000 Albemarle Street, NW, 5th Floor
Washington, DC 20016
202/686-7046

Aching muscles and bothersome joints are taken seriously at PMTI. Offering comprehensive programs in massage therapy and holistic health, PMTI sponsors a diverse selection of workshops, classes, and lecture series. Beginners may increase awareness of self and others through a one-time "Introduction to Massage" class, or they may enroll in a six-time massage course for a more thorough exploration of massage techniques. Classes start at $55.

Saint Mark's Yoga Center
Third and A Streets, SE
Washington, DC 20003
202/546-4964

Yoga classes on Capitol Hill meet Monday through Thursday during the evening and on Saturday mornings. Classes include 10 to 20 people, usually ranging in ages from 25 to 60. The Center sponsors occasional retreats and special events which have featured potluck suppers and group meditations. Class costs range from $10 each to $50 for any eight classes. The first class is free, beginners can attend any class.

The School of T'ai Chi Chuan (STCC)
P.O. Box 2064
Merrifield, VA 22116
703/845-0083

Two Northern Virginia locations are available to those interested in learning T'ai Chi - the "grandmother of martial arts". According to traditional Chinese medicine, this exercise of slow, flowing movements has been designed to reduce stress by concentrating the "chi", or vital energy we each possess. Founded in New York City in 1976, the STCC hosts a series of sequential classes around the world. Locally, the group meets at the Rock Spring Church Neighborhood Center in Arlington and the Tyson's Sporting Club. Entry level classes are scheduled four times a year, and participants receive a periodic newsletter, *"Rounds"*. STCC also offers films, lectures, and Hawaiian Swimming, or "T'ai Chi In Water".

Sunflower Yoga Company
1305 Chalmers Road
Silver Spring, MD 20903
Ms. Sarabess Forster
301/445-3882

Weekly yoga workshops and classes have been standard commodities at this company since 1980. In addition to workshops on diet, nutrition, positive thinking, and meditation, the Yoga Company also organizes occasional retreats to local and exotic destinations which have included Costa Rica and the Caribbean. Retreats include from 20 to 70 individuals who incorporate meditation, yoga, and other events into their vacation. Yoga classes are generally $5 to $12 and may be taken individually or in a series. Workshops and retreats costs vary. Sarabess is the producer and creator of the TV series, "The 20 Minute Yogi," which is now appearing on cable in Montgomery, Prince Georges, Fairfax, and Arlington counties. Home practice videos based on her award-winning TV series are available.

Unity Woods Yoga Center
4853 Cordell Avenue, Penthouse 9
Bethesda, MD 20814
301/656-8992

The Mid-Atlantic's largest yoga center offers classes for all levels of students in posture, breathing, and yoga philosophy. Classes are held in Bethesda, Woodley Park, Georgetown, and Annandale. The Center also offers discussion groups, workshops, weekend intensives, and seminars. Classes are generally $120 for 10 weeks.

For further information on other yoga classes in the area, contact:
Mid-Atlantic Yoga Association
P.O. Box 60
Cabin John, MD 20818
301/948-7167 ⚜

Photographic Washington
Capital Images

Metropolitan Washington and the surrounding regions offer photographers a wealth of scenery to explore. From the famous monuments shimmering in the Reflecting Pool, out to the nearby natural beauty of the Chesapeake Bay and Appalachian mountains, ample opportunities await amateur and professional photographers alike. The groups in this chapter explore local picturesque sites and also offer lectures and courses for novices and more experienced camera enthusiasts.

Camera Clubs

Washington camera clubs provide friendly forums for local photographers to meet at regularly scheduled events, which include competitions, lectures, and workshops. Group activities include outings to special exhibits, as well as local field trips for special night shoots of downtown Washington or overnight fall photo excursions in West Virginia. Some clubs have journeyed further, organizing trips to Yosemite and northern Italy. Newsletters provide valuable tips as well as updates on local courses, lectures, and exhibitions. Most clubs vary in skill level and medium, from beginner to advanced and from color slides to black-and-white prints.

Greater Washington Council of Camera Clubs (GWCCC)
11716 Teri Lynn Drive
Fulton, MD 20759
Mr. Clarence Carvell
301/725-0234

The GWCCC is the parent organization of camera clubs throughout the Washington metropolitan area. The GWCCC sponsors monthly meetings, seminars, workshops, and competitions, and provides current information on Washington's camera clubs. Two of the larger Maryland and Virginia clubs are profiled below, followed by a listing of others.

Bowie-Crofton Camera Club
P.O. Box 515
Bowie, MD 20718
Ms. Roz Kleffman
301/464-1867

Sky divers, canoers, and avid hikers who are members of the Bowie-Crofton Camera Club are adventurers in every way. Their monthly field trips have featured sky diving over the capital area, canoeing on the Patuxent, and hiking and biking along the C&O Canal. Other trips have yielded impressive photos of the capital skyline, Maryland small towns, and West Virginia's fall foliage. The club schedules three Monday meetings every month that include guest speakers, demonstrations, and photo competitions in novice, intermediate, and advanced categories. Members kick off the year in September with a potluck dinner and mini slide-show, and also enjoy an annual Fourth of July backyard potluck picnic. Other annual events include club dinners, Christmas parties, and an awards dinner to conclude the season. This is one of Maryland's largest camera clubs with 165 members. Members range in age from 14 to 78, although the average age is 40 through 50. The club is open to all interested shutterbugs, and about half of the members are residents of Bowie and Crofton. The club was founded 25 years ago, and today is a member of GWCCC, the Maryland Camera Club Council, and the Photographic Society of America. The club publishes a monthly newsletter, *Viewfinder*, and charges annual dues starting at $12 ($18 for a family).

Northern Virginia Photographic Society (NVPS)
Mr. Joshua Taylor
1210 North Quantico Street
Arlington, VA 22205
703/536-9112

More than 130 members belong to the NVPS, one of the largest camera clubs in Virginia. Three meetings per month from September through May feature outside speakers, competitions of members' work in both print and slide categories (members may enter two images in each category), and a forum meeting in which members sponsor programs of their work, demonstrate techniques, and present slide shows. The Society also sponsors workshops and field trips throughout the year. The club was founded in 1964 and publishes a monthly newsletter, *Fotofax*, from September through June. Annual dues start at $25.

The following camera clubs are open to the public, but keep in mind that club representatives change frequently. For updated information contact the GWCCC, profiled earlier.

Bethesda-Chevy Chase Camera Club
Mr. Roger Cole
301/320-3734

Fotocraft Camera Club (YMCA)
Mr. Frank Butler
202/526-3545

Gaithersburg Camera Club
301/977-4387

Manassas-Warrenton Camera Club
Ms. Andrea Shetley
703/635-6398

McLean Photography Club
Ms. Sally Carey
703/848-1738

North Bethesda Camera Club
Mr. Joshua Taylor
703/536-9112

Potomac Society of Stereo Photographers
(3-D photography)
Mr. Jim Roy
703/536-3926

Silver Spring Camera Club
Mr. Steve Stubits
301/593-5106

Vienna Photographic Society
Ms. Fran Livaditis
703/938-4317

Washington Society of Film and Video Makers
Mr. and Mrs. Wilt Weidler
301/421-4418

Photography Classes

At photography classes throughout the area, you can learn photo and developing techniques in fully-equipped classrooms, studios, and darkrooms that provide the media necessary for picture-perfect results. The Smithsonian Associates TSA (Resident Program), the Corcoran School of Art, the Montpelier Cultural Arts Center, Georgetown University's School for Summer and Continuing Education, and several other cultural institutions offer photography classes for all levels. Many adult education programs and community and recreation centers also sponsor a diverse selection of photography classes, from "Beginning Photography" to "Advanced Video: Field Production." For further information, consult the resources in *Arts* ("Visual Arts" and "Further Resources"), *Education*, and *Parks, Recreation, and Community Centers* for the classes nearest you.

Photoworks
Glen Echo Park
7300 MacArthur Boulevard
Glen Echo, MD 20812
301/229-7930

"Intensive, highly personalized learning experiences" are the framework for photography classes and workshops at Photoworks. Students can find beginning and advanced instruction as well as specialized courses such as Infrared Photography, Photojournalism, and Photographing People. An open darkroom, which is available on Saturday, Sunday and Monday, and is staffed by an experienced darkroom assistant, allows former and current students to develop film for $6 an hour. Classes run four to six weeks, are generally scheduled on weekends and weekday evenings, and often include field trips. Class costs range from $50 to $225.

Prince George's County Community College
Continuing Education and Evening Programs
301 Largo Road
Largo, MD 20772-2199
301/322-0878

If you've ever dreamed of doing a photo-shoot for a major magazine or producing a Hollywood film, this is your chance to learn how. Courses from Beginning Photography to Photojournalism are part of a foundation series which can lead to a "Vocational Photography Letter of Recognition." And if you progress to Advanced Video: Field Production, you and a team of amateur producers will accompany a professional production team to sports and entertainment events at area arenas. Courses are offered on weekends and weekday evenings in series ranging from two to 13 sessions. Fees vary considerably.

Washington Center for Photography
1731 21st Street, NW
Washington, D.C. 20009
202/234-5517

Professional photographers and serious photo enthusiasts should consider joining the Washington Center for Photography. The Center sponsors exhibitions of photographs by local and nationally known photographers, receptions, education programs, workshops, and a newsletter which reviews area photo events and members' exhibitions. Informal meetings and conversations are part of the process at the Gallery Talks and Meet the Masters Series, and workshops afford students the opportunity to work with professional photographers on polaroid image transfers or on-location photo "assignments." Membership dues start at $25. Some events are free, and others range from $7 to $150.

Washington School of Photography (WSP)
4850 Rugby Avenue
Bethesda, MD 20814
301/654-1998

If you are considering a career as a professional photographer or just looking to develop your technique, the WSP may be the place you're looking for. WSP offers classes and programs for those with a serious commitment to understanding the photographic process. WSP features small classes (usually an 8:1 student/teacher ratio) and highly qualified instructors. Classes are offered for beginners, amateurs, and freelancers in a variety of topics, which have included Photography Fundamentals, Portraiture, Sports Photography, Wedding Photography, and the Nude in Nature. Students produce their work both in studio assignments and on location, and are encouraged to build a professional portfolio and enroll in the Certificate Program in Professional Photography. WSP classes run for approximately eight weeks, and are generally scheduled on weekday evenings. Specialized Saturday workshops feature a variety of freelance techniques and occasionally include a catered lunch. Class costs range from $150 to $300. ⚜

Political and Civic Organizations
The Body Politic

From the epicenter of power on Capitol Hill, ripples of advocacy spread out through nearby states, counties, and communities where residents gather to take action on the issues that impact their lives. National and local partisan politics are well represented through traditional Democratic and Republican clubs at every level of government. For those intersted in local issues, thousands of civic associations and nonpartisan groups meet around the area to address concerns ranging from public education to recycling. All 50 states and six territories have societies in Washington which can serve as a connection to your home state through special events like the Louisana Mardi Gras Bash or a Hawiian luau. In this chapter you can get involved at the international, national, state, county, city, or neighborhood level of the political scene. The following information is meant to be a unbiased representation of the opportunities for political and civic involvement in the metro area.

Partisan Clubs

Both the Democratic and Republican sides of the political spectrum offer a plethora of clubs sponsoring programs for members to meet the candidates, elected officials, and one another through a host of political, cultural, and social activities.

National Partisan Clubs

Washington, as the center of political life, hosts the national headquarters for the country's most prestigious partisan clubs.

National Democratic Club
30 Ivy Street, SE
Washington, DC 20003
202/543-2035

Capitol Hill Club (Republican)
300 First Street, SE
Washington, DC 20003
202/484-4590

The National Democratic Club and the Capitol Hill Club are fairly exclusive organizations which generally cater to Washington's political elite. A potential member must be nominated by at least one current member, selected by an election committee, and pay initiation fees and annual dues. Each club sponsors a full calendar of breakfast and dinner meetings featuring prominent speakers. Other events include football brunches, cocktail parties, theater evenings, local excursions, special events, and golf and tennis tournaments.

Women's National Democratic Club (WNDC)
1526 New Hampshire Avenue, NW
Washington, DC 20036
202/232-7363

The WNDC, whose members include both men and women, sponsors a diverse selection of educational, cultural, and social programs. This organization hosts a weekly speaker and seminar series featuring lectures, discussions, and in-depth analyses of both international and national affairs. The WNDC also organizes frequent social events, local excursions, community outreach projects, holiday galas, and election night celebrations. In addition, the WNDC's Democrats for the '90s offers a unique program for young professional Washingtonians under 35.

National Federation of Republican Women (NFRW)
310 First Street, SE
Washington, DC 20003
202/547-9341

The NFRW focuses primarily on partisan advocacy. This strictly-women's organization works to "elect Republicans... promote Republican philosophies and initiatives ... and advance the participation of Republican women in all areas of our political system." Contacting the number listed above will put you in touch with NFRW clubs in the Washington area. One local club, Federal City Republican Women's Club, includes primarily young professional women in the metropolitan area (for more information on the Federal City Club write to Ms. Pamela Speka, 6000 St. John's Drive, Alexandria, VA, 22310).

Local Partisan Clubs

Local partisan organizations provide important community forums for grass roots advocacy at the local, state, and often national level. Several clubs feature monthly meetings addressed by public officials, political candidates, and other prominent speakers. Campaign and voter registration drives, candidate forums, fundraising events, election night parties, community service projects, local excursions, sports tournaments, and other special events are frequently included in club calendars as well. Generally, each county or jurisdiction has both a Democratic and Republican club. You'll also find several "young member" organizations, such as the Arlington County Young Republican Club; a host of women's clubs, including the Fairfax County Republican Cardinals; and a few Black, Hispanic, and Asian partisan clubs. Especially popular are local breakfast clubs which often politic over coffee and bagels. The sheer number of partisan clubs allows for vast differences in club size and activities. Annual membership dues also vary, although dues are generally under $25 for individuals and may include senior citizen discounts.

To illustrate just what partisan clubs have to offer, we have selected a few Democratic and Republican clubs to profile in each local jurisdiction. For further information about clubs in your area, contact the local Democratic and Republican Committees listed below.

WASHINGTON, D.C.
D.C. Democratic Ward Organizations

In each of the eight Wards in Washington, D.C. you'll find a Democratic club which sponsors voter registration drives, monthly meetings, guest speakers, and candidate forums. These clubs contribute to the policy development and implementation of the D.C. Democratic Committee. Below we profile the club in Ward I; call the Committee at 202/434-8732 for the club contact in your Ward.

Ward I Democratic Club
918 Westminster Street, NW
Washington, DC 20001
Mr. Romes Calhoun
202/745-0535

Housing and jobs are the critical issues in Ward I, which encompasses 12 to 15 communities including Adams Morgan and Shaw. Monthly meetings are generally attended by 20 active members, and provide a forum for discussion of social and political issues important to the Ward. Members also circulate candidate petitions throughout the community, schedule mock caucuses and straw polls, sponsor voter registration and education drives, and organize fundraising events such as the annual Hall of Fame Banquet in recognition of members who have made outstanding contributions to the community. Members, who are usually around 45 to 50 years of age, encourage interested residents to attend monthly meetings (except during the summer) scheduled on the third Tuesday of the month at the Third District police station. You may also call the number listed above to be placed on the Club's mailing list.

League of Republican Women of D.C.
1155 Connecticut Avenue, Suite 400
Washington, DC 20036
Ms. Ann F. Heuer, President
202/785-8534

The oldest Republican women's club in the country, the League of Republican Women of D.C. began as a critical lobbying group in the struggle for women's suffrage. Today, the all-women's League remains an active partisan club which sponsors receptions, luncheons, speakers, and political briefings at Washington embassies and throughout the metropolitan area. The club's 200 members include women from throughout the metropolitan area who range in age from 23 to 96. Membership is $25 annually.

MARYLAND

Bethesda-Chevy Chase Democratic Breakfast Club
7801 Maple Ridge Road
Bethesda, MD 20814
Mr. John Ward, President
301/656-6390

Bethesda Chevy Chase politicos meet on the first Monday of every month at 7:30 a.m. in the back room of the Hot Shoppes restaurant in downtown Bethesda. Governors, U.S. Senators, Congressional candidates, and others have addressed this group, whose members are generally over 35 years of age and active in the Democratic party. Annual fee is $10.

Montgomery County Democratic Action Committee (McDAC)
3720 Farragut Avenue
Kensington, MD 20895
202/682-7271

This organization of Montgomery County political and community activists has four main activities: organizing events, conducting community service projects, working on public policy issues, and participating in political activities to advance the goals of the Democratic party. McDAC members have run voter registration drives, phone-a-thons, and they continue to work and repair homes for the Association for Retarded Citizens, among other projects. Monthly meetings of the 20-35 year old members are often followed by an evening out at a local pub or watering hole. Annual membership is $15.

Montgomery County Republican Club
9083 Shady Grove Court
Gaithersburg, MD 20877
301/869-6951

The Montgomery County Republican Club organizes a host of activities which include monthly meetings, voter registration drives, and social events such as Baltimore outings to Orioles' baseball games. Membership starts at $15 and includes subscriptions to *The Republican Reveille*, an informative monthly newsletter featuring club news and articles of interest to Montgomery County Republicans.

Laurel Democratic Club
1004 Turney Avenue
Laurel, MD 20707
Ms. Nina Scardina, Treasurer
301/776-5290

There are nearly 30 Democratic clubs in Prince George's County, but this grassroots organization is especially active in the Laurel community. The original club was founded in 1960, and today includes over 100 members. Guest speakers and elected officials are invited to address the club's regular meetings, which are often attended by local and County delegates. The club's primary purpose is that of an educational vehicle to inform County residents about the candidates and their policies. Other Club events include election night parties, candidate forums, and community service projects, such as those with Help Laurel, a local organization which collects food and clothing for the needy. The $5 annual membership fee includes a periodic newsletter.

Prince George's County Republican Club
3443 Memphis Lane
Bowie, MD 20715
301/262-7657

Established in 1969, the Prince George's County Republican Club sponsors monthly meetings with prominent speakers and catered buffets at the Bowie Recreation Center. These meetings are announced in a monthly newsletter and attended by up to 185 people. The club's political forums are especially popular: a recent forum featured speeches by candidates for the U.S. Senate, a question-and-answer session, and a straw vote. This club also organizes several fundraisers and community service projects. Membership dues are $8 for singles, $10 for couples, and $5 for college students, with discounts for senior citizens.

Seneca-Potomac Democratic Club (SPDC)
11811 Enid Drive
Potomac, MD 20854
301/299-4316

Serving primarily as a social and informational organization for the Seneca and Potomac River Watersheds, the 25-year-old SPDC sponsors frequent meetings, political candidate forums, and periodic social events. Club functions are generally attended by small groups of 20 to 30 members who range in age from early 20's to late 70's. Membership is $10 annually.

South Prince George's County Republican Club
5100 Woodland Boulevard
Oxon Hill, MD 20745
301/423-2494

For over a quarter of a century, this 200-member club in the southern part of the County has organized voter registration drives, fundraisers, summer lawn parties, and monthly events which include a dinner, business meeting, and guest speaker. Up to 70 people may attend these events announced in the monthly newsletter. Annual dues start at $12.

VIRGINIA

Northern Virginia Democratic Club
6530 Oakwood Drive
Falls Church, VA 22041
Mr. Wayne Buckle, Treasurer
703/256-1806

Over 400 Northern Virginia Democrats in Alexandria and Arlington and Fairfax Counties belong to this social and educational partisan club. Founded over 25 years ago, this club sponsors fairly regular meetings from September until June, featuring dinners and notable speakers from the press, Congress, and the Washington community. These events, drawing from 50 to 200 members, are announced in club mailings. Annual membership is $10.

Virginia Young Republican Clubs
P.O. Box 5557
Arlington, VA 22005
Mr. James Parmelee, Chairman
703/534-6319

This statewide Republican group has clubs all over Virginia which schedule monthly meetings with guest speakers and candidate forums. These twenty and thirtysomething politicos campaign hard and also sponsor social events such as picnics, parties, and holiday celebrations. A monthly newsletter informs members of upcoming events. Call the main office to find out which club is in your area. Annual membership fee is $5.

Roosevelt Society
4620 Lee Highway, Suite 208
Arlington, VA 22207
703/528-8588

Named for former president Franklin Delano Roosevelt, the Roosevelt Society is a fundraising arm of the Arlington County Democratic Committee. Members sponsor two parties a year to benefit its coffers, and enjoy discounts to the Committee's special events such as the fall Gala, Jefferson/Jackson Day in the spring, and the January celebration of FDR's birthday. The 150 Democratic party members are requested to pledge $10 a month to join.

Note: If none of the clubs profiled above speak to your concerns or partisan affiliations, try the local partisan committees listed below. They either sponsor partisan club activities on their own, or will provide you with information on clubs in your area:

Alexandria Democratic Committee
4600 Duke Street Suite 1317
Alexandria, VA 22304
703/549-3367

Alexandria Republican Committee
1127 King Street, 2nd Floor
Alexandria, VA 22314
703/836-5090

Arlington County Democratic Committee
4620 Lee Highway, Suite 208
Arlington, VA 22207
703/528-8588

Arlington County Republican Committee
405 South Glebe Road
Arlington, VA 22204
703/685-2488

District of Columbia Democratic Committee
1200 G Street, NW Suite 800
Washington, DC 20005
202/434-8732

Fairfax County Democratic Committee
7245 Arlington Boulevard
Falls Church, VA
703/573-6811

Fairfax County Republican Committee
4321 Markham Street
Annandale, VA
703/256-0202

Montgomery County Democratic Central Committee
3720 Farragut Avenue
Kensington, MD 20895
301/946-1000

Montgomery County Republican Central Committee
15833 Crabbs Branch Way
Gaithersburg, MD 20877
301/417-9255

Prince George's County Democratic Central Committee
8507 Red Wing Lane
Lanham, MD 20706
301/552-1188

Prince George's County Republican Central Committee
9420 Annapolis Road Suite 105
Lanham, MD 20706
301/459-2580

State Societies

National Conference for State Societies (NCSS)
Box 180 Longworth Building
Washington, DC 20515

Do you miss cheering for your old home team in this city of avid Redskins fans? Do you long to meet other Nevadans or fellow Buckeyes? You can discover a network of fun and friends from your home state at the 50 state and five U.S. territory clubs known as state societies. These societies, which belong to the NCSS, sponsor educational, cultural, charitable, civic, and patriotic programs which include dinner parties, receptions, picnics, cultural activities, sports, local excursions, and community service projects. Most societies organize annual receptions with their respective Congressional delegates, although all are strictly non-partisan organizations. Always popular are "sports nights" at local bars and restaurants, where state societies from California to New York root for home teams from the Fortyniners to the Mets. Each state society also organizes its inimitably unique events: the Kentucky Society, for example, sponsors a "Kentucky Derby Night" at a local race track. NCSS is also the major sponsor of Washington's Annual Cherry Blossom Festival, a week of special spring events including perennial receptions, luncheons, Grand Ball and Banquets, and parades on Constitution Avenue. Members' ages range from early 20's on up, and most events are open to the public. Some events are free, others require ticket purchase.

The following profiles of state societies from Hawaii to Maine should give you an idea of their varied activities. For more information about the society from your home state or territory, call the number listed above.

California State Society
1523 New Hampshire Avenue, NW
Washington, DC 20037
202/745-1938

Displaced Californians will enjoy this society's annual events: February receptions with California Congressional delegates, spring Academy Awards Parties, June summer picnics, and "Fiesta de Navidad" Christmas parties. Many events incorporate distinctly California themes: the "California Beaches" picnic, for instance, included a guest appearance by the California Raisins, and "Take Me Out to the Ballgame" featured an auction of memorabilia donated by California's major league baseball teams. Happy hours are held quarterly, formal dinners honoring retiring members of Congress, chili cook-offs, and other events provide the perfect forum to meet your transplanted California neighbors. The Society is over 50 years old, and draws from 500 to 1000 Californians and others at its popular functions. The Board meets once a month to plan events, and mails out a periodic newsletter as well as an announcement for every event. Members range in age from early 20's to 60's, and pay $15 in annual dues. Some events are free, others cost up to $25.

Hawaii State Society
3067 North Oakland Street
Arlington, VA 22207
Ms. Lorna Daniels
703/841-1823

Luaus, leis, and ukeleles are featured at the Hawaii Society's annual June bash held in celebration of King Kamehaneha's birthday, a state holiday in Hawaii and "a good excuse for a big luau" in Washington. Colorful garlands of Hawaiian flowers are flown in from the Islands for the occasion, including those for the leis which are draped over King K's shoulders in the U.S. Capitol's Statuary Hall. The celebration also features Hawaiian food and music for the 400 to 500 attendees. Other Society events have included a Sushi making contest (with awards for the most beautiful and most original), lei-making and hula dance classes, and several community service projects including the popular annual chili cookout. The Society promotes the "Aloha spirit" and celebrates the state's ethnic diversity through its affiliation with a number of Asian/Pacific associations. Meetings are generally scheduled once a month, and the 300 members are kept informed of activities through its newsletter, *KA NUPEPA*. You must have some affiliation with the State of Hawaii to join, and membership fees vary.

Louisiana State Society of Washington, D.C., Inc.
227 Rocky Run Road
Falmouth, VA 22406
Mr. David Friedman, President
301/251-6717

"Laissez bon temps rouler" with the food, music, and festivals of the Louisiana State Society. For Louisiana expatriates who miss out on the annual New Orleans festivi-

ties, the Society sells 60 tickets to the Washington Mardi Gras, a three-day, black-tie extravaganza attended by 3000 people. Other annual events include June Crawfish Boils, Fall Picnics, and King Cake Parties complete with a King Cake jamabalaya, Cajun dancing, a King Cake, and the crowning of the Royal Couple. In May, corporate and congressional receptions honoring members who have made outstanding contributions to the state. Most events are open to the public and attended by up to 250 people. Call the number listed above to be placed on the mailing list, and you'll receive periodic newsletters which announce upcoming events. Annual dues are $15, and costs for events generally start at $20.

Other state societies in the area include:

Alabama: 202/224-4124
Alaska: 202/898-5673
Arizona: 202/224-2235
Arkansas: 202/224-4735
Colorado:202/682-4776
Connecticut: 202/226-7384
Florida: 202/225-5744
Georgia: 703/836-9221
Idaho: 202/224-2752
Indiana: 202/223-0964
Iowa: 703/998-4284
Kansas: 202/797-3393
Kentucky: 703/425-3718
Massachusetts:703/978-9377
Michigan: 202/225-3561
Minnesota: 703/573-6982
Mississippi: 202/638-3535
Missouri: 703/845-8984
Montana: 410/672-0186
Nebraska: 202/861-4625

Nevada: 202/624-5404
New Hampshire: 703/524-1385
New Jersey: 703/734-4738
New Mexico: 202/224-2522
New York: 301/530-6914
North Carolina: 703/719-7249
North Dakota: 202/737-5166
Ohio: 703/356-3771
Oklahoma: 202/225-2701
Oregon: 202/225-6730
Pennsylvania: 202/225-4315
South Carolina: 202/874-0624
Texas: 202/660-6278
Utah: 202/224-1344
Vermont: 301/868-5184
Washington: 202/547-7975
West Virginia: 703/971-0291
Wisconsin: 202/366-9349
Wyoming: 202/224-3424

Civic Associations

For many Washingtonians, civic associations provide the ideal opportunity to meet next-door neighbors and lend a voice to important community concerns. For others, involvement in a civic association is virtually a second career. In either case, these local organizations provide the perfect vehicle to open front doors, widen back yards, and reinforce a sense of community in a city otherwise dominated by national and international affairs.

Members meet at monthly speaker forums, testify before city officials and local representatives, and participate in standing committees and task forces to confront local issues such as homelessness, crime, development, public education, and recycling.

The thousands of community, civic, citizen, homeowner, and condominium organizations in the metropolitan area vary widely in operation and activity. Some are strictly neighborhood organizations, while others evolve from specific community concerns. As it is impossible to include a complete listing, we have profiled a few associations in order to provide a general impression of their role in civic affairs. However, we encourage you to contact the civic federations and other organizations listed below for information on the civic association in your neighborhood.

Media Alert!

Thursday's *Washington Post Weekly* features "News Near You," a profile of meeting dates, locations, and current concerns of many local associations.

Barcroft School and Civic League

800 South Buchanan
Arlington, VA 22204
703/521-0825

Since 1908, the League has been a center of neighborhood life for the former town of Barcroft, now bordered by Arlington Boulevard, Columbia Pike, George Mason Drive, and Four Mile Run. One of the League's chief goals at the turn of the century was to establish a neighborhood school (hence the current name). Today, the League owns a community house where 15 to 50 members attend monthly meetings devoted to topics of neighborhood interest, from crime prevention to the elimination of gypsy moths. The League's 450 members take pride in their community service projects, one of which is to maintain the area around where the Old Dominion Bike Trail crosses Columbia Pike. The League has also recently completed a 'blueprint' for the future of their neighborhood, the "Neighborhood Conservation Plan." This extraordinarily active community association organizes a Fourth of July Parade complete with barbecues, musical bands, and tug-of-war competitions, and a Christmas program featuring neighborhood musicians, carolers, and storytellers. A monthly newsletter includes a calendar of local events, neighborhood news, volunteer opportunities, and other articles of local interest.

Capitol Hill Restoration Society, Inc.

1002 Pennsylvania Ave, SE
Washington, DC 20003
202/543-0425

This 1000-member organization, founded in 1957, is both a civic and historical preservation association. The Society was instrumental in establishing the Capitol Hill Historic District. Its ongoing projects include tracking City Council legislation and proposals that may impact the neighborhood; and, on occasion, testifying before city agencies on issues such as zoning cases and historic preservation. Two issues of recent import have included escalated crime and the incursion of commercial and nonprofit organizations into residential districts. The society meets regularly with the police. The Society schedules monthly meetings attended by up to 70 members, and publishes a newsletter ten times annually. The Society's principal fundraiser, scheduled every Mother's Day, includes a Capitol Hill House and Garden Tour. This occasion features an evening candlelight tour and reception, a tour of ten houses in the Historic District, and an elegant Sunday afternoon tea.

Dupont Circle Citizen's Association (DCCA)
P.O. Box 18162
Washington, DC 20036
202/387-5312

Mayor Kelly recently spoke at a monthly meeting of the DCCA, a 350-member organization established in 1922. From 30 to 100 members attend the DCCA's monthly meetings on the first Monday of the month at St. Thomas Parish. The DCCA's major concerns are development and the environment, and one of the association's greatest successes has been the "17th Street Plan," which resulted in the planting of trees along 17th Street, upgraded sidewalks, and improved lighting. The DCCA sponsors a clean-up drive every spring with a local merchant association, and a fall House Tour on the third weekend in October. This annual fundraiser includes an evening candlelight tour and a Sunday afternoon tour through Dupont Circle's historic homes. Membership dues are $12 annually.

Greater Bethesda Chevy Chase Coalition
4310 Kentbury Drive
Bethesda, MD 20814
Mr. Anthony Czajkowski
301/656-7946

Trail vs. rail is the issue confronting this coalition. In keeping with its broad goal of preserving green space and creating parks in what has become a Bethesda-Chevy Chase metropolis, the Coalition is working for biking and hiking trails along the Georgetown Branch connecting the C&O Canal and Rock Creek Park, where the county plans to install a light rail line. The coalition welcomes local residents to join one of the thirty citizens groups which represent over 30,000 families in the area.

Piscataway Citizen's Association
P.O. Box 1098
Clinton, MD 20735 -1098
Ms. Vicki Tedder, President
301/292-3079

A large portion of southern Prince George's County is represented by this citizen's association, which takes its name from the Historic Village of Piscataway. Issues such as zoning, community service, and conservation of natural resources are on the legislative agenda submitted at the local, county, and state levels. Monthly meetings and newsletters ensure an active and well-informed community of citizens. Dues are $12 per year.

Civic Federations

Civic federations are the next tier on the ladder of citizen activism, and can often provide information on member associations in your neighborhood (civic associations send delegates to monthly meetings of the regional civic federations).

DISTRICT OF COLUMBIA

D.C. Federation of Civic Associations
P.O. Box 4549
Washington, DC 20017
Mr. Thomas J. Houston, President
202/723-5349

Crime, drug abuse, and the transition of the old administration to the new are the issues confronting this federation, founded in 1921. At the federation's monthly meetings, delegates from 59 member associations map out strategies to deal with these and other city issues.

Federation of Citizens Associations of the District of Columbia
938 Perry Place, NE
Washington, DC 20017
Mr. Dino Joseph Drudi, Secretary
202/526-0891
Mr. Stephen A. Kaczak, President
202/686-0953

This federation, made up of around two dozen member associations, works to encourage the District of Columbia government to provide good services and affordable taxes to the citizens of the nations capital, and often works closely with the D.C. Federation of Civic Associations (see above).

MARYLAND

Montgomery County Civic Federation
22330 Old Hundred Road
Ms. Karen Calla, President
202/675-7901

There are over 800 citizens' associations in Montgomery County, 80 of which belong to this federation. Growth and development, environment and transportation, and the budget are the primary issues of concern. Delegate meetings scheduled on the second Monday of the month are open to the public. Executive Committee meetings are scheduled on the third Thursday every month.

Prince George's County Civic Federation, Inc.
6004 Westchester Park Drive #102
College Park, MD 20740
Mr. Robert Callahan, President
301/513-9560

Fifty of the 200 civic associations in Prince George's County belong to this federation, which was founded in 1928 by homeowners and residents concerned about the increase in building and growth in the Washington suburbs. The only organization of its kind in the County, this federation meets on the first Thursday of every month at 8:00 at the Hyattsville Municipal Center on 4310 Gallatin Street to discuss concerns which include ethics in government, zoning and land use, and environmental and social/health concerns. Association dues are $25 annually.

VIRGINIA

Alexandria Federation of Civic Associations
P.O. Box 3613
Alexandria, VA 22302
Mr. Rod Kukro, President
703/548-1044

Common concerns unite the 70 civic, condominum, and residents' associations that belong to this Federation. Development, public education, traffic and transportation, fiscal issues, and the protection of neighborhoods are among the issues included at the Federation's monthly meetings. Members schedule public meetings and distribute information on candidates' positions during the months preceding city council and mayoral elections.

Arlington County Civic Federation
2607 North Wakefield Street
Arlington, VA 22207
Mr. David Foster
202/662-4517

Of the more than 200 civic associations in Arlington County, 61 belong to the Arlington County Civic Federation. Founded in 1916, this federation is the "civic voice" for Arlingtonians to broadcast their concerns on issues such as the county budget, school budget, and zoning for affordable housing. An issue of long-standing concern has been the noise generated by National Airport air traffic.

Fairfax County Federation of Citizen's Association (FCA)
3315 Mantua Drive
Fairfax, VA 22031
Mr. Gerry Connolly, President
703/204-0092

The FCA, one of the oldest and largest citizens federations in the area, includes over 200 citizens associations in Fairfax County. The three most important issues facing the FCA are diversifying the tax base to lessen the pressure on homeowners, regulating development while re-igniting economic growth, and increasing citizen control over legislative affairs.

Note: If, after contacting the federations profiled above, you are still unable to locate an association in your neighborhood, try the following resources:

WASHINGTON, D.C.

Washingtoniana
Martin Luther King Library
901 G Street, NW
Washington, DC 20001
202/727-1213

This repository on D.C. information has general information on civic and citizens associations in the District of Columbia.

MARYLAND

Montgomery County Community Relations Office
8787 Georgia Avenue
Silver Spring, MD 20910
301/495-4600

Call the number listed above, or visit your local library and ask for a copy of *Rainbow Directory*, published by the Montgomery County United Way, which lists several county civic associations.

Prince George's County Memorial Library System
Fairmont Heights Library
5904 Kolb Street
Fairmont Heights, MD 20743
301/925-9704

This is the location of the extension service which publishes a listing of county civic associations in the annual Directory of Organizations in Prince George's County, available at all public County libraries.

VIRGINIA

Alexandria City Hall
P.O. Box 178
Alexandria, VA 22313
703/838-4350

Fairfax County Office of Public Affairs
12000 Government Center Parkway
Fairfax, VA 22035
703/324-3187

Arlington County Board Office
#1 Courthouse Plaza
2100 Clarendon Boulevard, Suite 300
Arlington, VA 22201
703/358-3130

Finally, if you are still unable to contact a civic association in your neighborhood, contact:

Council of Presidents of
Metro Washington Metro Civic Citizens Federations (COP)
P.O. Box 22707
Alexandria, VA 22304
Mr. Mike Hicks
703/370-9363

Advisory Neighborhood Commissions (ANCs)
Board of Elections
441 4th Street, NW, Suite 250
Washington, DC 20001
202/727-2504

The monthly, public meetings of Washington, D.C.'s 323 ANCs provide a unique political forum for District residents. Created by law in 1973 and funded by the D.C. government, the ANCs are designed to assure government responsiveness to neighborhood needs and concerns. ANCs may advise the District government on "matters of public policy including decisions regarding planning, streets, recreation, social services programs, health, safety, and sanitation." With few counterparts found in other parts of the country, ANCs differ from civic associations in that the former are created by law and represent entire communities, while the latter are strictly volunteer organizations which may represent a singular interest group. In some instances, ANCs and civic associations may work closely together and even hold joint meetings.

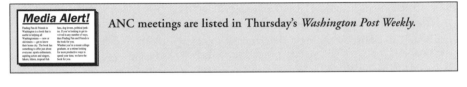

Media Alert! ANC meetings are listed in Thursday's *Washington Post Weekly.*

Non-Partisian Organizations and Activities
For a view of what goes on behind the national and local political scenes, you might want to explore the public programs of the city's many advocacy organizations, think tanks, research institutes, and universities. You can enroll in a monthly lecture series, take a class in public policy, or hear renowned speakers on a range of subjects from national health insurance to international diplomacy. Or you may choose a more hands-on approach by participating in work groups, round tables, brown-bag luncheons, and other activities to formulate goals and implement objectives.

Many dedicated residents contribute volunteer time to Washington's innumerable special interest organizations. Whether you support NARAL or the pro-life movement, handgun control or the National Rifle Association, or virtually any other current issue, you are bound to find a group of others who share your interests. From answering phones with fellow volunteers to organizing the next membership drive, your combined efforts are often critical to the life of the organization. *Washington: A Comprehensive Directory of the Key Institutions and Leaders of the National Capital Area* (Columbia Books, Inc., 1350 New York Avenue, NW, Suite 207, Washington, D.C., 20005) is published annually and includes complete listings of organizations involved in the following areas:

* National Government
* Local Government
* International Affairs
* National Issues

* The Media
* Business
* National Associations
* Labor Unions
* The Bar
* Medicine and Health
* Foundations & Philanthropy
* Science and Policy Research
* Education
* Religion
* Cultural Institutions
* Clubs
* Community Affairs

Note that this publication also profiles innumerable "professional clubs" in metropolitan Washington that accommodate the area's large corps of lawyers, economists, federal workers, business executives, foreign service members, journalists, and other urban professionals. These clubs are valuable resources for social events as well as career development and networking activities. Some clubs are exclusive, such as the "Gridiron" journalists who roast government officials and other celebrities in theatrical skits. Others, such as The National Lawyers Club, sponsor lectures, discussions, and other events for Washington's legal community.

The profiles below provide a sampling of organizations that offer a diverse range of non-partisan programs and educational activities. Within this group you will find a representation of all stripes of of the political spectrum. Most programs are open to the public, although a few are invitation-only for Washington's elite corps of scholars, policy analysts, diplomats, and other professionals.

American Enterprise Institute (AEI)
1150 Seventeenth Street, NW
Washington, DC 20036
Ms. Hillary Laytham
202/862-5830

This institute sponsors programs, seminars, and workshops such as the Bradley Lecture Series, a series of monthly evening lectures "devoted to enriching the debate in the Washington policy community through exploration of the philosophical underpinnings of current political controversies." These lectures by prominent AEI and other renowned scholars draw up to 200 people and cost $5 per lecture. AEI also sponsors an Election Watch series and nationally-renowned conferences on issues including the environment, international relations, and health and economic policy.

Amnesty International (AI)
Mid-Atlantic Regional Office
1118 22nd Street, NW
Washington, DC 20037
202/775-5161

This renowned human rights organization is part of an independent worldwide movement, with over 1,100,000 members whose work in the field of international human rights focuses on prisoners of conscience. The regional chapter includes approximately 15 community-based "working groups" comprised of eight to 25 members, who "meet regularly to write letters, organize and publicize actions on behalf of individual prisoners of conscience, work against torture and the death penalty, and participate in special human rights campaigns." These campaigns may include writing urgent-action letters on behalf of a political prisoner in South Africa or a long-term project focusing on children's rights. The regional office also sponsors symoposia, conferences, training sessions, and other events. Membership starts at $15 and includes national and local publications, invitations to special events, and a vote in board elections.

Coalition for Harmony of Races in the United States (CHORUS)
P.O. Box 59848
Rockville, MD 20859
301/948-8060

CHORUS is a grassroots effort started on May 6, 1992 in the wake of the civil unrest following the Rodney King verdict in California. CHORUS' goal is to promote positive race relations and to open communication across racial, ethnic, and cultural lines. The local branch of the group sponsors monthly meetings and participates in the annual Racial Harmony Ribbons Day. There are no dues or fees; the only requirement is a willingness to try to help "open up communications with other people and brainstorm ways to improve racial relations, eradicate racism, and unify America."

Congressional Quarterly
1414 22nd Street, NW
Washington, DC 20037
202/887-8620

The Congressional Quarterly's Professional Education Service sponsors non-partisan programs on the legislative, budgetary, and political processes. One and two-day sessions provide insider analysis for Washingtonians already involved in the federal government or trade and professional associations and corporations. Classes have included Congress and the Legislative Process, and Lobbying Techniques for the 90's: Strategies, Coalitions and Grass-Roots Campaigns.

George Washington University
Center for Career Education
2020 K Street, NW Suite B-100
Washington, DC 20052
202/994-5299

George Washington's classes and workshops held at satellite centers throughout the region offer degree and certificate programs in disciplines including legislative affairs, international affairs, criminal justice, and security policy studies. Two programs offer training in government relations: the Legislative Specialist Program and the Washington Representative Program. Both are "hands-on programs with practical political applications," offering new perspectives on government relations and the legislative process. Courses include Who Lobbies and How, and The Congressional Legislative Process. You can also get information on the "Washington Reps Network," which is a social and professional gathering of students, faculty and friends that meets monthly after work.

Institute for Policy Studies (IPS)
1601 Connecticut Avenue, NW
Washington, DC 20009
Mr. Wayne Tormala
202/234-9382

IPS, the nation's leading progressive think tank, serves as the home for much more than just thinking. Its Social Action and Leadership School for Activists (SALSA) seeks to train organizers to work more effectively in their communities. IPS periodically sponsors debates, conferences, and discussions on everything from nuclear disarmament to tax reform. A monthly brunch called the Breakfast Club brings together progressives who are in their 20's and 30's.

League of Women Voters (LWV)
National Headquarters
1730 M Street, NW
Washington, DC
202/429-1965

The LWV is a non-partisan organization founded over 70 years ago to "promote political responsibility through informed and active participation of citizens in government." It is the only citizen advocate organization working at the local, state and federal levels on issues including universal voter registration and campaign integrity, reproductive choice, civil rights, the environment, affordable housing and child care, and responsible federal fiscal policies. The League "monitors government activities from city councils and school boards to state legislatures and the U.S. Congress," and "sponsors candidate debates and public issue forums." The state, county, and local chapters throughout the metropolitan area offer outstanding opportunities for community political advocacy. These chapters sponsor voter registration drives and meetings, workshops, study groups, and symposia which address county and city concerns. Contact the numbers listed below for more information.

WASHINGTON, D.C.
LWV of Washington, D.C.
2025 I Street, NW
Washington, DC 20004
202/331-4122

MARYLAND

LWV of Maryland
200 Duke of Gloucester Street
Annapolis, MD 21401
301/269-0232

LWV of Prince George's County
P.O. Box 441455
Fort Washington, MD 20789
301/864-1016

LWV of Montgomery County
12216 Parklawn Drive
Rockville, MD
301/984-9585

VIRGINIA

LWV of Virginia
2805 McRae Road, A-5
Richmond, VA 23235
804/320-7528

LWV of Fairfax County
4026 Hummer Road
Annandale, VA 22203
703/620-4958; 703/280-2328

LWV of Alexandria
1103 Dartmouth Road
Alexandria, VA 22314
703/549-3240

LWV of Falls Church
325 Little Falls Street
Falls Church, VA 22046
703/534-5089

LWV of Arlington County
3102 6th Street North
Arlington, VA 22201
703/522-8196

Society for International Development (SID)
Washington Chapter
1401 New York Avenue, NW Suite 1100
Washington, DC 20005
Mr. Steve Von Oehsen
202/347-1800

SID is a professional association for people with an interest in international economic, political and social development. SID has members in 120 countries and territories that form a network of over 95 national and local chapters. Weekly brown bag luncheons, roundtables, and workgroup meetings (26 to choose from), as well as open houses and other special events, fill the calendar at this active chapter of SID. Events focus on regional and issue-specific topics. Membership fees start at $25.

United Nations Association, National Capital Area
1319 18th Street, NW
Washington, DC 20036-1802
202/785-2640

This organization studies and celebrates the United Nations and its program agencies through luncheons, dinners, festivals, seminars, and other special events. A busy calendar of almost daily activities has featured U.N. experts speaking on current issues, small study groups and new member meetings, and opportunities to participate in Global Policy Projects on themes such as "Collective Security." Special events have included a Human Rights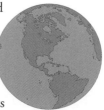

Day luncheon and U.N. Community Day, which featured an international market, cultural performances, workshops, and seminars. Over 1200 members belong to this non-partisan, non-profit organization. Membership begins at $35, with a special rate of $10 for students.

The Woodrow Wilson Center
1000 Jefferson Drive, SW
Washington, DC 20560
(Attn: Public Affairs)
Ms. Cynthia Ely, Coordinator of Special Events
202/357-2115

A monthly calendar announces a multitude of discussions, conferences, and seminars offered by the Woodrow Wilson Center. Timely international topics have included The New Journalism in Leningrad and Yugoslavia between Crisis and Tragedy. While some events are by invitation only, most are open to the public. For a copy of the calendar and/or newsletter, The Report, write to the address listed above. Please do not call for a copy of the newsletter.

World Affairs Council of Washington, D.C.
1726 M Street, NW
Washington, DC 20036
202/293-1051

The 1700 members of the World Affairs Council of Washington, D.C. enjoy free monthly lectures and programs on a diverse array of foreign policy issues. An audience of 300 to 500 Washingtonians attend lectures that have featured noted speakers such as Ambassador Thomas Pickering and former Secretary of State George Schultz. The programs are free for members, $10 for nonmembers. The Council also sponsors a separate monthly forum for young professionals ($13 members, $15 nonmembers). The annual membership fee is $40. ⚜

Volunteering
Lending A Hand

No single person can save the world, but each of us can make our own neighborhood a better place to live. The possibilities for service and involvement in the metro area are endless, and volunteering is a sure way to make new friends with a similar outlook. Virtually every non-profit organization depends on those who give their time and energy. Volunteering provides an opportunity to meet people from all walks of life and learn new skills while doing something truly worthwhile. In this chapter, we provide an overview of the many volunteer opportunities in the Washington area under the following categories:

* Volunteer Clearinghouses
* Just for Seniors
* Unique Volunteering Programs
* Community Service
* Environmental Releaf
* Volunteering: A Global Perspective
* Volunteering: Among the Animals
* Volunteering: Culture and the Arts
* Endnotes

Volunteer Clearinghouses

Local volunteer clearinghouses open doors to volunteer service by matching the interests and skills of prospective volunteers with the needs of thousands of community organizations in metropolitan Washington. Depending on your interests and talents, you may choose to volunteer at a local soup kitchen, tutoring program, or advocacy organization. You may wish to help as a hotline listener or a phonebank caller, or to volunteer with children, senior citizens, the disabled, or the homeless. Often one phone call can put you in touch with an organization where you can make a significant contribution. Whether you wish to volunteer after work, on your lunch hour, or on the weekends, once a month or once a week, in your neighborhood or near your office, the clearinghouse coordinators are trained to identify a volunteer program tailored to your interests and promote a happy marriage between volunteer and project.

The volunteer clearinghouses listed below provide the critical link between interested volunteers and community organizations. Several also publish frequent newsletters that detail upcoming events and programs, and all maintain comprehensive profiles of current volunteer opportunities. Areas of interest include: Advocacy/Legislative, AIDS, Animals, Arts/Culture, Children, Churches, Crisis/Counseling, Drug Related Issues, Education, Environment, Fitness, Homelessness, Hospitals, Housing, Human Rights, International Causes, Legal Systems and the Courts, Media, Medical Care/Mental Health, Nursing Homes, Physically Challenged, Seniors, Soup Kitchens, Tutoring, Urban/Community Development, and Women's Issues.

Alexandria Volunteer Bureau
801 North Pitt Street, Suite 102
Alexandria, VA 22314
703/836-2176

Arlington County Volunteer Office
#1, Courthouse Plaza, Suite 314
2100 Clarendon Boulevard
Arlington, VA 22201
703/358-3222

Volunteer Center of Fairfax County
10530 Page Avenue
Fairfax, VA 22030
703/246-3460

Montgomery County Volunteer and Community Service Center
401 Fleet Street, Number 106
Rockville, MD 20850
301/217-4949

Prince George's County Voluntary Action Center
6309 Baltimore Avenue, #305
Riverdale, MD 20737
301/779-9444

Just for Seniors

Retired Senior Volunteer Program (RSVP), a national volunteer clearinghouse program, has five local chapters that pair senior citizens (you must be over 55) with hundreds of volunteer organizations in the metropolitan area. RSVP's dual mission is to encourage seniors' participation in the community while effectively utilizing their years of expertise and experience. Seniors work in local hospitals, hospices, nursing homes, public libraries, animal shelters, and other non-profit organizations. In an especially popular program, groups of senior volunteers create arts and crafts projects for children, the homeless, and hospital residents. Volunteers also borrow residents from local animal shelters for afternoons of patting and chatting with seniors living in nursing homes. RSVP's social events include annual recognition luncheons, fundraisers, and picnics. The Northern Virginia chapter sponsors a series of tea and coffee parties, organizes annual tours of the White House and other local sites, and publishes a periodic newsletter, *The Link*, featuring updates on current volunteer projects. Contact the chapter in your area and ask for the Volunteer Coordinator.

Washington, DC RSVP
929 L Street, NW
Washington, DC 20001
202/289-1510

Montgomery County RSVP
401 Fleet Street, Room 106
Rockville, MD 20850
301/217-4940

Northern Virginia RSVP
1108 Jefferson Street
Alexandria, VA 22314
703/838-4840

Prince George's County RSVP
6420 Allentown Road
Camp Springs, MD 20748
301/248-6606

Unique Volunteering Programs

A number of volunteer organizations are so broad in scope and involvement that they defy categorization, and offer local samaritans a limitless agenda of volunteer opportunities in community service, environmental conservation, and cultural programs.

American Youth Hostels (AYH)
Potomac Area Council
1108 K Street, NW, Lower Level
Washington, DC 20005
202/783-0717 Office
202/783-4944 Activities hotline

The AYH volunteer program offers adventurous opportunities to explore the area's back roads and unusual places. Through the Adopt-a-Hostel Program, AYH volunteers paint, clean, repair, rake, and garden at hostels in Harper's Ferry, the Chesapeake Bay region, and the Blue Ridge Mountains. Volunteers also accompany inner-city youth on hiking, rock climbing, rafting, and horseback riding outings. Those who choose to stay closer to home can paint walls at local youth shelters, repair low-income homes, and serve food at soup kitchens. The social side of AYH offers something for every one: outdoor adventurers choose from hiking and biking excursions, sports fans compete in AYH athletic tournaments, and others join hostelers from around the world at Bastille Day Celebrations and outings to Chinatown. Membership is not required to volunteer. AYH members receive the *Calendar of Events* and other publications listing local AYH activities and global travel opportunities, and enjoy access to over 5000 hostels worldwide including those in Washington, D.C., Maryland, and Virginia. Membership starts at $25, is open to all ages, and includes discounts on international travel. While some AYH events are free, others vary considerably in cost (also see *Athletics and Outdoor Adventures*).

Washington National Cathedral
Massachusetts and Wisconsin Avenue, NW
Washington, DC 20016-5098
202/537-8990 Coordinator of Volunteers

The Washington National Cathedral, chartered by Congress in 1893 as a "House of Prayer for all people", fosters cooperation across lines of denomination and faith through an extensive volunteer program. Nearly 1000 volunteers choose from over 40 opportunities in cultural, historical, and educational programs: volunteers lead tours, usher at services and special events, ring English peal bells, and assist in the All Hallows Guild gardening programs and the Medieval Workshop's craft activities. Other volunteers work with local community service agencies to renovate housing projects, serve and distribute food at homeless shelters, and tutor at area literacy programs. Volunteers enjoy a flexible commitment of monthly, weekly, or full-time volunteering. They receive *The Volunteer Voice* and the *Cathedral Calendar,* which provide updates on new volunteer opportunities and special events. Volunteers also enjoy orientation sessions and periodic social activities such as informal potluck luncheons and suppers. In addition to public tours, films, lectures, concerts, craft demonstrations, receptions, and open houses, the Cathedral sponsors special programs strictly for volunteers. A recent lunchtime program for volunteers and staff included a screening of *The Stone Carvers*. Vincent Palumbo, a master carver who worked on the Cathedral, was on hand to answer questions and demonstrate his craft. Membership is not required to volunteer; dues start at $20 and include a subscription to Cathedral Age. Also see *Education*.

Note: Churches, synagogues, temples, and other houses of worship throughout metropolitan Washington offer similar volunteer opportunities. Consult the resources in "Religious Organizations" in *Personal Growth*.

Community Service

Whether we realize it or not, each of us can help make a difference in the community. People who are "good with their hands" can lend their expertise to projects building and working on low-income homes. Those who dream of someday constructing their own home can learn by doing: there are year-round volunteer projects underway in the metro area. Soup kitchens and the homeless need wannabe chefs to cook for them. And perhaps the most urgent need - thousands of young people could use your encouragement and enthusiasm a few hours a week. Whatever your education, no matter what skills you think you have to offer, you are needed. We hope the groups profiled here inspire you to get involved. Contact the volunteer agency nearest you for local opportunities to make a difference.

Media Alert!

Finding Fun & Friends in Washington is a book that is useful in helping all Washingtonians — new or old-timers — get to know their home city. The book has something to offer just about everyone: sports enthusiasts, aspiring actors and singers, hikers, bikers, tropical fish fans, dog lovers, political junkies. If you're looking to get involved in any number of ways, then Finding Fun and Friends is the book for you. Whether you're a recent college graduate, or a retiree looking for more productive ways to spend your time, we have the book for you.

The *Washington Post* updates community service volunteer opportunities every other Thursday in the Weekly and every Saturday in "Anne's Reader Exchange." Local papers such as the *Uptown Citizen* also announce volunteer opportunities and often profile volunteer organizations.

The Washington, D.C. Volunteer Guide is an impressive publication written by Andrew Carroll. According to Carroll, "even ordinary acts of kindness can produce extraordinary results." An extraordinary accomplishment of its own, the *Volunteer Guide* profiles hundreds of community organizations that offer a wide variety of volunteer opportunities. Check your local library or call your volunteer clearinghouse for further information.

The Emergency Food and Shelter Directory provides a comprehensive listing of food and shelter programs throughout the metropolitan area. This guide is divided into five major sections — emergency food, soup kitchens, shelters, medical services, and day shelters — and includes locations in Washington, D.C., Alexandria, and Arlington, Fairfax, Montgomery, and Prince George's Counties. For your free copy, send a self-addressed, stamped business-size envelope with 75 cents postage to Interfaith Conference of Metropolitan Washington, 1419 V Street, NW, Washington, DC, 20009, (202/234-6300).

Volunteer Networks

For those in the area who want to actively help alleviate some of the suffering found in the city instead of offering spare change on the streets, the selection of organizations needing volunteers can be overwhelming. "Volunteer networks" have been formed to coordinate community projects by pairing interested volunteers with non-profit agencies. Here's how it works: potential volunteers receive free, monthly newsletters that detail upcoming projects and project leaders. Volunteers may call project leaders and sign up to help as often as they wish. On the day of the event, groups of volunteers spend a weekend morning or weekday afternoon restoring low-income homes, serving food to the homeless, accompanying homeless children on local outings, or participating in other volunteer activities at soup kitchens and food banks, clinics and hospitals, schools and community centers, homeless shelters, transitional homes, and elderly housing co-ops.

doingsomething
1500 Massachusetts Avenue NW, Suite 448
Washington, DC 20005
202/393-5051

doingsomething is an all-volunteer network which stresses flexibility. Nearly 2,500 area residents participate in activities as often as their individual schedules allow, with no time commitment required. A monthly newsletter details 35-45 volunteer projects available to members and friends. There are no dues or mandatory orientation sessions. Projects range from work with at-risk children through field trips and special events, low-income housing rehabilitation and renovation, food collection, preparation, and distribution, and environmental clean-up and restoration projects.

Examples of projects include: working on home construction and cleaning with Habitat for Humanity or at Barry Farms neighborhood; taking homeless children from the Carpenter's Shelter in Alexandria to the Children's Museum, delivering meals to the homeless on the streets with McKenna's Wagon or the Grate Patrol, or planting trees along the Anacostia river with the Anacostia Watershed Society.

doingsomething volunteers are generally of the 20-30 something generation. Monthly social get-togethers are organized for volunteers, and several fundraising events are held annually to provide the bulk of their resources. The events focus on the agencies that doingsomething serves: a "Shoe-In" brought in more than 1,600 pairs of shoes for area shelters, "Plant-It Earth" focused on environmental programs, "The Wild Thing" at the U.S. Botanical Gardens garnered more than 1,000 children's books for an area literacy program.

Greater D.C. Cares
2300 N Street, NW Fifth Floor
Washington, DC 20037
202/663-9207

Founded four years ago, D.C. Cares built an outstanding reputation as a valuable way to participate in community service. Its statistics are impressive: since merging with the Volunteer Clearinghouse last year, this network grew to more than 6,000 volunteers working with hundreds of community service organizations on approximately 130 events every month. Most events are one-day activities, such as housing renovation projects involving 10 or 15 volunteers. Among the most popular activities are children's field trips, in which groups of up to 30 volunteers accompany children to baseball games, nature hikes, museums, theater productions, and festivals. Other volunteers prepare and serve meals at homeless shelters, and sort food for distribution to over 150,000 shelter residents. The monthly Activities Calendar and quarterly newsletter inform volunteers of all upcoming events. Volunteers may participate in one-time events, or join flexible project teams which staff a project sponsored by a particular community service organization at least once a month.

Every two months, Greater D.C. Cares' educational series offers opportunities for informal gatherings, such as an inspiring theater production performed by group of homeless men, women, and children. The organization also holds an annual May event called the Serve-A-Thon, where volunteers who have gathered pledges from sponsors meet at the base of the Washington Monument for an assignment somewhere in the Metro area. The Greater D.C. Cares volunteers then fan out around the city to complete their service project.

Homelessness

An unsettling sight for most Washingtonians is the huddled form in a doorway, the bodies resting on park benches, the makeshift shelters on top of the metro vents.

More than ten thousand homeless men, women, and children are thought to live in the District of Columbia. Hundreds of local organizations rely on volunteer efforts to prepare food, maintain shelters, tutor, and assist with other necessary programs for the city's homeless. In addition to the programs described below, refer to other organizations profiled in the following pages, contact your local volunteer clearinghouse, or research the "Media Alerts" in this chapter.

Anacostia/Congress Heights Partnership for the Prevention of Homelessness
2307 Martin Luther King, Jr. Avenue, SE
Washington, DC 20020
202/889-2102

With a mission to prevent at-risk families from joining the growing numbers of the homeless, this organization recruits volunteers to tutor at the Partnership's after-school and evening programs, to assist at special events that include a Back-to-School Bash and picnic, and to organize environmental projects such as creating community gardens, planting trees, and initiating recycling drives.

Coalition for the Homeless
1234 Massachusetts Avenue, NW
Washington, DC 20005
202/347-8870

The Coalition for the Homeless provides two emergency shelters, four transitional homes, and 10 family apartments that offer housing and support services for homeless men, women, children, families, and veterans. The Coalition offers a range of volunteer opportunities that include serving food, tutoring, informal counseling, renovation and yard work, and accompanying children on outings.

Other organizations that offer volunteer opportunities to assist the homeless include:

Bethany Women's Center
1226 Vermont Avenue, NW
Washington, DC 20005
202/483-3739

Community for Creative Non-Violence
425 2nd Street, NW
Washington, DC 20001
202/393-4409

Father McKenna Center
19 Eye Street, NW
Washington DC 20001
202/842-1112

Georgetown Ministry Center
1041 Wisconsin Avenue, NW
Washington, DC 20007
202/338-8301

House of Ruth
Administration and Volunteer Programs
501 H Street, NW
Washington, DC 20002
202/6173

Martha's Table
2114 14th Street, NW
Washington, DC 20009
202/328-6608

Samaritan Ministry
3640 Martin Luther King Jr. Avenue, SE
Washington, DC 20032
202/562-3096
-and-
1516 Hamilton Street, NW
Washington, DC 20011
202/722-2280

Hunger

Washington volunteers serve three million meals a year to the city's needy, according to a recent survey. These volunteers have discovered that you don't have to be a professional chef to sort donated food, distribute meals, prepare sandwiches, or serve dinners. A number of agencies coordinate convenient volunteer opportunities to accommodate nine-to-five schedules. While many of the area's soup kitchens are housed in Northwest Washington, you'll find a number of similar programs at other metropolitan locales. Volunteers also work with agencies such as Meals on Wheels and Food and Friends to deliver meals to the homebound elderly and AIDS patients. Consult the volunteer clearinghouses and "Media Alerts," described above, for volunteer opportunities at soup kitchens, food banks, churches, community centers, and other sites that provide for the hungry in your area.

Capital Area Community Food Bank
645 Taylor Street, NE
Washington, DC 20017
202/526-5344

This 48,000 square-foot warehouse collects and organizes food donations from wholesalers, retailers, restaurants, and the general public. Volunteers help sort the food on Saturday mornings from 8:30 a.m. to 1:30 p.m., and on Wednesday evenings from 6 to 9 p.m. The boxed food is sorted into canned and dry goods, beverages, glass, and other miscellaneous categories. The food is then distributed to 500 local shelters, emergency grocery bag programs, soup kitchens, and other providers.

So Other Might Eat (SOME)
71 O Street, NW
Washington, DC 20001
202/797-8806

Initially a soup kitchen in a church basement on North Capitol Street, SOME first served a handful of people a simple meal of soup and bread. Today, a large network of volunteer 'chefs' serve over 1200 breakfasts and lunches daily from 7 to 9:30 a.m. and 11 a.m. to 2 p.m. (convenient times for before work and during lunch hours). Volunteers serve food, assist in the kitchen and dining room, and socialize with the homeless. SOME also offers volunteer opportunities in building renovation and repair, clothing drives, fundraising programs, and health, social, and support services.

Other programs that offer volunteer opportunities to serve the hungry:

Bread for the City
1606 7th Street, NW
Washington, DC 20001
202/332-0440

Dinner Program for Homeless Women
945 G Street, NW
Washington, DC 20005
202/737-9311

Serves dinner Sunday through Thursday
from 4:00 p.m. until 8:00 p.m.

Food and Friends
P.O. Box 70601
Washington, DC 20024
202/488-8278

Loaves and Fishes
1525 Newton Street, NW
Washington, DC 20010
202/232-0900

Martha's Table
2114 14th Street, NW
Washington, DC 20009
202/328-6608

Housing

During the week, a number of Washingtonians are masters at faxing, word processing, and other feats of office technology. On the weekends, however, many of these same people have perfected the use of chain saws and electric drills in renovating area homes for low-income residents. From light restoration to total gutting and rebuilding, these efforts serve to upgrade and improve the living conditions of the community's less fortunate residents. For further information about shelters in your area, contact your local volunteer clearinghouse or consult the resources listed above in "Media Alerts."

Foundry Housing Corporation
c/o Foundry Methodist Church
1500 16th Street, NW
Washington, DC 20016
202/234-5224

Established in 1976, Foundry Housing Corporation seeks to provide safe, healthy accommodations for the elderly poor in Washington, D.C.'s Zone 2. Over 110 volunteers of all ages and skills meet one or two Saturdays a month at Zone 2 homes to clean, paint, put up dry wall, replace locks, and deliver furniture. While most volunteers are members of Foundry Methodist Church, anyone is welcome to participate.

Habitat for Humanity

In early 1990, D.C. Habitat for Humanity and a corps of volunteers broke ground in Congress Heights for the construction of two low-income homes. Ever since, D.C. Habitat and its local affiliates have discovered that even the most seasoned pencil pusher can manipulate a hammer and power tool. Every weekend, Washington office dwellers and others form teams of 15 to 40 volunteers who continue work on projects throughout the area. Washingtonians will find plenty of opportunity to help with carpentry, plumbing, electrical work, masonry, landscaping, painting, and cleaning. The general camaraderie is continued at frequent impromptu get-togethers, monthly committee meetings, and an annual volunteer night. Local affiliates of Habitat for Humanity include:

D.C. Habitat for Humanity
P.O. Box 27316
Washington, DC 20038-7316
202/347-3077

Montgomery County Habitat for Humanity
114 West Montgomery Avenue
Rockville, MD 20850
301/647-2355

Prince George's County Habitat for Humanity
P.O. Box 306
Riverdale, MD 20738
301/779-1912

North Virginia Habitat for Humanity
601 North Vermont Street, Suite 203
Arlington, VA 22203
703/276-3520

Hands on Housing (HOH)

c/o Holy Trinity Church
3513 N Street, NW
Washington, DC 20007
202/337-2840

Hands on Housing, sponsored by Georgetown's Holy Trinity Church, has renovated or helped renovate 17 homes for sale to low income families in the past four years. More than 100 volunteers organized into teams work on weekends to improve or build homes with non-profit development groups such as MANNA and the North Capitol Neighborhood Development Corporation. Their "sweat equity" helps reduce the purchase cost to families qualifying for home ownership in D.C. Skilled and unskilled volunteers work on Saturdays from 9-3:30. Lunch and on-the-job training are provided. Currently HOH is working on the Nehemiah Project, site of the 1960's riots, located near 14th Street and Florida Avenue.

Special Note: Christmas in April
3408 Wisconsin Avenue, NW Number 212A
Washington, DC 20016
202/362-1611

Once a year, skilled Santas arrive in homes all over the area to repair and rebuild the houses of elderly, handicapped, low-income, and other needy metropolitan residents. One of the first such organizations in the city and extraordinary in its scope and achievement, Christmas in April sends over 2500 volunteers into the field to shore up back porches, install new floors, plaster, hang drywall, paint, repair basements, renovate brickwork, caulk and weatherstrip windows, clean yards, overhaul electrical systems, and install new stoves and cabinets. Volunteers also work year-round to help with office work, fundraising, and special activities. Companies and organizations often provide groups of volunteers, but other teams are formed by interested individuals. Programs are coordinated throughout the Washington area; call the number above for the office nearest you.

Health

Hospitals, clinics, hospices, and local medical centers welcome volunteers who can offer administrative, counseling, and clinical assistance. Volunteers work in community clinics, intensive care unit rooms, and hospital gift shops. They provide a variety of services which include registering patients, comforting boarder babies, measuring blood pressure, and serving as nurse's aides. For further information about health care volunteer opportunities in your area, contact your local volunteer clearinghouse or consult the resources listed in the "Media Alerts".

Planned Parenthood of Metropolitan Washington
1108 16th Street, NW
Washington, DC 20036
202/347-8500

Volunteers assist at Planned Parenthood's administrative office and centers throughout the Washington area as receptionists and counselors. Volunteers also staff booths at area health fairs, work in the Montgomery County Thrift Shop, and work on other Planned Parenthood projects. Planned Parenthood's Choice Action Night is every Wednesday at 6 p.m. for volunteers who want to become more involved in advocacy/public affairs issues. Call the number listed above for the Planned Parenthood center nearest you.

Whitman Walker Clinic
1407 S Street, NW
Washington, DC 20009
Volunteer Coordinator
202/797-3576

The Whitman Walker Clinic — now a model for similar clinics in San Francisco and New York — was founded in 1973 and is now D.C.'s primary gay and lesbian community-based provider of AIDS services. Of the 1700 volunteers, approximately 65% are gay and lesbian. The Clinic requires a three-hour orientation, a private interview, and a two-day training session. Each volunteer signs an agreement stressing confidentiality and committing to a full year of service. After this extensive introduction to the Clinic, volunteers are assigned to teams of 20 people who provide administrative, counseling, and clinical support for the Clinic's varied services at locations throughout D.C., northern Virginia, and the Maryland area. Volunteers also participate in community outreach and educational programs. Monthly meetings provide supervision, support, and updates on volunteer opportunities. Social opportunities include frequent, informal get-togethers and an annual banquet.

Zacchaeus Medical Clinic
1606 7th Street, NW
Washington, DC 20001
202/265-2400

Zacchaeus was founded in 1974 as the first (and for some time, only) free, primary health care clinic in Washington, D.C. Nearly every evening and weekend, eight to 10 volunteers arrive at Zacchaeus Medical Clinic to provide health care for the uninsured, homeless, and working poor of metropolitan Washington. Volunteers who serve as patient advocates take patients' vital signs, order lab work, and assist with exams and counseling. Volunteers also work in general intake services and as pharmacy or lab technicians (after a training period). Additional opportunities exist to help with screening and treatment for pre-natal care and childbirth education, housing and legal assistance, and counseling. Flexible evening and weekend hours are available. Generally, half of Zacchaeus' volunteers are doctors, nurses, and medical students. Other volunteers receive training to assist the medical staff.

Mentors, Tutors, and Literacy Programs

The area abounds with volunteer opportunities at tutoring and literacy programs. Mentors meet with individuals or groups of children to lend a supportive ear or an enthusiastic pat on the back. Volunteers may read aloud to a child at a homeless shelter, assist a teacher in an English as a Second Language (ESL) class, or tutor someone to acquire a General Education Diploma (GED) certificate at an adult education center. We have profiled only a few programs below; be sure to contact the volunteer clearinghouse in your area for information on a program that suits your interests and schedule.

Carlo Rosario Adult Education Center
35th and T Streets, NW
Washington, DC 20007
202/282-0140

Formerly Gordon Junior High School, this center now teaches ESL and GED classes to adult students of many nationalities. Volunteers are welcome to help instructors with classes on Tuesday, Wednesday, or Thursday evenings from 6 to 9 p.m.

Concerned Black Men of D.C., Inc.
1511 K Street NW, Suite 1100
Washington, DC 20005
202/783-5414

This DC chapter of the national organization began in 1982 and is dedicated to their motto "Caring For Our Youth." Volunteers work with groups of children to provide positive male role models and build stronger channels of communication between adults and children in the metropolitan area. 200 active members participate in a variety of programs to promote the educational, cultural, and social development of the young people.

Martha's Table
2114 14th Street, NW
Washington, DC 20009
202/328-6608

Join the over 200 volunteers who have contributed to Martha's Table literacy program on Monday, Tuesday, Wednesday or Thursday evenings from 6 to 7 p.m. during the school year and summer. This program matches prospective volunteers with children from ages six to 16 years old. Volunteers read aloud to children and tutor them in schoolwork, help parents with GED, ESL, and specific subject classes, and assist both parents and children in the organization's family learning program.

New York Avenue Presbyterian Church Community Club
1313 New York Avenue, NW
Washington, DC 20005
202/484-8626

Since 1962 this mentoring program has been assisting 7th-12th grade students from forty schools in the District of Columbia. Supportive adults are assigned a student for the Thursday evening sessions following an orientation. Prospective tutors should be available for the school year. More than 150 thirty-something professionals assist with the mentor program; tutors often socialize after the Thursday sessions which last from 6:45-8:15.

Washington Literacy Council
1799 Swann Street, NW
Washington, DC 20009
202/387-9029

Patient literacy tutors (who can make a one-year commitment) are needed to meet with adult new readers one hour a week to improve their reading and writing skills. After attending an 11-hour workshop, members qualify as Nationally Certified Literacy Tutors. Grant proposal writers, as well as those interested in public relations, fundraising events and assisting with community outreach programs are welcome to participate. Membership with tutor certification is $25 per year, non-tutoring members pay $15.

Environmental Releaf

Outdoor enthusiasts can take to the trail, the park, or the zoo to improve the environment through volunteer activities that include trail maintenance, recycling efforts, river and beach clean-ups, and community outreach projects.

Media Alert!

Finding Fun & Friends in Washington is a book that is useful in helping all Washingtonians — new or old-timers — get to know their home city. The book has something to offer just about everyone: sports enthusiasts, aspiring actors and singers, hikers, bikers, tropical fish fans, dog lovers, political junkies. If you're looking to get involved in any number of ways, then Finding Fun and Friends is the book for you. Whether you're a sworn college graduate, or a retiree looking for more productive ways to spend your time, we have the book for you.

MetNet Calendar/Newsletter
c/o Joe Libertelli
645 Morris Place, NE
Washington, DC 20002
202/544-5125

This publication is billed as "Metropolitan D.C.'s Most Comprehensive Calendar/Newsletter of Local, Regional, and National Environmental Events and Issues." First published in July 1990 as a response to the first Earth Day, MetNet continues to provide a communication link between local and national environmental groups that list their volunteer opportunities in MetNet's monthly publications. Almost-daily projects include trail restoration, river clean-ups, recycling fairs, and tree plantings. Call the number listed above for a subscription ($15 for 12 monthly issues), or purchase MetNet at food co-ops, bookstores, and other organizations throughout the metropolitan area.

Anacostia Watershed Society
5110 Roanoke Place, Suite 101
College Park, MD 20740
301/513-0316

With a mission to START! — Stop Trashing the Anacostia River Today — the Anacostia Watershed Society sponsors two events per month that have included tree plantings, hikes, and canoe clean-ups.

Chesapeake Bay Foundation (CBF)
162 Prince George Street
Annapolis, MD 21403
301/269-0481

CBF is the largest nonprofit organization working to "Save the Bay." Founded in 1967, CBF organizes hundreds of their 85,000 members into three major volunteer programs: Environmental Defense, Environmental Education, and Land Management. CBF's most visible activities include Storm Drain Painting and Stream Cleanup Projects: you may have noticed CBF's "Don't Dump: Chesapeake Bay Drainage" stencils on storm drains throughout the area. CBF Baywatchers also protect the natural resources of the Chesapeake Bay watershed by visiting public officials to discuss legislation, preparing CBF Action Alerts, repairing work boats, and planting trees. "Volunteer Project Alerts" inform members of action issues, activities, and events in the area. Members also receive *BayWatcher Bulletin*, a newsletter that describes more specific issues and opportunities for action.

Friends of the Earth
1025 Vermont Avenue, NW Third Floor
Washington, DC 20005
202/783-7400 Volunteer Information Line

Washingtonians interested in after-hours grassroots activism should stop by Friends of the Earth on Wednesdays between 6 and 8 p.m., when groups of volunteers assist staff members in preparing Action Alerts and press releases, responding to inquiries about the environment, and helping to educate Congress about issues such as ozone depletion, water pollution, toxic waste, tropical deforestation, energy conservation, environmental taxes, and corporate accountability. Volunteers enjoy refreshments and friendly company while fulfilling the organization's credo, "helping the Earth fight back."

Garden Resources Of Washington (GROW)
1419 V Street, NW
Washington, DC 20009
Ms. Judy Tiger
202/234-0591

GROW offers a cornucopia of gardening opportunities. A number of GROW volunteers help others to establish self-sufficient community gardens at private lots, public housing, church grounds, senior citizens' centers, homeless shelters, and park lands. Volunteers are also encouraged to coordinate special events and to teach informal workshops on organic gardening and food preservation. If you're not up to organizing a new gardening effort, GROW welcomes volunteer "Gardening Angels" to install, design, and work regularly at local gardens with children and seniors.

Izaak Walton League of America
1401 Wilson Boulevard, Level B
Arlington, VA 22209
703/528-1818

This nationwide conservation organization is named for the 17th-century biographer and naturalist whose love and respect for the outdoors continues to inspire modern environmental enthusiasts. There are several thousand Izaak Walton League members who belong to more than 100 chapters in the metropolitan area. Programs include tree planting, recycling, trout stocking, building wood duck nesting boxes, planting food patches for wildlife, and projects with the Save Our Streams program. Many chapters sponsor training courses in hunting, firearms safety, and environmental issues. Membership fees, projects, and facilities vary with each chapter. Call the number above for information about the chapter in your area.

National Park Service (NPS)
Volunteer-in-Parks Program for the National Capital Region
1100 Ohio Drive, SW
Washington, DC 20242
Mr. David Larson, Program Coordinator
202/619-7077

The national parks in the metropolitan area offer a diverse and unusual range of volunteer opportunities. The more than 2000 NPS volunteers conduct clean-ups along the Potomac River, C&O Canal, and Mount Vernon Bike Trail. They improve park trails for hiking enthusiasts and maintain nesting boxes for wood ducks. NPS volunteers also participate in gardening programs, archaeological digs, and ecological studies. One-day projects include massive clean-ups after holidays, festivals, and special events (on a recent July 4th, 500 volunteers collected over 3 tons of aluminum). Volunteers also serve as guides at popular attractions such as the Vietnam Veterans Memorial and the White House. At the Antietam National Battlefield, volunteers dress in period costume and demonstrate the latest in cannon-firing techniques. The Wolftrap Farm Park for the Performing Arts offers one of the most popular NPS volunteer programs: every night during the summer season, 150 to 200 volunteers usher at Wolftrap's outdoor performances and enjoy free concerts under the summer stars. For more information about what's currently underway for NPS volunteers, call the number above and ask for the VIP (that's Volunteer-in-Parks) Coordinator for any of the parks listed below.

* Antietam National Battlefield
* Chesapeake and Ohio Canal Park
* George Washington Parkway
* Harper's Ferry
* Manassas National Battlefield
* National Capital Parks East
* National Capital Parks Central
* President's Park
* Rock Creek Park
* Wolftrap Farm Park for the Performing Arts

National Audubon Society (NAS)

At the turn of the century, George Bird Grinnell mobilized a group of bird preservation clubs to protest the slaughter of plumed birds, whose elegant feathers were used to decorate "fashionable" hats. He named these clubs the "Audubon Societies" after artist and naturalist John James Audubon. Today the Audubon Society includes 550,000 members nationwide who have expanded the scope of their movement to include wildlife conservation, pollution control, land and water management, and development of public policy. Volunteer opportunities in science, land management, education, and action programs at NAS' local chapters are described below. Annual NAS membership starts at $20 and includes national publications and membership at local chapters. Also see "Birdwatching" in *Athletics and Outdoor Adventures.*

Fairfax Audubon Society (FAS)
P.O. Box 82
Vienna, VA 22183
703/256-6895 Ms. Meredith Compton, Volunteer Coordinator
703/642-0862 Packard Center, Annandale Community Park

Environmental volunteer opportunities at FAS include conservation and recycling programs, wetland reclamation, Accotink Creek clean-ups, stream monitoring, planting trees, building and monitoring bird houses and nest boxes, conducting eagle surveys, and staffing the State Park's Visitor Center. Find out more about these programs and others by attending FAS meetings on the third Tuesday of every month, September through May, at the National Wildlife Federation.

Prince George's Audubon Society (PGAS)
P.O. Box 683
Bowie, MD 20718
Mr. Tom Loomis
301/937-2257

This 1000-member Audubon Society sponsors trail maintenance and other volunteer projects at the Fran Uhlur Natural area, a wooded wetland area featuring nature trails and bluebird houses. A cadre of 25 active members organizes several other activities, such as birdwatching field trips, monthly meetings, lectures by expert naturalists, and other special events highlighted in the PGAS newsletter, *Bluebird.*

Nature Conservancy, Maryland Chapter
2 Wisconsin Circle, Suite 600
Chevy Chase, MD 20815
301/656-8673

The Nature Conservancy of Maryland owns and manages 29 nature preserves, where volunteers clear trails, clean shorelines, and build benches, boardwalks, and observation platforms during regularly-scheduled "workdays." From 15 to 20 volunteers, generally in their 20's and 30's, attend each workday and on occasion participate in biological research, conservation monitoring, and administrative projects. Conservancy members receive a national magazine, chapter newsletter, and volunteers receive a monthly newsletter that highlights upcoming projects. The Nature Conservancy also sponsors local field trips open to members for $7.50. For the more adventurous naturalist, other chapters sponsor educational tours including bear watching in Alaska, ranching in Arizona, and rafting in Oregon. Membership starts at $25. For further information, you may also contact the membership development office at the Conservancy's national headquarters, 1815 North Lynn Street, Arlington, Virginia, 703/247-3720.

Potomac Appalachian Trail Club (PATC)
118 Park Street, SE
Vienna, VA 22180
703/242-0693 Office
703/242-0968 Activities Information

Serious hikers and mountaineers will appreciate rigorous outdoor volunteering with PATC. Founded in 1927 to assist in building the 2099-mile Appalachian National Scenic Trail (that stretches from Georgia to Maine), PATC now oversees 240 miles of the Appalachian Trail through Virginia, West Virginia, Maryland, and Pennsylvania. PATC also maintains over 600 miles of nearby trails, including those in Washington's Glover Archibold Park. PATC's weekly "worktrips" feature trail, trail shelter, and cabin maintenance and construction: volunteers prune trees, rebuild waterbars, construct shelters, and restore cabins, and enjoy afternoon breaks at nearby swimming holes. Anyone is welcome to join these worktrips, which range from a two-mile picnic hike to an overnight backpack trip. PATC volunteers also organize conservation projects such as recycling drives and tree plantings.

Of course, there's more than just work to be done. Outings staffed by trained volunteer leaders include Sunday Strolls and Circuit Hikes in Shenandoah National Park, Natural Sciences Trips, Civil War Hikes, and Backpack Trips Beyond the Shenandoahs. PATC also organizes hiking trips to the Adirondacks, and weekend cycling in the Blackwater Wildlife Refuge. Although no special requirements are necessary for worktrips or outings, a few events are described as "hiking odysseys" for "fast, tireless hikers." PATC's 1400 members also enjoy picnics and barbecues, an Annual Meeting, Seafood Festival, Fall Pig Roast, and Massanutten Weekend. Membership starts at $25. New members must be sponsored by a current member of at least one year's standing. Get to know a member/sponsor by visiting headquarters or joining an activity. Members receive a monthly newsletter, *Potomac Appalachian*, that provides worktrip and outing schedules. Worktrips are free; other events may require fees. (See *Athletics and Outdoor Adventures*).

Sierra Club
404 C Street, NE
Washington, DC 20002
202/547-2326 Activities Information
202/547-5551 Membership Information

Naturalist John Muir founded the Sierra Club over 100 years ago to preserve the rugged, ageless beauty of the Sierra Nevadas. Today, the Sierra Club remains at the forefront of environmental political action. Volunteers gather at the downtown headquarters to join Wednesday evening volunteer projects, and participate in Conservation, Legal, and other standing committees at the local chapters. These chapters also organize local environmental clean-up drives, high-school education outreach projects, and "Inner City Outings," in which 10 to 12 volunteers accompany homeless children on day and overnight wilderness adventures.

Weekend recreational and educational hikes, downtown lunch break socials, moonlight walks along the C&O Canal, and monthly meetings are also featured in several chapters' weekly calendars. At 'monthly socials' volunteers present lectures, demonstrations, and slide shows of Kenya safari trips, 'earthwatch expeditions' to Costa Rica, and Shenandoah canoeing excursions. Snacks, beverages, or small donations are requested and space is limited to the first 20 to 30 callers. Call the Membership Information number listed above for the contact person at your local chapter. Membership in most chapters starts at $15, and benefits include subscriptions to Sierra and chapter publications. Volunteers may receive a calendar of events for a small fee by calling the numbers listed above. (Also see *Athletics and Outdoor Adventures*).

Tree Action
P.O. Box 1306
Herndon, VA 22070
703/471-4337

An environmental advocacy group in Herndon, Virginia, Tree Action sponsors tree plantings, landscaping projects, and "environmental literacy" programs in area schools. Its large volunteer corps — from 200 to 300 members — receives frequent newsletters with updates on volunteer opportunities.

And A Final Note ...

Community centers and local departments of park and recreation are also in need of volunteers to assist with a range of programs, that include conservation and horticultural projects, historic preservation, community outreach projects, children's sports, swimming programs, senior trips, programs for disabled individuals, classes and workshops, arts activities, and festivals and special events (see *Parks, Recreation, and Community Centers*).

Volunteering: A Global Perspective

Washington is not only the nation's capital but an international center of diplomacy, trade, and business. Ambassadors, professionals, students, refugees, and others who arrive from all corners of the globe often rely upon the hospitality of Washington's volunteers to open the channels of cultural exchange. In the profiles below, we describe a few of the organizations that offer volunteer opportunities with Washington's international community.

The Hospitality and Information Service (THIS)
1630 Crescent Place, NW
Washington, DC 20009
202/939-5622

Those who would like their contact with the international community to extend beyond brief encounters with diplomatic license plates may join the more than 275 active volunteers of The Hospitality and Information Service. THIS serves over 2500 diplomatic families by easing their adjustment to life in America. Volunteers organize and conduct tours, book discussion groups, English conversation classes, cooking classes, family activities, and special events for all ages. Many volunteers have been involved with the U.S. Foreign Service, have lived abroad, or speak foreign languages. An application, interview, and training program is required of each volunteer. THIS, organized in 1961 at the request of the United States Chief of Protocol, strives to encourage a better understanding, greater rapport, and a closer relationship between the resident members of the Diplomatic Corps and the Washington community. It is affiliated with Meridian International Center, the site of several THIS activities. Renowned for promoting international and intercultural understanding through the exchange of people, ideas, and the arts, Meridian International

Center sponsors world affairs lectures, seminars, and exhibitions. These events are open to the public, and announcements are sent to supporters and volunteers.

United Jewish Appeal Federation of Greater Washington (UJA)
6101 Montrose Road
Rockville, MD 20852
Ms. Karen Bernstein, Human Resources Development
301/230-7200

Washingtonians interested in helping Jews from the (former) Soviet Union to re-settle in the U.S. should contact UJA Federation. This organization sponsors a community resettlement program to acclimate those who have recently arrived on our shores. UJA Federation also sponsors a Jewish Information and Referral Service and several community outreach programs. As a national fundraising organization, UJA Federation organizes several special events such as the Super Sunday dial-a-thon and the spectacular black and white gala, as well as frequent luncheons, cocktail parties, and happy hours.

Meridian International Center
Training and Visitor's Services
1630 Crescent Place, NW
Washington, DC 20009
202/939-5544 Volunteer Office

The Meridian International Center offers professional programs and orientation training for thousands of foreign visitors arriving in the U.S. from abroad. The center operates through a network of community organizations and more than 450 local volunteers, who must be available during the day to meet visitors, lead tours, and attend events. Volunteers also attend workshops, seminars, lectures, and exhibitions.

Youth for Understanding International Exchange (YFU)
3501 Newark Street, NW
Washington, DC 20016-3167
Ms. Karen Yoho, Director of Volunteer Services
202/966-6800

One of the oldest and largest international youth exchange programs in the country, YFU began in 1951 with 75 German exchange students as part of the post-World War II effort to rebuild international friendship. Tens of thousands of exchange students have since been chosen by a corps of volunteers who evaluate high-school exchange applicants and participate in a group selection process. During the fall and spring sessions, over 200 area volunteers meet in groups of eight to 15 to screen and discuss applicants for the Congress-Bundestag, Japan-U.S. Senate, Finland-U.S. Senate, Sports for Understanding, and Corporate programs. Volunteers must attend orientation and training meetings and commit to three to six hours per week for a full session. A wide range of volunteer opportunities also includes recruiting students and host families, assisting in orientations, providing support services, fundraising, and media relations.

Volunteering: Among the Animals

For those who do not own pets, but would welcome the chance to care
for a furry friend part-time, the organizations in this section need you. Exotic possibilities await the adventurous who want to assist the zoo keepers or help out in the labs at the National Zoo. Owners of traditional pets will find opportunities to share their animals with those confined to health care facilities in this section. Please refer to the Animal chapter for detailed information on working with horses and the theraputic riding programs.

Friends of the National Zoo (FONZ)
Office of Volunteer and Educational Services
The National Zoological Park
Washington, DC 20008
202/673-4955

Washingtonians can escape the urban jungle and retreat to the wilds of the National Zoological Park as a FONZ volunteer. Over 800 active FONZ volunteers choose from 16 FONZ programs in education, conservation, and research. Volunteer positions include park guides and educators, "hands-on" lab volunteers, and zoo keeper aides. Time commitments depend entirely on the program: park guides attend four-week training classes and escort school groups twice a week, and volunteers at community festivals help out as often as their schedules permit. FONZ volunteers also manage busy social calendars that include champagne breakfasts with zookeepers, educational programs, field trips, and special events such as ZooNight, and ZooFari. While membership is not required, volunteers receive up to 20% discounts on FONZ membership dues which start at $24. FONZies enjoy members-only tours and events, exhibit previews, discounts on classes, and FONZ publications. Some programs are free and open to the public (also see *Education*).

PETS-DC
2001 O Street, NW
Washington, DC 20036-5955
202/234-PETS (7387)

Volunteers for PETS-DC serve the needs of pet-owning people with HIV/AIDS. The goal of the organization is to keep the pets healthy and with their owners as long as possible, and volunteers provide in-home pet care, foster care, pet grooming, pet food and supplies, veterinary care, pet care financial assistance, aid in long term planning, and assistance in placement of pets when the human companion dies or can no longer maintain the pet. Volunteers must complete an application and a training and orientation program, and all volunteers are invited to a Volunteer Drop-In Night on Mondays, which is a relaxed and fun opportunity to get to know other volunteers and to help out in the office.

Shelters and Helping Organizations

The following organizations need volunteers in various capacities: for cleaning, feeding, walking, and cuddling their residents. Call them for details.

District of Columbia Animal Shelter
1201 New York Avenue, NE
Washington, DC
202/576-6664

Washington Animal Rescue League
71 Oglethorpe Street, NW
Washington, DC 20012
202/726-2556

Washington Humane Society
7319 Georgia Avenue, NW
Washington, DC 20012
202/333-4010

Montgomery County Animal Shelter
14645 Rothgeb Drive
Rockville, MD 20850
301/279-1823

Prince Georges County Animal Control
8311 D'Arcy Road
Forestville, MD
301/499-8300

Animal Welfare League of Alexandria
910 South Payne Street
Alexandria, VA 22314
703/838-4775

Fairfax County Animal Shelter
4500 West Ox Road
Fairfax, VA 22030
703/830-1100

People-Animals-Love (PAL)
4832 MacArthur Boulevard, NW
Washington, DC 20007
202/337-0120

PAL is a non-profit volunteer organization that uses people and their pets to brighten the lives of institutionalized individuals. Volunteers bring their pets to visit children in hospitals, as well as residents of nursing homes and hospice programs. PAL also has a newly evolving program that utilizes animals to positively influence the lives of young people who are at risk. PAL volunteers also come together for an annual December holiday party and for a summer picnic, both of which give them the opportunity to socialize with other volunteers and swap stories. There is no membership fee; the only requirement is a willingness to make visits to sick and/or elderly individuals with a well-mannered, healthy pet.

Volunteering: Culture and the Arts

Virtually every theater, museum, concert hall, and arts and cultural center in metropolitan Washington recruits volunteers as ushers, docents, stagehands, visitor and information aides, and research and curatorial assistants. Many volunteers also contribute their business or legal expertise to Washington's dynamic arts community. Often, volunteer contributions are rewarded with membership benefits and invitations to special events. Contact any organization profiled below, (or in *Arts*, especially those profiled in "Fan Clubs"), and you're bound to find an interesting way to explore the vibrant cultural life of the nation's capital.

Arena Stage
6th and Maine Avenue, SW
Washington, DC 20024
202/554-9066

Over 1800 volunteers have ushered at Arena Stage's renowned productions. Volunteers are also welcome to lead tours, organize opening night parties, and work in the theater office. Volunteers are frequently invited to attend Arena's symposiums on current productions as well as other Arena special events.

Business Volunteers for the Arts/Washington (BVA)
Cultural Alliance of Greater Washington
Stables Art Center, Suite 600
410 Eighth Street, NW
Washington, DC 20004
202/638-2406

"There's an art to business. Share it." So claims the BVA, a program of the Cultural Alliance that matches art organizations with the interests and talents of business professionals in the Washington area. The BVA's matchmaking program encourages business professionals to experience the arts as insiders, find opportunities to utilize their talents in a challenging new context, and participate directly in the operation of arts organizations. Over the past three years, more than 200 Washington area corporations and arts groups have participated in the program. Volunteers have contributed their expertise to the Folger Shakespeare Theatre, the Friends of the Torpedo Factory Art Center, the Virginia Chamber Orchestra, the Prince George's Choral Society, and the KanKouran West African Dance Company. Projects have included the development of management and personnel, installation of computer information systems, and assistance with membership drives.

Members of the BVA team have worked cooperatively to present management workshops and design a variety of resource materials for their arts clients. In addition to meeting other business people who share an interest in the arts, BVA volunteers enjoy an ongoing series of backstage events from special performances to artist receptions and exhibition openings. Outstanding volunteers are honored at the BVA Recognition Luncheon. BVA welcomes applications from professionals with three or more years of experience in their fields who agree to contribute an average of two hours per week over a year's time. Volunteers may work intensively on one project or take on several short-term tasks. Call the BVA number listed above for an application.

Hexagon, Inc.
P.O. Box 3952
Frederick, MD 21701
Mr. Terry Matthews
301/431-6516

"If your artistic or charitable instincts need an outlet, you are warmly invited to join Hexagon," proclaims the membership brochure. Hexagon produces an all-original, political, satirical annual comedy revue, and everyone connected with the production — "from director to stagehand to usher" — volunteers his or her talents. Proceeds from the show are donated to a local charity. Members collaborate December through March on the annual revue, and keep in touch during the remainder of the year via the monthly newsletter and several scheduled parties.

The John F. Kennedy Center for the Performing Arts
Washington, DC 20566-0003
202/416-8000

The Kennedy Center offers unique opportunities to volunteer behind-the-scenes at one of the country's most prolific arts centers.

Volunteers participate through Bravo!, Friends Assisting the National Symphony, Friends of the Kennedy Center, the National Symphony Orchestra Association, the Washington Opera Guild, the Washington Performing Arts Society, and a host of other membership organizations. See "Fan Clubs" in *Arts* for further information. Depending upon level of contribution and/or volunteer commitment, members of these organizations enjoy access to private lounges at designated performances, receive members-only invitations to "meet-the-artists" receptions, and attend roundtable discussions, backstage tours, dress rehearsals, cast parties, and other special events. Members' annual dues start at $30 and include publications and discounts on the educational and cultural programs of Kennedy Center Performance Plus (see *Education*).

Opera Theatre/Opera Guild of Northern Virginia
2700 South Lang Street
Arlington, VA 22206
703/549-5039

The Opera Theatre presents three operas each season in English, including one suitable for children. Volunteers are needed to assist with set building, prop gathering, and other backstage work, as well as ushering and box office assistance during performances.

The Opera Guild (703/536-7557) offers members a diverse menu of social, educational, cultural, and support activities with congenial music lovers and performers.

National Building Museum
401 F Street, NW
Washington, DC 20001
202/272-2448, Volunteer Coordinator

This museum celebrates all aspects of building, including architecture, engineering, building crafts, and urban planning. Its volunteer program features opportunities to work behind-the-scenes on exhibitions, educational programs, collections management, and development. Volunteers also staff the Information Desk and Museum Shop, or serve as docents for walk-in visitors, scheduled tours, and school groups. Those who help receive automatic membership in the National Building Museum that includes invitations to openings, special events, and festivals, as well as discounts on tours, workshops, and museum shop purchases.

Smithsonian Behind-the-Scenes Volunteer Program
Smithsonian Institution
Visitor Information and Associates' Reception Center
Washington, DC 20560
202/357-2700

Ardent art lovers can volunteer behind-the-scenes at any of the Smithsonian's museums. Volunteers work with the libraries, photo archives, natural sciences and aviation projects, history and art museums, and translation services. Assignments are generally available Monday through Friday between 9 a.m. and 5 p.m., and require a minimum commitment of six hours per week. Docent and visitor assistance programs are also available in most of the Smithsonian museums.

Volunteer Lawyers for the Arts
918 16th Street, NW Suite 400
Washington, DC 20006
202/429-0229

Lawyers in the Washington area interested in finding rewarding ways to use their legal skills should contact the Volunteer Lawyers for the Arts. This organization pairs the legal needs of individual artists and low-budget arts organizations with the talents of local attorneys. Quarterly seminars are conducted for both attorneys and artists. The organization's 50 or so members are part of a national network of lawyers interested in the arts.

Wolftrap Farm Park for the Performing Arts
1551 Trap Road
Vienna, VA 22182
Volunteer Coordinator
703/255-1893

During the summer season at Wolftrap Farm Park — the only national park dedicated to the performing arts — 800 to 1000 volunteers usher and assist backstage at evening performances and enjoy free concerts under the summer stars. Daytime opportunities exist for volunteers at the Theater in the Woods. Applications are accepted for ushers from the fall through the spring, not during the summer performance season.

Special Events
You'll also find a creative array of volunteer opportunities at local arts festivals and celebrations, where dedicated volunteers organize, coordinate, and staff virtually every aspect of the special events. For further information, contact your local arts councils and commissions listed at the end of *Arts*.

Endnotes
A number of advocacy organizations in the area schedule weekly "volunteer nights" for interested Washingtonians to collate, mail, phone, and participate in other nec-

essary tasks that contribute to the life of the organization. These 'afterhour' volunteer opportunities often include refreshments and the friendly camaraderie of fellow advocates. You may also consider volunteering with a local charitable organization at an upcoming bike-a-thon, phone-a-thon, or other fundraising benefit. And animal lovers will discover a host of opportunities to take care of felines and canines at their local animal shelter. To locate these and other volunteer opportunities, contact your local volunteer clearinghouse. ⚜

Miscellaneous

Occasionally in life we encounter items that defy categorization. This catch-all chapter includes something old, and something very, very new. For those who haven't found their niche in the previous fifteen chapters of organizations and programs, we offer the following possibilities for your exploration:

American Radio Relay League
6903 Rhode Island Avenue
College Park, MD 20740
301/927-1797

This group is the national membership organization for ham radio operators. More than 50 amateur radio clubs dot the Baltimore-D.C. area. They hold annual Hamfests (flea markets) and sponsor scholarships for licensed radio amateurs and classes and exams. Events are held throughout the metro area and there is no membership fee.

Computing: The Electronic Connection

Thousands of area residents are plugged into electronic billboard bulletin services (BBS) and communications are flying across the region's telephone lines between computer users who are "On-Line". Getting online at home requires a personal computer (usually IBM or compatible) equipped with a modem; nowadays many families are getting into the act. Instead of the telephone being a source of contention, teens and parents are arguing over who needs to use the computer!

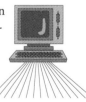

Capital P.C. User Group
51 Monroe Street
Plaza East Two
Rockville, MD 20850-2421
301/762-9372 Voice
301/738-9060 BBS

This organization of nearly 5,000 members is dedicated to the support and education of personal computer users. The group is a forum for IBM and compatible micro-computer owners from the novice to expert level. Monthly meetings featuring product demonstrations and lectures by leaders in the field are held at the National Institutes of Health in Bethesda, Maryland. Annual memberships are $35 (for a single/or the entire family). The fee entitles members use of the BBS for up to two hours/day, and includes a subscription to *The Monitor*, a monthly magazine chock full of information.

Media Alert!

Finding Fun & Friends in Washington is a book that is useful in helping all Washingtonians — new or old-timers — get to know their home city. The book has something to offer just about everyone: sports enthusiasts, aspiring actors and singers, bikers, hikers, tropical fish fans, dog lovers, political junkies. If you're looking to get involved in any number of ways, then Finding Fun and Friends is the book for you. Whether you're a recent college graduate, or a retiree looking for more productive ways to spend your time, we have the book for you.

Computer Digest
15215 Shady Grove Road, Suite 305
Rockville, MD 20850
301/921-8216

This free monthly tabloid offers 50,000 p.c. users in the Baltimore-D.C. area the latest developments in the regional computer industry, as well as a calendar of computer-related events user group listings, and a listing of local BBS's.

D.C. On-Line! Magazine
P.O. Box 2045
Stafford, VA 22555
703/899-0932

This new monthly newspaper is geared towards users of the fun and hobby-type bulletin boards in the area. Those new to the on-line experience will find this free publication at area computer stores and some bookstores.

Department of Juggling
Chevy Chase Community Center
5601 Connecticut Avenue, NW
Washington, DC 20015
703/360-6023 Coordinator
202/282-2204 Community Center

Of all of the agencies and departments in Washington, perhaps none have managed the balancing act quite like the Department of Juggling. These 10 to 25 juggling devotees meet from 7:30 to 9:30 on Friday evenings at the Chevy Chase Community Center auditorium, where they continue what is one of oldest professions in the world by tossing around their treasured collections of clubs, balls, and rings. These jugglers insist that exceptional coordination and razor-edge dexterity are not juggling prerequisites, and to prove it they offer free lessons to interested beginners. Their weekly meetings begin with a brief update on the club calendar and juggling events around town, and often follow with a visit to a local pub. The club welcomes any interested or would-be jugglers to stop by, but recommends that you call the club coordinator first. This group is an official affiliate of International Jugglers Association and requires no fees. The average age of most members is mid to late-20's, but ages vary from 10 on up to the 70's. Children under 16 should be accompanied by a parent.

Salon Network of Greater DC
P.O. Box 2774
Kensington, MD 20891
301/961-4679

The concept of salons originated during the early 17th century in Paris, when the upper classes would gather writers, artists, philosophers, and musicians for conversation or for an intimate musical soiree. Today the salon concept has become a small gathering of people, usually with a focus to their discussion, although each salon is very different. The Salon Network is a loose coalition of more than 30 area salons that support the growth of salons and helps people find an open salon through both a directory and a voicemail referral system. Three times a year the Network sponsors a meeting to introduce salons to each other and to potential new members.

Shillelagh Travel Club
8027 Leesburg Pike #413
Vienna, VA 22182
703/556-8646

Founded in 1964 as America's first air travel club, Shillelagh Travel Club sponsors everything from Virginia wine festivals to exotic trips to Kenya and Costa Rica. This club organizes foreign and domestic travel and social events for Washington area residents. The club's more than 1600 members live in the District, Maryland, and Virginia, so you're bound to find fellow travelers who continue to get together on home turf. Annual membership dues start at $35.

Toastmasters
District 36
District and Maryland Membership
301/322-3143

District 27
District and Virginia Membership
703/506-4717

If standing up to address a group signals the butterflies in your stomach to begin soaring, joining Toastmasters should keep them away. This international professional organization provides a supportive, learning environment in which to develop communication and leadership skills. Most of the area's 150 Toastmaster clubs are sponsored by metropolitan firms and companies, but some clubs meet after hours at community centers and local restaurants. Meetings are generally held twice monthly. Members may prepare four to six speeches per year, and receive training and evaluation as they progress up the Toastmaster hierarchy from Competent to Distinguished. Annual dues vary at each club.

U.S. Chess Federation (USCF)
186 Route 9W
New Windsor, NY 12553
914/562-8350

 If this ancient intellectual sport is your game, you'll be interested to know that Washington is home to an entrenched network of avid chess enthusiasts. The local chess clubs profiled below invite new players to drop in, pull up a seat, and join in a game. Everyone is welcome, from the absolute beginner to the professional player. For a free listing of additional chess clubs in the area, call the USCF, listed above. USCF members participate in chess games and tournaments throughout the nation, receive the monthly magazine *Chess Life*, and additional benefits for annual dues of $30.

Arlington Chess Club
6942 North 28th Street
Arlington, VA 22213
703/534-6232

The Arlington Chess Club, the largest chess club in D.C. area and the "grandfather of local chess," boasts 300 members. Players arrive at the Cherrydale Senior Adult Center in St. Andrew's Episcopal Church on Friday nights at 7:00 p.m. for ladder tournaments, "action chess" (three games in one night), casual games, or chess instruction.

D.C. Chess League
c/o Mr. David Mehler
1501 M Street, NW
Washington, DC 20005
202/857-4922

The D.C. Chess League meets in the largest chess facility in the nation, the U.S. Chess Center, which sponsors league competitions and classes for all levels of play and serve as a clearinghouse for information on local chess clubs. Write to the address above for further information.

Laurel Colonial Corner Chess Club
Harrison Beard Building, 8th and Montgomery
P.O. Box 113
Laurel, MD 20707
Mr. Allan Beadle
301/776-0488

The Laurel Chess Club meets Friday nights; call for further information.

New Carrollton Chess Club
7414 Riverdale Road
New Carrollton, MD 20784
301/459-6900 New Carrollton Public Library

Join this club on Saturday afternoons at the New Carrollton Public library.

Reston Chess Club
2310 Colts Neck Road
Reston, VA 22091
703/476-4500 Reston Community Center

This club meets Thursday nights at the Reston Community Center snack bar.

Rockville Chess Club
12517 Greenly Street
Wheaton, MD 20906
301/881-0100 Rockville Jewish Community Center
301/933-1410 Coordinator

Anyone is welcome to join in these chess games on Wednesday nights at the Rockville Jewish Community Center.

For other chess opportunities, visit the stationary chess tables in Dupont Circle and in Lafayette Park, where chess players co-exist with granite figures who sit in frozen concentration day and night. ♣

to order more copies...

Finding Fun & Friends is a perfect gift for newcomers and longtime residents alike. People have given the book for birthdays, holidays, housewarmings, and even weddings! If you would like to order a copy, send a check (payable Piccolo Press) with this form to:

Piccolo Press
901 King Street, Suite 102
Alexandria, VA 22314

Call 703-519-0376 for further information.

Yes, I'd like to order more copies of *Finding Fun & Friends in Washington.* Please send my order to the address below.

Name _____

Address _____

City _____ State _____ Zip _____

Telephone _____

Number of Copies _____ x $14.95   =   _____

VA residents add .67 per book   =   _____
(state sales tax)

Shipping & Handling @ $2.00   =   _____

Total   =   _____

Bulk discounts are available. Please call us for details.
To use this book for nonprofit fundraising, please call 703/519-0376.

Index